THE
PRINCE
IN THE
TOWER

The Short Life & Mysterious

Disappearance of Edward V

MICHAEL HICKS

TEMPUS

Cover Illustrations:
Front: The Princes in the Tower, by Sir John Everett Milais, courtesy of Royal Holloway, University of London.
Back: Edward V in his garter robes, a previously unknown portrait discovered in the Black Book (Garter Register). By permission of the Dean and Canons of Windsor.

This edition first published 2007

Tempus Publishing Limited
Cirencester Road, Chalford,
Stroud, Gloucestershire, GL6 8PE
www.tempus-publishing.com

© Michael Hicks, 2003, 2007

The right of Michael Hicks to be identified as the Author
of this work has been asserted in accordance with the
Copyrights, Designs and Patents Act 1988.

British Library Cataloguing in Publication Data.
A catalogue record for this book is available from the British Library.

ISBN 978 0 7524 4386 7

Typesetting and origination by Tempus Publishing Limited
Printed and bound in Great Britain

CONTENTS

PREFACE

When Jonathan Reeve of Tempus Publishing suggested that I should fill in the histories of English monarchs with a biography on Edward V, I was incredulous. There was a very good reason for the gap. Edward V had lived for only twelve years, reigned for only eleven weeks, and then vanished. It could not be done. Reflecting at leisure on the extraordinary proposal, itemising what I already had at hand, and planning further searches for the other sources that ought to exist (but regrettably do not), I took on the task. It has been illuminating for me. Jonathan Reeve was right: there is a book in the subject. Thank you Jonathan. I hope that *Edward V* makes a lively, informative and rewarding read; I believe that it also adds significantly to our understanding of his era.

This book has taken advantage of (and rather taken for granted) the immensely fruitful labours of Keith Dockray, James Gairdner, Rosemary Horrox, Paul Murray Kendall, Tony Pollard and Charles Ross on Richard III, whose career interacted so crucially with that of his nephew Edward V. Insufficiently acknowledged below, they are gratefully thanked here. Fortunately I myself had worked over the last thirty years on so many aspects of the subject and had notes and references aplenty, all of which I have revisited in the original. I have tried not to repeat myself or unthinkingly to contradict myself, although in places I have had to alter my stance. Revisiting old haunts demonstrated once again the value of biography: what appears to work from one angle may not when studied from another. I have been repeatedly forced to reconsider possibilities that I thought I had ruled out. I have been successful in only some of my efforts to find evidence that I am sure once existed and may still exist, somewhere. The subject is certainly not exhausted: if David Lowe trawled thoroughly through most of the Prince's records for certain purposes, I have merely sampled them for others. There is much more to be done.

This book would have been difficult indeed without the context supplied by Cora L. Scofield, Professor Charles Ross – author of the standard biographies of both Edward IV and Richard III – and, on Wales, of Professor Ralph Griffiths. John Ashdown-Hill's ground-breaking article on Eleanor Butler demonstrated the practicality of further studies of Edward IV's mistresses, long ago abandoned prematurely by myself as futile, and Professor Nicholas Orme's paper on Edward V's education was invaluable. Michael K. Jones' *Bosworth, 1485: Psychology of a Battle* (2002) has proved stimulating and complementary. Anne Sutton and Livia Visser-Fuchs have opened much heraldic and literary material to me. Geoffrey Wheeler devised and supplied the illustrations and also passed me some crucial references that I would certainly have missed. The central chapters rely heavily on the work of others, in particular Professor Orme and the late lamented David Lowe (d.1980), whose important research into the Prince's estates in Wales and the Wydevilles generally was so regrettably cut short. Our friend and mentor T.B. Pugh (d.2002), historian of the nobility, the marcher lordships and the House of York, has been often in my thoughts.

This is my book and my interpretation: I often differ from my predecessors. All errors are my responsibility. All quotations have been rendered into modern English. All books are published in London unless otherwise indicated. Documents at the Public Record Office have been cited by their call numbers.

My last two family holidays were shaped by this book and the search for illustrations, several of which – some photographed by my wife – have made it into the book. Writing books can be a lonely business, both for the author and for his family, and this has never been truer than in 2002. Thank you once again as always

Cynthia, for your patience and support and for your critical reading, as also to my son Ralph. I dedicate the book to my father, Gilbert Edward alias George Hicks, who was not a historian, but who always supported me and even read all my books.

Winchester, November 2002

I

WHY EDWARD V?

Who Was Edward V?

King Edward V reigned more briefly than any English king since the Conquest. His reign lasted for only the seventy-seven days from 10 April to 25 June 1483. His coronation was twice post-poned and he was never crowned. Only twelve years old and under-age, he succeeded automatically, but never ruled. Others governed on his behalf, his guardians, councillors and Lord Protector. He was then discarded and deposed. He was declared illegitimate and was thus disqualified from kingship. He was not rightly king and never rightly reigned. Yet other bastards had been kings. Like Edward VIII, who abdicated, but unlike Lady Jane Grey, queen for nine days, Edward V retained his place in the roll of English monarchs. His reign barely interrupts the succession to the two Yorkist brothers, his father King Edward IV (1461–83) and his uncle and supplanter King Richard III (1483–85). Later in 1483, the year of three kings, he disappeared permanently from sight. Most probably he perished. A child so briefly king, so rapidly and ruthlessly erased from the pages of history, is a curiosity and symbol rather than the stuff of which history books are written. How much more ludicrous, surely, is a biography of Edward V than even one on Lambert Simnel, about which Dr Ian Arthurson once heard 'a well-known historian' chortle: 'A book on Lambert Simnel! What next? One on Perkin Warbeck?'[1]

Yet Arthurson's *Perkin Warbeck* became a substantial book. Confidence trickster Warbeck may have been, yet his pretence to be Edward V's younger brother, Richard, brought him international attention and a royal marriage; threatened the fledgling Tudor regime with invasions and undermined it with plots; and cost many lives including his own. It was not what he was that mattered, but what he was thought to be. Where Perkin was a curiosity and symbol, Edward V was the real thing. From the moment of his birth, in sanctuary at Westminster, he was the symbol of Yorkist resistance to the Lancastrian government. He was still a babe in arms when recognised and invested as Prince of Wales, proof of the male succession and the seal of permanence to the dynasty of York, and still a toddler when despatched as figurehead to quell disorder and instil better governance in the principality and marches of Wales. Still a child when his father died, he succeeded automatically and was recognised everywhere. All agreed publicly on his coronation, which would – at twelve years old – have passed him the actuality of power as well as the mere panoply. His usurpation was high political drama of fundamental importance. Though still politically inactive and personally impotent, he was the figurehead for those who rejected his uncle's regime, too dangerous to let live, for Richard III – or indeed for Henry VII, had Edward lived so long. He died for what he stood for and for what he might have been, not for what he was. His fate, real or imagined, destroyed his uncle's reputation, made possible the accession of Henry VII, and underpinned a century of Tudor rule.

Yet Edward V is a household name. Not perhaps as King Edward V, as Edward Prince of Wales, or as Prince Edward, the eldest son of Edward IV. Only those ageing survivors of the old kings of England style of English history that Sellar and Yeatman ridiculed seventy years ago in *1066 And All That*, historians and students of the Wars of the Roses, and aficionados of Richard III can place him with any confidence. No, the epithets that ring almost everyone's bells are the 'Two Little Princes in the Tower', most probably equated with Millais' famous painting, and the 'Babes in the Wood'. Few can locate the princes to the appropriate century and fewer yet imagine that a historical reality lies behind the nursery story. A mere handful, surely, can name either 'Little Prince' or 'Babe'. The stories are instructive, archetypal and eternal, utterly independent of their original context and as relevant to the third millennium experience as ever. They originated, however, in concrete events, the most heinous and unforgivable crimes that an earlier age could conceive of and which rank alongside the child abuse, suicide bombings and war crimes of today. That Edward V was born to be king and was wrongfully brought down deeply impressed subsequent generations. He is one of history's greatest victims. Contemporaries compared his fate automatically to the greatest crimes known to them, King Herod's murder of the Holy Innocents and Judas Iscariot's betrayal of Jesus. Subsequent generations agreed. Today he stands unnamed alongside Anne Frank, the Holocaust victim whose autobiography every schoolchild reads, and an endless stream of child victims whose atrocities have yet to stand the test of time. Perhaps they are more obviously relevant to us today. Yet every child encounters and every adult remembers the 'Two Little Princes in the Tower' and the 'Babes in the Wood'. Edward V mattered in his own time. He has mattered ever since. He matters today. Beware wicked uncles everywhere!

A Biography of Edward V?

Assessment of Edward's significance and the kaleidoscopic changes in his fortune is indeed the stuff of history and a subject worthy of historical articles, chapters and this book. Whether it is a biography is, of course, a matter of opinion. Why bother to write the biography of a king who scarcely lived and about whom so little is known? 'The childhood and education of Edward V necessarily make up the whole of his biography', writes Professor Orme.[2] Of sex, of violence – except as victim – of appearance, actions, spoken words, and the thoughts that most biographies contain we can know barely anything. Cannot what is known of Edward V be safely left to the biographies of his father Edward IV and his uncle Richard III, as indeed it normally has been? Of course it can. Yet something is lost in the process. It is an outside job. Such books regard Edward V merely as an object, from the point of view of others. Every individual, past and present, has a different relationship with those about them. Examining even the most well-known events from another point of view forces us to reassess them. Approaching familiar scenes previously analysed and discussed in other books from this particular vantage point has compelled this biographer to plumb new sources, to recognise new insights, and to revise his interpretations. What previously was so obvious cannot have been so. *He* cannot have said or thought *that*. With all the dangers of empathy, of the biographer identifying himself with his subject, this extra dimension recreates the complexity of the past and revives the contribution of the individual. Historians can do this – better, undoubtedly, with well-documented cases – but sufficiently well to make the attempt worthwhile. This book seeks, therefore, to perceive Edward V's troubled life from the point of view of Edward V, which has not, to the author's knowledge, been attempted thus far.

Of course the standards of biography against which *Edward V* and *Perkin Warbeck* are measured are unrealistically high. Few if any medieval characters, however striking and dominant, can offer the scope for psychological or even psychiatric investigation, for study of self-image and interaction with others so commonly provided by the diaries and sheaves of letters of modern notables, or even for the concrete investigation of upbringing and education, sexuality, careers and recreations that are normally taken for granted today. Extant evidence even for the greatest churchmen and politicians, Edward V's uncles Clarence and Gloucester, great-uncle Warwick, grandfathers York and Rivers, and great-great-uncle Cardinal Bourchier is seriously deficient in most of these ways. Kings do better. We know about most aspects of Edward IV, though never enough, and rather less of Richard III and Henry VII. Twelve years a prince and eleven weeks a king, Edward V has left much more behind him than other boys of his time. Our problem is, however, that it falls into two parts: what should have been rather than what actually was and what was done in his name, to which he may have contributed, rather than what he himself did. We have to be grateful indeed for those few glimpses of the real lad that contemporaries have transmitted to us. Edward himself was a living, breathing reality, to whom others related and around whom the future was planned. It was because of what he was, as well as who he was, that some founded their hopes upon him and others feared and destroyed him. As always, Edward was partly genetic and partly shaped by his environment, both of which are worthy topics for the biographer and can indeed be studied, if only up to a point.

Edward V only lived to be twelve. Of course he was capable of acting for himself, of influencing those about him – don't good and naughty boys do that today? – but it is hard to detect his individual contribution. His short life was shaped less by who he was than by what he represented. He was a symbol – a whole series of symbols – and consequently what he represented varied as he symbolised different things at different times. This book considers each of these symbols in turn. What he was, however, was determined not merely by what was happening at the time, but by what had preceded it. To an extraordinary extent, a life of Edward V has to take issue with the baggage he was born with. Much of Edward's life was preconditioned: events, relationships, attitudes that preceded his birth influenced his life up to its end and beyond. Like Lawrence Sterne's *Tristram Shandy*, much of Edward V's biography comes before his birth. That legacy resurrected itself twelve years later to destroy him.

2

THE LEGACY FOR EDWARD V

The Crown of England

The kingdom that Edward V was born to rule consisted of the England and Wales we know today and several dependencies: Ireland, with its capital Dublin and its own central government, presided over most commonly by a royal absentee as lieutenant and an Anglo-Irish earl as deputy, always a FitzGerald; Calais, under a captain; and the Channel Isles. Scotland was a separate and usually hostile realm. The Scottish frontier, the northern marches, were contracted out to aristocratic wardens, sometimes subject to and co-ordinated by a king's lieutenant: Edward's cousin Warwick in the 1460s and his uncle Gloucester in the 1480s were the prime examples. Two centuries after its final conquest, Wales was still partitioned into the principality in the west and north-west and independent self-governing marcher lordships everywhere else. The greatest marcher lords had been the dukes of York as earls of March. The lords marcher and the three earls palatine of Chester, Lancaster and Durham exercised regalian rights, ruling like kings within their domains. Away from such franchises and its Cornish, Welsh and Scots speaking peripheries, the kingdom was a unit, subjected to a single central government and a common law that operated through a uniform system of local government – county and sheriff, hundred and wapentake – that was already more than five centuries old. Everyone was subject to the single sovereign, the king, whose commands and allegiance overrode those of even the greatest aristocrats. The counties palatine and marcher lordships were accumulating in royal hands and even the independence of the rest was being whittled away by subtle combinations of coercion, blackmail and patronage.

The crown that Edward V was born to wear demonstrated his supremacy within his kingdom. Distinguished from everyone else by such symbolic attributes of monarchy as orb and sceptre, throne, crown and cap of estate, and dignified with titles unique to themselves, English kings were anointed with holy oil and crowned with great religious ceremony, as befitted God's lieutenant on earth. Semi-religious, they were able henceforth to cure scrofula, 'the king's evil'. In theory kings of England were absolute, their power unfettered, subject only to obligations to perform God's will, as befitted his representative; to operate within the constitutional limitations agreed by their predecessors and themselves; and to conform to established convention and political realities. In practice fifteenth-century English monarchs were hedged about by constraints. As Christians, they were bound by Christian standards. Kings were as liable to damnation for their sins as anyone else and subject to many more opportunities and temptations. They could not even take women by force, as Edward IV found. God's representatives were bound to rule according to Christian standards and, in particular, since government had been created for the benefit of the governed, to rule in the public interest for the common good. Kings succeeded not to the absolute power of the first ruler, but to what remained after concessions made by earlier kings, such as Magna Carta, had been deducted. It was to this attenuated inheritance that Edward V was heir. Every law to which kings gave their assent limited their freedom of action in the future. Past precedents, customary procedures and conventions dogged each step. Kings should not act alone, arbitrarily or impulsively, but with deliberation and advice, both seeking counsel and, crucially, following it. Counsel was expressed institutionally through the king's council, which he chose himself from the sober, serious and experienced; the great council of notables who selected themselves; and parliament, which included delegates from the localities, urban and rural. Whatever the theory, kings needed the moral and financial support of parliament to exercise their sovereignty, in waging wars, making laws and raising the necessary taxes. Parliament, moreover, was a reminder that sovereign power lay not in the king himself, but in his capacity, through consent, to harness the energy and resources of his subjects. Not to do so, as Henry VI found, spelt failure. No king could stand against his subjects. Those who tried, from Edward II in 1327 to Edward IV in 1470, were defeated, deposed and, usually, destroyed.

Edward V was heir to a huge and unrivalled, if archaic, administrative machine. His ministers and judges presided over his central departments of state – chancery, exchequer, privy seal and the central courts – and over an established network of local government founded on sheriffs, escheators, coroners and justices of the peace. The royal household or court dwarfed and overawed the greatest of his subjects. The greatest of provincial rulers, backwoodsmen like the Mowbray dukes of Norfolk and the Percy earls of Northumberland, were mere supplicants at court, soliciting favours and intercession with the king from royal ministers or household officers. Edward IV's uncle and long-time treasurer, Henry Earl of Essex, who had a daily audience with the king, and his intimate and household chamberlain William Lord Hastings, who controlled access to the royal apartments, rated much more highly at court than they did in their home counties. It was sometimes easy to forget that the pecking order at court need not apply throughout the kingdom. Overmighty subjects, though sometimes court magnates, were powerful provincially because of their vast estates, the great wealth and the thousands of dependants, which they could bring to bear when required. Decisions at court were diluted the further away they were exercised. Implementation depended on the co-operation of those of local standing, whose wishes carried local weight. Locally and nationally, as a class and as individuals, the aristocracy really mattered, particularly those sitting in the House of Lords (the peerage) and especially the highest nobility, predominantly dukes and earls of royal blood, who were political heavyweights. Yet the people could never be ignored. The Wars of the Roses was a time when they were repeatedly aroused against governments, any governments, and several times swept them away. Nor was England an island, except in a geographical sense. The great powers of northern Europe, France and Burgundy, frequently intervened in English affairs, by invitation of disgruntled Englishmen or as active puppeteers: four times invaders forcibly removed the ruling regime. To suppose that court and government represented political reality was dangerously complacent. Several times Edward V's father Edward IV fell into that trap.

Monarchy was hard work. A king had to be everything: a military and political leader, able to organise, command and inspire; an assiduous administrator, possessing both an overview of the whole range of government and a mastery of detail; politically adept, able to buy support with sparing distribution of patronage, to require it by coercion and to know when each was appropriate; and personally impressive, demanding respect and yet able to mix amicably with the aristocratic class to which he belonged.

Edward IV, an imposing figure well over 6ft tall, came close to this ideal on occasions, yet he was inclined to let things drift and fell short of the moral lead that some expected. An impossible job was yet more difficult for a minor, whose councillors could take no permanent decisions, although much was allowed in the hope of something better. This was the challenge faced in 1483 by Edward V, a twelve-year-old king: a challenge that he was denied the opportunity to surmount.

Governments were absorbed with routine. They sought to keep things going, not to change them. That was difficult enough. It was the king who was responsible for law, order and justice – for keeping the peace. Crimes against his subjects were regarded as offences against himself: it was his task to wreak revenge on behalf of the whole community – the king versus the culprit: vengeance and the bloodfeud were banned. For this he relied on his law courts at Westminster; the assizes and quarter sessions in the localities; and local law-enforcement officers. It was not enough. Too often crime exceeded local control, indeed, not infrequently local officers were the criminals or were suborned, and the king had to intervene, compelling local potentates to submit and obey. Similarly routine foreign relations were often overthrown by circumstances beyond English control: trade embargoes, the alliances and wars between third parties and Charles the Bold's destruction by the underrated Swiss. Long-term policies, if seriously planned, were often overturned. It was the king with whom the buck stopped, who had to take remedial action, though normally – and fortunately – it was his evil councillors that paid the price. Kings, in the last resort, were protected by their sovereignty, the overriding duty of allegiance owed by all, and the draconian treason laws. Kings were always given a second chance: until 'in 1483', when, as Professor Pollard says, 'uniquely, deposition was used as a weapon of first resort'.[1] Edward V was to be the victim.

York, Mortimer and Neville

Edward V had the chance to reign because he was the eldest son of King Edward IV and Queen Elizabeth. Kings were selected by hereditary right from those members of the ruling clan, which was just beginning to be called the Plantagenets, who combined political power (conquest) and popular assent (election or acclamation). Might could be right and election could be fixed, but inheritance could not be. Richard III's attempt to fix all three achieved only the briefest acquiescence. The hereditary right that Richard's nephew Edward V possessed and that Richard's niece Elizabeth made good was only a generation old.

It had been Edward V's father, Edward IV, who was the first king of the House of York. He was the eldest son of Richard, third Duke of York (d.1460),[2] and his consort Cecily Neville (d.1495), both descendants of King Edward III (1327–77). York was the grandson of Edward III's fourth adult son Edmund of Langley, 1st Duke of York, and a Castilian princess. Besides his dukedom and its substantial endowments, such as Sandal (Yorks.) and Fotheringhay (Northants.), Duke Richard was heir through his mother Anne Mortimer, secondly and most importantly, to the earldoms of March and Ulster. Together these made him the greatest landholder within the kingdom after the king: greatest above all in the marcher lordships of Wales. Ludlow (Shrops.) was his principal seat. York was the premier duke in England. He was well aware of his royal blood, his pre-eminence within England and of ties with other royal houses abroad. He lent his leadership to calls for reform against the governments of his cousin, the Lancastrian King Henry VI (1422–61). Three times, in 1454–55, 1455–56 and in 1460, York was appointed by parliament as Lord Protector when King Henry was mad or otherwise politically exposed. York's grandmother Anne Mortimer herself had been descended from Edward III through another senior line, that of the king's second adult son Lionel Duke of Clarence (d.1368). Thirdly and finally, Edward IV traced his royal descent via a third, Beaufort, line through Cecily Neville. This marriage knit Edward to the most fertile and well-connected clan in contemporary England, the Nevilles, whose numbers, wealth and connections made up for the sparse kinsfolk of York's own. Warwick the Kingmaker was his cousin. All these, one generation removed, featured on Edward V's pedigree also.

The name Mortimer had much more significance than this. It had been for promoting the Mortimer claim to the crown that York's father had been executed in 1415. Albeit through two females, this Mortimer line was senior to that of the three Lancastrian kings, descendants in the male line of Edward III's third adult son John of Gaunt, Duke of Lancaster (d.1399). Getting rid of Richard II had been the priority in 1399, when the Lancastrian Henry IV was of age and the Mortimer claimant a mere child. The name of Mortimer was repeatedly a talisman for conspirators up to 1450, when the rebel Jack Cade acquired the pseudonym, and almost by itself the surname sufficed to destroy an obscure kinsman in 1423.[3] Not until 1460, after a decade of faction-fighting and repeated public denials of any further ambitions, did Richard Duke of York dare to assert his claim to the throne. He presented to parliament his pedigree from Duke Lionel as his justification. His title was accepted by the House of Lords, but was not to take effect at once. Instead Henry VI, already a king for thirty-eight years, was to continue for life, York to rule on his behalf, and York himself would succeed on his death. Whilst this *Accord* proved unacceptable to many, including Henry VI's Queen Margaret of Anjou, it actually provoked civil war and cost many lives including that of York himself, resulting in 1461 in the accomplishment of the change of dynasty that York had proposed the previous year. Although Henry VI still lived, it was nevertheless York's eldest son Edward IV, then aged only nineteen, who was elected king on 4 March 1461 and thereafter made his title good on the battlefield of Towton. The most successful general of the Wars of the Roses, King Edward was to re-assert his right against several more rivals over the next decade, to withstand all challenges, and to pass his kingdom on peacefully to his son Edward V in 1483.

Edward IV was not an only child. He was, in actual fact, York's second son, the first-born Henry having died in infancy. Edward's next brother Edmund Earl of Rutland, only one year his junior, fell with their father at the battle of Wakefield (1460), but he had two more brothers and three sisters. The eldest remaining brother George (d. 1478), aged twelve at his accession and heir presumptive until Edward had children of his own, was created Duke of Clarence: a highly symbolic title that deliberately recalled the dynasty's origins. Richard (d. 1485), aged eight, was created Duke of Gloucester. Edward's two eldest sisters Anne (d. 1476) and Elizabeth (d. 1504) were already married to the dukes of Exeter and Suffolk: Henry Duke of Exeter (d. 1475), regrettably, was a Lancastrian, who was never to live with his duchess again. Suffolk had sons and Exeter a daughter. Edward's youngest sister Margaret of York, already fifteen, was a beautiful diplomatic pawn eventually bestowed in marriage in 1468 on Charles the Bold Duke of

Burgundy, one of the three great powers of northern Europe. She recurs later as Margaret of Burgundy (d. 1503), partisan of the Yorkist pretenders after 1485.

Apart from the Duchess Cecily, the king's mother, and the luxuriant Nevilles, the House of York was completed by the king's aunt Isabel (d. 1483), her children and grandchildren, and her husband Henry Bourchier, Earl of Essex (d. 1483), repeatedly Lord Treasurer and brother of Cardinal Bourchier, primate of all England for the duration of the dynasty. The Nevilles, in contrast, were legion. Older and more experienced than the young king, they did everything for him: not surprisingly the years 1461–67 have been dubbed 'The Rule of the Nevilles'. Besides his Neville allies and mentors, the young Edward IV relied heavily on York's former connections, several of whom he ennobled. Prominent amongst these were: William Lord Hastings, who was chamberlain of his household – right hand man and friend – throughout the reign and eventually the dominant figure in the east and north Midlands; Humphrey Lord Stafford of Southwick (Earl of Devon, 1469) and John Lord Dynham, his agents in the West Country up to 1469 and after 1478; and William Lord Herbert (Earl of Pembroke, 1468) and his brother-in-law Walter Lord Ferrers of Chartley in south and mid-Wales. It was to York's Mortimer connection that Edward always looked to manage south and central Wales, first to the Herberts and then to the team orchestrated by the Wydeville-dominated council of Edward V.

Not everyone accepted Edward's title. Lancastrian resistance was to continue for a further decade. A new king and a new dynasty were initially shunned by foreign powers accustomed to the Lancastrians. The most valuable tool of diplomacy was the young king's hand in marriage, which several monarchs sought for their kinswomen. Edward's choice of an English gentlewoman served none of these purposes. It was left to his sister Margaret to fill the diplomatic gap. His new queen could, however, secure the dynasty by speedy provision of a male heir – Edward V. At first Elizabeth fell short. Though undoubtedly fertile, she initially produced only daughters: useful politically and diplomatically, but themselves no guarantee for the future of the dynasty. Elizabeth, Mary and Cecily preceded Edward V in 1470. A second son Richard in 1473, the third short-lived George in 1477, and yet more daughters, seven in total, of whom five outlived their parents. The House of York had come to stay. Prince Edward, the boy born to be king, duly succeeded in 1483. His existence helped make his father's second reign (1471–83) much more peaceful and secure than his first (1461–70).

The Sexuality of the House of York

The legacy of the House of York consisted not merely of its royal blood, status, crown, titles and connections, but of its licentiousness. Church and law recognised the legitimacy only of children born within wedlock, to husbands and wives within marriage. In an age when inheritance was the key to wealth, rank and status, it was only the legitimate who could inherit anything. Other children existed, born to the unmarried and to those married to others, but these were the product of lechery or lust, a deadly sin, of fornication or adultery, both of which were punished by the Church in those of humble status. Such natural, but illegitimate, children were bastards – a technical term as well as today's casual insult. The House of York was notorious for its practice of lechery: it offers examples in plenty of adultery and fornication actual and suspected, and it spawned numerous bastards. Apart from the twelve brothers and sisters born to his married parents and the two uterine brothers of his mother's first marriage, Edward V had at least three illegitimate siblings who were acknowledged, and probably many others who were not.

Perhaps the dynasty's promiscuity originated with the first duchess, the illegitimate daughter of Pedro the Cruel of Castile by his mistress. Doubts were cast over the legitimacy of her second son Richard Earl of Cambridge, Edward IV's grandfather. Could he actually have been begotten, as T.B. Pugh long ago suggested, by Richard's half-brother, John Holland Earl of Huntingdon, a serial seducer? Cambridge's sister Constance Lady Despenser was of dubious morality: she had a daughter by Edmund Earl of Kent (d.1408), and perhaps also an affair with Thomas Earl of Arundel (d.1417).[4] No such adventures are known for Richard Duke of York, but his son Edward – the future Edward IV – was supposedly fathered by some other man. That aspersion was cast on him and his mother only in the 1460s,[5] when York – who had always acknowledged his son – had long been dead. It was vigorously denied. Englishmen, from pure chauvinism, often doubted the legitimacy of those born abroad, like Edward IV at Rouen and his brother George at Dublin. Very recently Dr Michael K. Jones has argued that Edward was indeed a bastard. The itineraries of duke and duchess do not appear to coincide at the right time for them to have conceived Edward together and the christening was rather low-key, in the castle chapel rather than the cathedral of Rouen.[6] We cannot be altogether sure, however, where both parents were at the crucial times, the pregnancy was neither impossibly long nor short, and the christening was respectable enough.[7] Illegitimacy, therefore, is feasible, not proven. In the next generation, the youngest, the future Richard III, does not seem to have secured the dispensation needed to validate his marriage and to legitimate the children born to him by his duchess and future queen Anne Neville.[8] Richard's natural daughter Katherine, who was at least fourteen at her wedding in 1484, was born before Richard's own marriage (c.1472), but his son John of Pontefract (Yorks.), 'the lord bastard', was presumably born later – after 1471, when Richard secured access to Pontefract as chief steward of the north parts of the duchy of Lancaster.[9] York's eldest daughter Anne divorced her exiled husband, remarried to Thomas St Leger, and bore him a daughter during her first husband's lifetime. There were also doubts about the virginity (and even childlessness!) of his youngest daughter Margaret,[10] who was unusually mature, at twenty-two, when first wedded to Charles the Bold.

Women were expected to be chaste, since inheritance and succession depended on the provision of undoubted heirs. Women's honour, once impugned, could not easily be repaired – mud stuck. Men were different. This was the age of the double-standard. Although sinful, there was no *social* discredit attached to their sexual liaisons and extra-marital affairs. Princes and noblemen were expected to have other partners, to father bastards, and to acknowledge them. All three of Henry V's brothers fathered bastards. Several individuals were known to contemporaries, in shorthand, as the bastards of Clarence and Fauconberg. Both Edward IV and the future Richard III fathered bastards. Ten post-conquest kings had mistresses and bastards and five of these including Edward IV far exceeded normal expectations. He was a libertine.[11] Indeed, he indulged most of the sins of the flesh to excess, and perhaps thereby expedited his death. Like his grandson, the future Henry VIII, the strikingly handsome prince was corpulent by his middle age, as the Burgundian Philippe de Commynes maliciously pointed out.[12]

Lust and its various expressions were of course sinful, to be answered for at the Last Judgement, and popular opinion was less forgiving than high society. Richard III was to find political mileage in charging his Wydeville opponents with immorality and denounced the personally innocent Henry Tudor as a bastard on both sides.[13] The Church also disapproved. Wrestling with the fate of his master's soul, the Crowland Continuator, a churchman who had known Edward IV and served him since the 1460s, described his faults with regret. 'A gross man so addicted to conviviality, vanity, drunkenness, extravagance and passion', he writes, 'in his own day he was thought to have indulged too intemperately his own passions and desire for luxury'. The Gregory Chronicler of the 1460s merely records the contemporary surprise that the king was so long unmarried and contemporary fears that he was not 'chaste of his living'.[14] Marriage to a beautiful woman in 1464 who was to bear him ten children did not stop the king looking elsewhere. By 1472 he had fathered, acknowledged, and was supporting a lord bastard, who was supplied with clothes by the Great Wardrobe.[15]

By the 1480s, and doubtless earlier, Edward's sexual prowess was notorious. An Italian visitor in 1483 was able to record that:

he was licentious in the extreme: moreover it was said that he had been most insolent to numerous women after he had seduced them, for, as soon as he grew weary of dalliance, he gave up the ladies much against their will to other courtiers. He pursued with no discrimination the married and unmarried, the noble and lowly: however he took none by force. He overcame all by money and promises, and having conquered them, he dismissed them.[16]

Affairs with ladies, wrote Commynes, was a facet of Edward's single-minded pursuit of pleasure. 'The King was a man who would readily cast an eye upon young ladies', recalled Polydore Vergil, 'and love them inordinately'.[17] Similarly Sir Thomas More, forty years later, wrote of 'his wanton lust and sinful affection ... He was in his youth greatly given to fleshly wantonness'. Buckingham in 1483, he reported, had denounced 'the King's greedy appetite' as insatiable:

and everywhere over all the realm intolerable. For no woman was there anywhere young or old, rich or poor, whom he set his eye upon, in whom he any thing liked either person or favour, speech, pace, or countenance, but without any fear of God, or respect of his honour, murmur or grudge of the world, he would importunely pursue his appetite and have her, to the great destruction of many a good woman, and great dolour to their husbands, and their other friends, which being honest people of themselves, so much regard the cleanness of their house, the chastity of their wives, and their children, that they were liefer to lose all that they have beside, than to have such villainy done them.[18]

It was also under Henry VIII that *Hearne's Fragment* recalled that this 'lusty prince attempted the stability and constant modesty of divers ladies'.[19] His pursuit of ladies, so Commynes said, went beyond reason.

Given that kings lived in palaces, the royal quarters including the bedchamber being stuffed with staff at all times and access being strictly controlled, Edward's courtships, liaisons and seductions must have been perfectly well-known within the court and, perhaps, so commonplace as normally to occasion no remark. His staff would have reacted very differently had he married any of his courtesans! The reduced formality of the hunting season eased his *amours*, observes Commynes.[20] Vergil touches on one such half-remembered scandal with more potentially serious consequences. The king had 'assayed to do some unhonest act in the earl's house': he was supposed to have seduced some woman in Warwick's household.[21] 'The King would say', so More reports,

> that he had three concubines, which in three divers priorities diversely excelled: one the merriest, another the wiliest, the third the holiest harlot in his realm, as one whom no man could get out of church lightly to any place, but it were to his bed. The other two were somewhat greater personages, and nevertheless of their humility content to be nameless and to forebear the praise of those properties. But the merriest was this Shore's wife, in whom the King therefore took greatest pleasure.[22]

More had actually met William Shore's wife Elizabeth, known to history as the 'vile and abominable strumpet' Jane Shore, who was frequented towards the end of the reign by the king, his stepsons, Hastings and other 'promoters and companions in his vices'. The other two are unnamed; however More elsewhere writes of Elizabeth Lucy. More also knew of one of Edward's bastards, Arthur Plantagenet, who served in the households of his half-sister Queen Elizabeth of York until her death, of her widower Henry VII, and of his nephew Henry VIII. From 1523 Arthur was Viscount Lisle.

The record evidence for all these liaisons is poor. We know by name only of the mistresses mentioned by More and of a handful of possible bastards: Arthur, who initially surnamed himself Wayte and was connected to the Hampshire Waytes,[23] was acknowledged by his half-sister Queen Elizabeth of York; the 'lord bastard' of 1472 if different from him; Mistress Grace, apparently adult and unmarried in 1492 at Queen Elizabeth Wydeville's funeral;[24] Elizabeth Lucy's bastard, if different from the above; and the Margaret (not Elizabeth, as wrongly reported from the 1530s on), natural daughter of Edward IV, who was married to Sir Thomas Lumley by 1480, when 'our most excellent and dread prince and lord King Edward IV' induced Bishop Dudley to grant them a licence.[25] The King's involvement and her forename suggest that she was his bastard by Margaret Lucy, problematically short though the generations are. These could be as many as five bastards or as few as three: an unimpressive total when set alongside the 30 mistresses, bastards, and grand bastards organised upon a regional basis of Edward's contemporary Philip the Good, Duke of Burgundy. In an age before genetic finger-printing, the offspring of liaisons within marriages counted as those of the husbands. No doubt there were penalties for repudiating the bastards of kings. The King's exalted rank and favour may have eased the offence felt by husbands just as it enticed their wives to surrender. Nothing could be done about the women's honour: no subject could challenge his King to a duel. 'Not presuming to touch the King's concubine', honest William Shore 'left her up to him altogether'.[26] It was only single women, spinsters and widows, who were left holding the baby and who may have needed their kingly paramour to take on responsibility. Regrettably we lack Edward's privy purse expenses, which presumably included gifts and payments to his mistresses. The patent roll and its warrants do not record any sexual orientation lying behind royal grants and appointments. Mistresses and bastards, even royal ones, seldom occur in conventional historical records, are rarely explicitly identified, may lack surnames, had no rights of inheritance, and hence are difficult to study. I have been little more successful in finding answers than my predecessors. Besides the few bastards that are acknowledged, we ought perhaps to suppose there were rather more whose paternity was concealed.

Edward started early. We know of no liaisons before his accession aged 19, but the years 1461-4 were clearly sexually active ones. Nothing was set down at the time. The generalisations of the chroniclers are based on rumours circulating later or at the time and/ or specific instances known to themselves. Regrettably we cannot tell which was which. We do know of three stories, two recorded much later, which seem to bear out what Mancini and More wrote: they may, of course, have been generalising from these very instances. They relate to Dame Elizabeth Lucy, to Lady Eleanor Butler, and to the Queen. The first two were first recorded late in relation to the precontract alleged in 1483, the story that Edward had been committed to another lady before marrying his Queen, and therefore that his marriage was invalid and any resultant children illegitimate. This features in *Titulus Regius* (1483), which justified Richard III's accession by discrediting the claims of his nephews, and in narrative accounts of his usurpation. Very little is known about either of the first two ladies, even about their identities, let alone about their relationship with Edward. The tales might be entirely fabricated but contemporaries found them at least briefly credible.

Richard III's *Titulus Regius* identifies Eleanor Butler as a daughter of the military hero John Talbot, 1st Earl of Shrewsbury, defeated and slain in the last battle of the Hundred Years War at Châtillon in 1453, by his second wife Margaret (d.1467), daughter of Richard Beauchamp Earl of Warwick and sister of Duke Henry (d.1446).[27] Born about 1436 (and thus somewhat older than Edward IV), she was married about 1450 to Sir Thomas Butler (Botiller), son and heir of Ralph Lord Sudeley (d.1473): such a notable match, into a ducal family, signalled that the Butlers had arrived and was the culmination (and inspiration) of both surviving Butler genealogies.[28] Jointure was settled on the young couple and their unborn heirs. There were to be no children. Thomas was a Lancastrian and was killed in battle against Edward IV at Towton. Subsequently, so the story runs, sometime between Towton and Edward's marriage, 'King Edward was and stood troth plight to one

Dame Eleanor Butler, daughter of the old Earl of Shrewsbury, with whom the said King Edward had made a precontract of matrimony'. They had contracted to marry, perhaps married, and, Edward IV being Edward IV, had consummated the match with sexual intercourse. Commynes fleshes out the story. The king 'pursued a lady of England because he was anxious to have his pleasure of her'. Hence the marriage. 'And for this promise he had lain with her, and did it only to deceive her'.[29] She calculated, we must surmise, that a mutual exchange of vows in the present tense – *per verba legitime et presenti,* the contemporary phrase – and secured by intercourse was as binding as a marriage in the eyes of the Church, and could not be set aside. That was the law, as the infuriated Norfolk family of Pastons found when Margery Paston betrothed herself to their bailiff Richard Calle. Such a contract invalidated any later marriage to anyone else.

But in this case, Eleanor Butler was never recognised as Edward's spouse. Having secured such a promise, surely she must have pressed her case, unsuccessfully? Why else the exchange of vows? Surely because Edward calculated, as Commynes says, that she could not prove his promise: she presumed, wrongly, that the King would keep his word. If the story is authentic, perhaps there were no witnesses to the promises, in which case Edward could simply deny it had happened: both parties had to confirm an exchange of vows. 'If one or both secret spouses deny the marriage', writes Professor Kelly, 'it cannot be enforced without proof that it took place'.[30] Such proof could be provided by witnesses. But what if they refused to testify? Thirty years on Commynes reports that Robert Stillington, Bishop of Bath and Lord Privy Seal in 1461-4, had admitted twenty years later that he had actually married them. Supposedly, Stillington told the future Richard III that King Edward IV, being most anxious for a lady in England, promised to marry her provided that he lay with her and she agreed. The bishop said that he had married them: nobody was there except him and her. He was a courtier and had not revealed it and had helped make the lady keep quiet.[31]

Apparently he told her that the King would deny it, that he himself would not testify in her favour, and that it would be futile for Eleanor to claim to be married to the King. To have done otherwise would presumably have incurred the King's wrath and terminated Stillington's career. Commynes points out that, since then, the bishop had fallen from favour, had actually been imprisoned, and thus wanted vengeance. How much credence should be attached to a report of an allegation by someone with an axe to grind about something he had apparently previously concealed and hence perjured himself? If the story is true and if Stillington was the source – two very big 'ifs' – Edward must surely have denied that any vows had taken place and indeed made his promises merely to get Eleanor to bed. As far as we know, there was no pregnancy.

Whilst there is no surviving record evidence, Eleanor's position is suggestive. Of the Lancastrians at Towton, 113 were attainted by parliament and forfeited their lands; another 24 listed by pseudo-Worcester in fact escaped, probably by striking a deal with the government; and yet others like Sir William Plumpton paid fines not to be attainted. Thomas Butler could have been attainted and his lands forfeited. Eleanor was wholly dependent on her join-ture, Grove and North Dorset (Warks.), but this had apparently been settled on her without licence and was liable to be cancelled and to revert to her father-in-law Ralph Lord Sudeley. Whereas Sudeley had provided the lands at his own expense to support his heir, now that there was none, he felt disinclined to honour the agreement. The marriage that had seemed such a coup when his splendid pedigree rolls were drawn up, to the daughter of the great Talbot and the niece of a duke, was now an embarrassment. He persuaded her – blackmailed her? – to surrender one of her two manors. Eleanor may well have needed the King's favour to fore-stall her husband's attainder and/or to overlook the absence of a licence. Whether it was her disadvantage that Sudeley's sister Elizabeth Lady Say was the King's godmother, we cannot say. In such circumstances, Eleanor may well have been amongst those war victims who needed the King's favour, Edward may have tried it on, and Eleanor may have given way in return only for a promise of matrimony that proved to be misplaced. Apparently she did secure her jointure of one manor and held it at her death in 1468, when her father-in-law recovered it.[32] How she could afford to patronise Corpus Christi College, Cambridge, as supposedly she did, must remain a mystery.

Not having read *Titulus Regius*, Sir Thomas More presumed that the lady of the precontract was the Dame Elizabeth Lucy, 'a proud high-minded woman' of dubious loyalty, of whom he had heard. More reported that Edward had seduced her and had already fathered a child by her before his marriage, when the King's mother the Duchess Cecily claimed that Edward 'was sure' to her and 'her husband before God'. She was therefore Edward's real wife. An investigating tribunal interviewed her. She said that Edward's sweet-talk had encouraged her to hope of marriage and had brought her to bed, but admitted that no actual promises had been made.[33] More's story is rather vague. For a start, who was she? Was Lucy her birth-name or her marital name? She cannot have been the Dame Elizabeth Lucy around in More's day, who married three times before dying in 1536 and was still bearing children in the 1510s, fifty years after the supposed contract. The Elizabeth Lucy (née Wayte), who was perhaps the daughter of the Hampshire squire Thomas Wayte, does not appear to exist. Nor can she have been the daughter of the childless Sir William Lucy of Richards Castle in Herefordshire and Dallington (Northants.) (d.1460). No doubt there were daughters of the Lucys of Charlecote (Warks.) called Elizabeth, though this was the Christian name of the wives of neither William Lucy the elder (d.1466) nor younger (d.1495) of Charlecote. An obscure commoner will not do, since More classes Edward's mistress among 'somewhat greater personages' – ladies of birth and rank. Most probably our problem arises because she was not called Elizabeth – this was a mistake of More's, a natural confusion with the notorious lady around in his own day – but Margaret.

Dame Margaret Lucy was born soon after her parents' marriage in 1432 as the eldest daughter of Sir Lewis John (d.1442) by his second wife Anne Montagu (d.1457), daughter of John Earl of Salisbury (d.1400) and subsequently Duchess of Exeter. Apart from siblings by her mother's first Hankford marriage, Margaret had three younger whole sisters – Alice, Elizabeth Wingfield and another Margaret. The Duchess Anne chose her great-nephew Warwick as her supervisor in 1457: he had her and her daughters included in the *Salisbury Roll* in 1463.[34] In 1453 Margaret became the second wife of Sir William Lucy of Dallington (Northants.), who was killed on the Lancastrian side in battle in 1460 almost next door outside Northampton. There were no offspring. Sir William's heirs were his nephew Walter Hopton, also slain at Northampton, and his great-nephew William Vaux, who was attainted at Edward IV's first parliament, so the reversion of half and perhaps all his estate (including Margaret's dower and jointure) belonged to the crown. Her husband too had settled her jointure without a royal licence. Margaret's dower was not authorised for sixteen months, until 24 November 1461, and was not assigned until March 1462, when the coheirs strangely declined to partici-pate.[35] Her brother Sir Henry Lewis had also been attainted. Perhaps, therefore, we have here another Lancastrian widow in her late twenties needing royal favour to secure her rights.

Margaret, however, may have had a succession of sexual liaisons and was the object of slander and ill-fame. Pseudo-Worcestre claims that John Stafford, her husband's killer, married her. Any connection must have been temporary, however, since Stafford was killed nine months later at Towton, and informal, certainly not amounting to marriage, since it passes unremarked in her pardon of 5 February 1462. Warwick was then one of her addresses, suggest-ing that she was in the earl's household and perhaps also that it was she that the King supposedly essayed there. She required royal favour for her pardon.[36] It was in 1461-2, therefore, that any liaison with the King and consequent pregnancy belongs. Next she was courted by a rich lawyer Thomas Danvers, servant to Bishop Waynflete, her brother Sir Henry Lewis first acting as go-between in January/February 1463, about the time that he himself was pardoned and restored in blood. Whatever happened (and evidently Margaret requited *some* of her suitor's affection), Danvers fancied 'that he loved the said Margaret as [much as] was possible for any earthly man to love a woman', that they were actually married (*per verba legitime et presenti*), and that the contract was secured by promises (never legally enforceable recognisances) from Lewis and her servant Thomas Pachet of £1,000 in default. Danvers accepted, however, that their match was a mésalliance in the eyes of her high-ranking kin, most notably her cousin Warwick the Kingmaker, and needed to be concealed. Whether her ardour cooled or she never saw it that way, she resisted, 'marvelled greatly that he could find in his heart to trouble, defame, or spread wrongful rumours about her' and complained of his 'slanderous labour'. She married instead, publicly and with the full backing of friends and kinsmen, Thomas Wake of Blisworth, a prominent Northamptonshire squire, formerly sheriff, and a Warwick retainer. Danvers sued for confirmation of his marriage and the annulment of Margaret's new one in the church courts: the Bishop of Lincoln delegated the case to Warwick's brother Lord Chancellor Neville, perhaps by November/December 1464, when Pachet was bound to appear before him. Alleging the power of Thomas Danvers, Margaret appealed to Rome, whence the case was referred back to be settled by three English bishops (23 August 1465). About the same time Danvers sued in chancery for payment of the promises of £1,000. Lewis appeared, admitted much of the story, but denied any binding contract. Wake, Lucy and Pachet evidently defaulted, ignoring subpoenas from chancery, so a commission was issued from Archbishop Neville's palace of Cawood (Yorks.) on 8 October 1465 to arrest them and bring them to chancery.[37] We do not know what ensued in either suit. When Margaret died on 4 August 1466, still only about thirty and apparently at her family's home at Horndon in Essex, she left an infant son twelve weeks old (and *her* heir) called John Wake, presumably conceived about August 1465. Although her magnificent brass at Ingrave (Essex) calls her Margaret Wake, neither writs nor inquisitions post-mortem call her other than Margaret late the wife of Sir William Lucy, so she may not have been confirmed as married to Thomas Wake. His heir Roger Wake, already adult in 1476, was his son by an earlier marriage.[38] Perhaps Edward IV and another bastard lie in between. Warwick would certainly have found the Danvers connection disparaging. And later dealings with her brother Richard FitzLewis indicate that Richard III may have known her history.

His Parents' Marriage

Edward V was the product of Edward IV's marriage to another widow, Dame Elizabeth Grey (née Wydeville). Unfortunately contemporaries regarded this match in much the same light as the King's illicit liaisons. 'One of the ways he indulged his appetites was to marry a lady of humble origin', wrote Mancini. 'He had not so much married as ravished her'.[39] The marriage came as a complete surprise. The great council at Reading Abbey in September 1464 was convened to discuss the coinage. Instead Edward's marriage became its principal business. In the fifteenth century only those without property paired off for love. The higher ranks did not marry to please themselves. Arranged marriages, that yielded concrete benefits to all parties, were what all expected. This was even truer of kings, whose marriages were of the utmost public importance. After deliberating which of the available foreign princesses their King should marry, the assembly pressed him to choose. They pressed him so hard that he could procrastinate no longer. His reply, that he could not marry any of them because he was already wed, astounded them.

Still more amazed were they to learn that his choice had fallen on Elizabeth Grey, the widowed daughter of Richard Lord Rivers and his wife Jacquetta of Luxembourg, Dowager-Duchess of Bedford, sister of the Count of St Pol and descendant of Charlemagne. Elizabeth failed all the usual tests for a potential queen. She was already Edward's subject, not an equal partner.

Respectable certainly, hailing from and married into the baronage, Elizabeth was aristocratic rather than royal. Descent via Jacquetta to the international European nobility counted for little in England. Elizabeth's father Richard Lord Rivers was a 'knave's son' and a mere esquire made good by marriage, so Edward IV himself as earl of March and the other Yorkist earls had forcefully informed him at Calais in 1460. It had been presumptuous for Rivers to 'have such [critical] language of lords being of the King's blood'.[40] Equally was it so, by the same standards, for his daughter to marry that same earl, now a King. So Edward's mother Cecily and brother Clarence, in public, supposedly declared, and his brother Gloucester may have covertly agreed. Thirteen years later the proposal of Elizabeth's brother (now a Queen's brother) to Mary of Burgundy was greeted by Commynes with derision: 'For he was a mere earl, and she the richest heiress of her time'.[41] Royal connections alone could not suffice.

Moreover Elizabeth brought with her neither the enormous dowry nor any of the usual diplomatic advantages of a Queen, of particular importance for a new dynasty in search of international recognition. It was 'not princely to marry his own subject'. It was to Edward's 'honour, profit and surety also', so More attributed to the King's mother, 'to marry into a noble progeny out of his realm, whereupon depended great strength to his estate by their kinship and great possibility of increase of his possessions'.[42] With his hand in marriage, Edward had relinquished his principal diplomatic asset, which might have neutralised a foreign foe and won him a powerful ally, and had left instead his kingdom exposed to further French-backed invasions. The well-known criticisms that Elizabeth was a widow and not the customary virgin reported by Mancini were apparently current at the time.[43] She was older than the King, not younger. Her husband had been only a knight – moreover a Lancastrian knight, killed fighting the Yorkists, whose death aroused speculation.[44] She had many English kinsfolk, it later appeared, to embroil her in English faction-fighting and to provide for at public expense. In return, she offered only fecundity and the capacity to bear Edward an heir, not yet apparent of course; blameless virtue, the common currency of eligible damsels; and sex appeal, notoriously available to Edward elsewhere and seldom a prerequisite in marriage. The love match was not then the ideal that it is today – if indeed Edward was in love rather than merely lustful. 'And the King fell in love with his wife when he dined with her frequently', Weinreich innocently explained.[45] After this, 'with immoderate haste, the King', a monk of Crowland writes, 'prompted by the ardour of youth and relying entirely upon his own choice, without consulting the nobles of the kingdom, privately married the widow of a certain knight'.[46] He was 'so fervently enamoured', reports the *Great Chronicle*, 'that he married her without advice and counsel of any of his lords secretly'. Elizabeth 'had been ravished rather than espoused', Buckingham reportedly said.[47] Everyone wondered, so Vergil later claimed, and

> the nobility truly chafed and cast out open speeches that the King has not done according to his dignity. They found much fault with that marriage, and imputed the same to his dishonour, as the thing whereunto he was led by blind affection, and not by the rule of reason.

Worse could not be said. Not only had he allowed his passions to rule his intellect, his heart to rule his head, like a beast or one of the lower orders of humanity devoid of the godlike faculty of reason, he had also acted without the counsel that all kings were bound to seek and take. Moreover, it soon emerged, his marriage to Queen Elizabeth had failed to interrupt his search for sexual satisfaction elsewhere. Further bastards were being added to Edward V's siblings up to the end of his father's life.

Edward and Elizabeth's marriage was secret, in a private place, and had been successfully concealed, who knows for how long. Hence we have no eyewitness accounts or wholly reliable evidence. It is usually stated that Edward and Elizabeth were married at Grafton Regis in Northamptonshire, the Wydeville seat, early in the morning of 1 May 1464. 'At which marriage were no persons present, but the groom, the bride, the Duchess of Bedford (her mother), the priest, two gentlewomen, and a young man to help the priest sing'. This was nevertheless a larger congregation than for Eleanor Butler's marriage! Edward then consummated the match. 'After which spousals ended, he went to bed [with her], and so tarried there upon three or four hours, and after departed to Stony Stratford', where he pretended that he had been hunting and none were the wiser. A day or two later he came to stay at Grafton, staying for four days, 'she nightly to his bed was brought, in so secret manner, that almost none but her mother knew of'.[48] Polydore Vergil also denies that her father Lord Rivers knew anything about it. This account is the fullest and most circumstantial, but it is also, as is so often the case, one of the latest and decidedly second-hand. It was the work forty years later of the chronicler Robert Fabian, who was a child, most probably an apprentice and in London at the time, and decidedly not a witness, yet historians have tended to rely on it. What Fabian wrote cannot be refuted and may indeed be authentic: long ago Cora L. Scofield showed that the King's route from London to Leicester enabled him to stay over the night of 30 April/1 May at Stony Stratford, so the King could indeed have been at Grafton that morning before journeying on to Northampton.[49] The second visit is impossible and none of the story can be authoritatively confirmed. It could be true, however. Rival versions of what happened were in circulation thirty years before Fabian wrote and his account is difficult to square with other evidence, not about the marriage but nevertheless related to it.

Fabian records a proper marriage service, admittedly secret, but sung by priest and clerk with five witnesses present, and presumably therefore in the household chapel or oratory at Grafton. Much later it may have been depicted as a conventional church wedding in a triptych of dubious provenance. Within an architectural setting, the centre panel shows the joining of hands of the royal bridegroom and bride in front of a bishop and reredos, two gentlemen and two males, one a courtier and the other a priest, in attendance. The side panels contain two ladies and three gentlewomen fashionably attired as courtiers.[50] Even if Edward's wedding is indeed the subject, the altarpiece nevertheless exaggerates greatly the formality, publicity and the numbers attending. In contrast, Richard III's *Titulus Regius* of 1483 states that it took place

> without the knowing or assent of the lords of this land . . .
> privately and secretly, with[out] reading of banns, in a private
> chamber, a profane place, and not openly in the face of the
> church, after the law of God's church, but contrary thereunto,
> and the laudable custom of the Church of England. [51]

All sources concur that the agreement was a marriage, not merely a betrothal. Two claim to know who the priest was. About 1471, one source incidentally records that Master John Eborall, 'a good man and a great preacher', rector 1443-70 of Paulerspury (Northants.), had offered to intercede for Robert Catesby of Newenham (Northants.) in a land dispute with the Queen and had indeed done so, 'supposing that he might have done good in the matter, forasmuch as he was then in favour because he married King Edward and Queen Elizabeth together (as he then affirmed)'.[52] His church of Paulerspury is only just up the Great North Road from Grafton and Stony Stratford. We do not know where Eborall was buried and hence whether he was the priest interred before the high altar at the London Minories to whom *Hearne's Fragment* attributes the marriage.[53]

There were at least three earlier variants of the story. First of all, there is the love story, that Edward wanted to bed Elizabeth and that she resisted. She said that she was too good to be a concubine, a knife was put to her throat, variously by Edward and herself, and she said that she would rather die than say yes. That version was circulating orally in Venice not later than 1468, perhaps even in 1466, when it was included with twenty-seven others in the unpublished manuscript *Of Admirable Women* by Antonio Cornazzano.[54]

Elizabeth's virtue and constancy were already legendary. The dagger story recurs in 1483 in Mancini's account, most probably encountered in England but possibly in France or Italy. The preference for death over dishonour, indeed almost the same words, in More's *History*, can only derive from an English source.

None of these mention the other romantic feature, common to the Gregory, pseudo-Warkworth, and other London chronicles, that the marriage occurred on the first day of May – already associated with love and romance. 'Fresh May', old January's love in Chaucer's *Merchant's Tale*, 'like the bright morrow of May' was 'fulfilled of all beauty and pleasure'. 'The month of May', declares the *Book of Alexander*, was

> a glorious time,
> When the birds create a wonderful sound,
> The fields are clothed in beautiful attire,
> And the unwed maiden sighs.[55]

Mayday, the feast of the apostles Philip and James, was when Edward, like other suitors, was expected by courtly convention to declare his love for his lady, without entering any binding contract. Was this a coincidence in date or an unhistorically romantic addition to a story whose early stages had been secret? Whilst the Gregory chronicler lived through and wrote up the years 1453-70, his account is unlikely to be earlier than that of Cornazzano; the *Short Latin Chronicle* was not written before 1471. All could have the same oral source.

Thirdly, there was a counter-interpretation, supposedly common and public knowledge in 1483, that the marriage was procured by 'sorcery and witchcraft committed by the same Elizabeth and her mother Jacquetta, Duchess of Bedford'. Although this charge is not recorded at Jacquetta's sorcery trial in 1469-70, the duchess was accused of possessing statuettes of the King and Queen, presumably to put them in love with one another.[56] Far from being an exemplary tale, in this version the marriage was unnatural, sinful, and procured by the black arts. 'What obloquy ran after of his marriage, how the King was enchanted by the duchess of Bedford, I here pass over', wrote Fabian.[57] Clearly he had come across such obloquies.

Not all these legends can be true. All apparently were circulating by 1470. Though writing long afterwards, under Henry VIII, More fleshes out the beginnings of the story with what seems to be an authentic tradition. Dame Elizabeth Grey was another of those unfortunate ladies victimised by the Wars of the Roses who petitioned the King to relieve her loss. Her father had contracted with Edward Lord Ferrers of Groby (d.1457) for her to marry his eldest son Sir John Grey, heir to the Ferrers of Groby barony. John and Elizabeth had two sons, Thomas and Richard, uterine elder brothers to the future Edward V. But John was slain on the Lancastrian side at the second battle of St Albans in 1461. As he died before inheriting, Elizabeth had no entitlement to dower. During the lifetime of her mother-in-law Elizabeth Lady Ferrers, she was dependent solely on the modest jointure worth 100 marks ($£66$ 13s 4d) – the three manors of Woodham Ferrers (Essex), Brington and Newbottle (Northants.) – settled in trust on her and her husband. Now married again to Sir John Bourchier, Lady Ferrers denied her daughter-in-law even these, conveying them in 1461 to a London vintner, most probably for resettlement on herself. Hence, writes More, 'this poor lady made humble suit unto the King that she might be restored unto such small lands as her late husband had given her in jointure'. Four bills survive from interlocking chancery suits: the future Queen's suit for the lands against the trustees, who were subpoenaed on 5 February 1462; her father Rivers' suit against Lady Ferrers and her second husband (subpoena, 12 May 1463) to desist from lawsuits for payment of the bonds for Elizabeth's dowry of 500 marks ($£333$ 6s 8d) that he had already paid; and the latters' denials that the lands were in trust for Elizabeth at all. No verdicts survive. However since two of the three surviving trustees confirmed that they held the three manors to Elizabeth's use, the other being noncommittal, it seems more likely that she won without recourse to the King. The relevant subpoenas are dated to 1462-3, not 1464, Elizabeth certainly held her jointure in 1466-7, when Queen,[58] and her possession is implied in her agreement with Hastings in 1464.

Recovery of her jointure, however, was only half the battle, for her son Thomas should have already inherited his grandfather Lord Ferrers' own Astley inheritance, which was to pass instead to his second son (and Thomas' uncle) Edward Grey of Astley (Warks.). The Ferrers of Groby inheritance itself actually belonged to Elizabeth's mother-in-law Lady Ferrers. In 1462 she settled Groby (Leics.) itself and the other principal properties jointly on herself and her second husband for life. He was not to die until 1495, twelve years after his wife, and there was a risk that the properties might thereafter be entailed away from Thomas.[59] Given that Sir John Bourchier was son of the King's uncle Lord Treasurer Essex, who continued to back him, Elizabeth had good grounds for alarm. It was to secure Edward's favour over those properties that Elizabeth still needed royal support in 1464 and hence access to the King.

There are two significant pieces of evidence. First of all, Elizabeth contracted with her distant kinsman William Lord Hastings for the marriage of her eldest son Thomas (or Richard should he die) to the eldest daughter born to Hastings, his brother or sister in the next five years. If any Astley or Ferrers lands were recovered, Hastings and Elizabeth were to share the proceeds until the heir came of age. Hastings was to pay 500 marks (£333 6s 8d) for the match, but if the boys died without issue, Elizabeth was to repay half. He had secured a potentially valuable husband for an as yet unborn daughter or niece and a share of any proceeds that fell in. Elizabeth was giving up her most valuable asset, her heir's marriage and indeed half of any revenues accrued, in return for help in securing the boys and for the hard cash: 500 marks was a reasonable matrimonial valuation for Thomas. Elizabeth was willing to enter into such an unequal match, we may deduce, because, in his capacity as the King's chamberlain, Hastings had influence with the King and controlled access to him. The date for this transaction, 13

April 1464, was only nineteen days before her supposed marriage to the King.[60] It shows that Hastings, the King's closest intimate, did not anticipate the marriage. Possibly Edward kept it secret from his closest friend. Surely Hastings could not have demanded nor would Elizabeth have conceded such an unequal agreement had her betrothal been concluded? Had she met the King, still more if she had dazzled him, no such contract with Hastings would have been needed. Hence it was as a result of this agreement that Edward and Elizabeth met and that she was able to exploit her attractions. On 13 April, therefore, no marriage was intended. If one occurred on 1 May, it was indeed on impulse.

Elizabeth and Hastings were apparently successful in recovering at least some of the Astley lands, for on 10 August Hastings was granted the wardship of Elizabeth's son Thomas, now a royal ward, as kin and heir of Edward late Lord Ferrers, the custody of any properties that Thomas had inherited, and the marriage of Thomas. The King signed the warrant himself:[61] a favour to Hastings, not the Queen. Once the lands were secured and Thomas thereby became a royal ward, Hastings could have been double-crossing Elizabeth to secure the lot; more probably he intended implementing their contract and allowing Elizabeth her cut as agreed. It could be that Elizabeth had extracted this concession in return for her hand. But surely she had no need for such a deal once married to the King and would have preferred to hang on to her son herself. Likewise the King would not have given up the custody and marriage of his stepson to Hastings: indeed, once his marriage was made public, Hastings' grant lapsed and Edward IV bought a much better match for Thomas. Furthermore Hastings would not have proceeded further had he known of the marriage. The extremely tough deal driven by Hastings may partly explain the hostility of the Queen thereafter. Unless we presume that Edward was so anxious to conceal his marriage that he hid it even from his most trusted friend, which is feasible, and was prepared even to flout the interests of his new wife and stepchildren, which is not, it seems that the marriage cannot yet have been concluded.

There is one other piece of circumstantial evidence to the same effect. The county of Chester was normally reserved for the crown prince. Its grant during pleasure on 30 August 1464 to Edward's brother Clarence was surely made in his capacity as the King's heir apparent.[62] The grant never took effect, because of changed circumstances, the marriage of the King, any progeny from which would take precedence. The grant implies that no marriage was intended as late as 30 August – a mere three weeks before his fatal announcement – or that as late as 30 August Edward did not expect his sex-oriented ceremony to ensnare him in matrimony. In short the Mayday marriage may be a myth. If a ceremony happened then, Edward did not intend to be bound by it. His marriage – or his realisation that he was stuck with it – most probably dates after 10 and probably 30 August and before 20 September. And if Mayday is a myth, what about the location at Grafton? Circumstantial evidence in its favour is the King's itinerary and the proximity of Eborall's parish.

Cornazzano may not have erred as much as Dr Fahy supposed. If the marriage may not have happened at Grafton, it could indeed have taken place in the City where the King held court at a palace accessible by water, obviously Westminster. Reading Abbey was also alongside the Thames. That the King and Queen's first child was born in February 1466 is not conclusive proof that Elizabeth was not with child since live births are not the only consequences of pregnancy. Moreover the King's passion may well have been common knowledge to the courtiers, certainly to Hastings who introduced them, and he may well have been able to keep the actual wedding secret, since such passions were commonplace, frequently resulted in intercourse, and had not hitherto resulted in marriage. The King may have made promises on earlier occasions to get his way. In this scenario, Elizabeth was introduced by Hastings to the King, who conceded her demands relatively early in the relationship. It was later, after 10 August, either that marriage proved essential to bed her or that he found himself committed to her. The long secrecy described by the chroniclers, with 1 May in mind for the marriage, was perhaps a few weeks or even a few days. Yet secrecy there was, both to pre-empt hostility to the event and afterwards, presumably to defer criticism. That made sense to Edward and delay was perhaps a small price for Elizabeth.

One cannot help wondering, however, whether marriage was really what Edward intended. Fabian passes over tales that 'after he would have refused her'.[63]

It appears likely that Edward had made promises and even gone through a form of marriage before to get his way, to Eleanor Butler and others, but in privacy, without witnesses prepared to testify or before witnesses who were willing to perjure themselves. Whilst a verbal exchange of vows made a binding contract, what if one party denied it? God may have known, but Man could not. Such promises could be dangerous, as Commynes said.[64] Did Edward really conduct his clandestine marriage so publicly, with so many witnesses, for which Fabian is our only source, rather than the privacy of *Titulus Regius*?[65] Or did Elizabeth's mother recruit people willing to testify (or mis-testify) to events? Did Edward intend this to be merely another seduction secured by a false marriage but found himself held to contract? Claims of a previous marriage would have stymied any diplomatic match. And what was the implication of any pregnancy: did Edward seize the opportunity for a son and heir and, like his grandson Henry VIII, rush ahead with marriage to make the forthcoming bastard legitimate? The contrasting fates of Mary Boleyn, mother to Henry VIII's bastard Richmond but unmarried, and her sister Anne, who held out for a promise of matrimony, are instructive.

Our only strictly contemporary source is a newsletter from Milanese merchants at Bruges dated 5 October 1464. 'The espousals and benediction' were already complete, they reported. 'The greater part of the lords and the people in general seem very much dissatisfied with all this', they continued, 'and for this sake are finding means to annul it. All the peers are holding great consultations in the town of Reading, where the King is'. How could the match be annulled, other than by refuting its validity, and how could that be impugned, both parties assenting, other than by an earlier marriage? Does not this report imply the Lucy tribunal to which More referred, especially as any such efforts failed? The match had been accepted by Michaelmas (29 September): it took a week for the news to reach Bruges.[66] The report indicates that there was doubt about the validity of the marriage of Edward V's parents from the start and hence about the legitimacy of the offspring, the future Edward V included. The blame rests firmly with Edward V's father, whose dishonourable conduct, faithlessness and duplicity, as much as his sexual immorality, was two decades later to place in doubt the title of a son who had not then even been born.

The Rise of the Wydevilles 1464-69

Once the King's marriage was public, it had to be accepted. Edward's mentor Warwick, who had been negotiating for the French king's sister-in-law, had been made to look foolish. Clarence, the King's brother and heir, was one of those who looked down on Elizabeth and her family. Both were obliged on Michaelmas day (29 September 1464) to lead their new Queen into the chapel of Reading Abbey for her public acceptance by the great council. If the Duchess Cecily bewailed the match, as several sources report, and tried to thwart it by pleading a precontract,[67] the attempt failed. What could she achieve, when the King denied it anyway? Was it not her word against his? Loyally denying that the marriage caused a rift, the Crowland Continuator pointed out much later how Elizabeth's title had been solemnly accepted by the political elite at the time.[68] Of course it was. What else could they do? Politics and foreign affairs alike had to take account of the new situation. But disapproval at Edward's choice and its subsequent repercussions endured and coloured the lives of both them and their offspring.

In the short term the match testified to the young King's growing independence of the Nevilles, who had managed many of his affairs in his early years, and contributed to the breach with them and especially with Warwick, now head of the family. This took time to develop, a key stage being the dismissal as chancellor of his brother Archbishop George Neville in 1467, and broke into civil war in 1469. A monk of Crowland attributed the breach between the King and Warwick to the King's marriage, which the authoritative Yorkist civil servant, who continued the chronicle, denied: the rift arose from differences in foreign policy.[69] Most historians, including the present author, have accepted his guidance. The monk, however, was not alone in his belief. Of the same mind were Waurin and pseudo-Warkworth.[70] Clearly many contemporaries saw Edward's marriage as the root cause: if Warwick did not object, perhaps many thought he should. Moreover the difference in foreign policy, in which Warwick's Francophile stance was rejected for a pro-Burgundian one, was fostered by the Wydevilles themselves, who made the most of Jacquetta's Burgundian links. The Queen herself was the patroness and her brother Anthony Lord Scales her champion in the celebrated London tournament in 1467 with the Grand Bastard of Burgundy that paved the way to the marriage of Edward's sister Margaret to Charles the Bold, Duke of Burgundy. Other domestic frictions also mattered.

Edward IV was the most generous of kings. Since he was the best endowed, with the principality of Wales, duchies of Cornwall, Lancaster, and York, the county of Chester, the Queen's lands, and the copious forfeitures of attainted Lancastrians, he could afford to be. By 1464 he had given away all the forfeitures and had moved on to Lancaster and Chester to endow his brothers on the scale he thought appropriate for royal princes: £4,400 a year for Clarence in 1467, three times that of the original duke of York. Endowing a queen at that level, the conventional amount, was a strain.

Her household and estates offered job opportunities and rewards to her cousins, the Hautes for instance. The King had not only his Queen to provide for, as was the case with foreign brides. She had a father, four brothers, five sisters and two sons, all of them ill-provided for according to the standards that Edward thought appropriate. Rivers was created an earl, appointed constable and treasurer of England, with revenues to match. The Queen's sisters were married to the duke of Buckingham, the heirs of the earls of Arundel and Essex, and to those of Lords Grey of Ruthin and Herbert. The latters' fathers were also created earls of Kent and Pembroke, since Edward evidently considered that for any of his sisters-in-law to be less than countesses was to disparage them. The King paid for these matches, in titles, in cash, in remission of wardship and in endowments of land. Herbert, now the Queen's in-law, was able to capture other wards for his other daughters and was confident of recovering their forfeited inheritances from royal grantees, notably the Nevilles.

The contract with Hastings having been set aside, Edward's stepson Thomas Grey was married instead to the King's niece Anne Holland, daughter of his sister Anne and heiress of the duchy of Exeter: for this the King paid 4,000 marks (£2,666 13s 4d). When in 1469 his own eldest daughter was betrothed, her husband was created a duke:[71] had all seven of his daughters been provided for in this way, the peerage would have been packed and the crown impoverished! Moreover sons were anticipated, who would need to be endowed as royal dukes.

Seeing former Lancastrians and those 'of mean calling' so advantaged was no doubt irritating to stalwart Yorkists, the 'old noble blood' and 'old royal blood' of the realm. In these years (1464–69), moreover, it was the King's new favourites Rivers, Stafford of Southwick and, much more important, Pembroke who most influenced the King. Edward was entitled to take counsel from whom he chose. Circumspection, however, was advisable: perhaps more circumspection than he chose. Finding advancement for his new in-laws inevitably denied it to others; indeed some properties formerly given to Warwick and the archbishop were taken back. Worse was to come if Pembroke was to recover Richmond honour and the Percy inheritance for his prospective sons-in-law. Many of the marriages that had already happened were apparently to Warwick's secret displeasure, not least because he too had heirs to marry and Edward had snapped up all the eligible parties. Warwick's male heir was George Neville, son of his brother John, who was to have married Anne Holland and to have secured the dukedom that the Nevilles so coveted before Edward snapped her up for his stepson. Probably Buckingham had been intended for one of Warwick's daughters. And Warwick's alternative proposal, to marry his two daughters to the King's two brothers, was vetoed: Edward wanted to arrange their marriages for himself. It is therefore understandable, if constitutionally inexcusable, that Warwick determined in 1469 to take matters into his own hands. If not strictly the cause of the crisis, the Queen's family were certainly the principal victims.

The Crisis of the Dynasty 1469-71

The 1469 uprising was launched by Warwick, his brother the archbishop and the King's brother Clarence, lately married to Warwick's eldest daughter Isabel. It culminated in the defeat of Edward's favourites on 27 July at Edgecote near Banbury, after which Earl Rivers, grandfather to the future Edward V, his son Sir John Wydeville, Pembroke and Devon were eliminated. Scales' estates were ravaged and Jacquetta was charged with sorcery. Queen Elizabeth's former brother-in-law, Sir Edward Grey of Astley, was on Warwick's side. King Edward was imprisoned first at Warwick, then at Warwick's Yorkshire castle of Middleham. The earl ruled in Edward's name. A parliament was summoned to meet on 22 September at York, where Warwick felt strong, but it was cancelled to enable Warwick to quell Lancastrian rebellion. To achieve this, he had to release the King, who resumed his rule, reconciled himself with his erstwhile opponents in a great council at Westminster in 1469-70 and reconstructed the aristocratic foundations of his regime to ensure that there was no repetition.

The rebels' manifesto had drawn ominous parallels between Edward's rule and that of former bad kings, who had been deposed, had denounced the King's favourites for evil counsel and had declared their intention to provide good governance themselves. Historians, including the present author, have presumed an intention to follow the precedent of Richard Duke of York and to have Warwick declared protector. One wonders, however, what was their fall-back position, if Edward would not co-operate, or if indeed the plan was to depose him. We cannot now demonstrate conclusively that allegations of Edward's bastardy circulating in 1469 originated with Warwick: later Louis XI alleged that Edward was the son of the Duchess Cecily and a French archer.[72] The English were always inclined to doubt the legitimacy of princes born abroad, like Edward at Rouen. Nor does the rebuttal of the charge of sorcery formally lodged against the Duchess Jacquetta in council at Warwick in August explicitly accuse her of using magic to bring about Edward's marriage.[73] Allegations of bastardy would have undermined Edward's right and allegations of witchcraft those of his daughters (and any future sons), thus clearing the way for York's second surviving son Clarence, who had, not coincidentally, just married Warwick's daughter. Next year the Lincolnshire rebels promoted Clarence's candidature. Moreover the involvement of Thomas Wake, who actually made the sorcery charge, is suggestive in other ways. As we have seen, he was a Warwick retainer, the widower of Margaret Lucy, and a native of Northamptonshire well-placed to know about Edward's wooing of Elizabeth Wydeville, particularly as he (or his father), as feoffee, had presented Eborall to his living of Paulerspury. Wake was shortly to become the second husband of Elizabeth Lady Latimer,[74] the sister of Margaret Countess of Shrewsbury and hence aunt of Eleanor Butler. A relationship already existed. Her husband was an idiot, in Warwick's custody, and her son and son-in-law had died for Warwick at Edgecote. Jacquetta is the source of much of what we know at this time. She appealed Wake among others for her husband's death. We know of the sorcery charge he levelled at her only because she wanted herself cleared and had her acquittal certified.[75] There may have been charges and rebuttals also about the King's bastardy and precontract, but, ignorant of the future loss of the council records, nobody had them exemplified. Arguments from silence are always dangerous. What was rejected in the past due to the absence of evidence now appears possible: that 1469 was a preview of 1483, when Edward V was the victim, and that it was the model for Richard Duke of Gloucester, an observer from the other side in 1469?

Edward's reconstruction included the betrothal of his eldest daughter Elizabeth, aged three, to the four-year-old George Neville, Warwick's male heir, the son of his brother John. John became Marquis Montagu and George was created duke of Bedford. It was a key ploy to provide for Montagu in non-material ways, to supply a partner of appropriate rank and a duchy for George, to give the Nevilles an alternative, legitimate, route to the crown – for George mattered as much to Warwick as his daughters – and to provide Elizabeth with a husband who was already a great heir.

Of course it involved conceding the succession – and England's most important diplomatic asset – but Edward intended Elizabeth's title in due course to be superseded by a son. It also, and crucially, committed Montagu to the legitimacy of Edward's marriage and his children born and unborn, including the future Edward V. With Edward back in charge, Jacquetta's sorcery case was brought to trial, Wake failed to substantiate his accusations, and the charges were quashed. But not forgotten. *Titulus Regius* in 1483 claims them still to be notorious.

Edward had miscalculated. Warwick and Clarence rebelled once more in the spring of 1470 and fled into exile. The King refused any further concessions. Desperate, they combined with Lancastrian exiles and with Louis XI of France and invaded in the autumn. Montagu wanted more material benefits and drove Edward IV into exile.

Henry VI reigned again. This was his Readeption. Yorkist supporters were executed like the Earl of Worcester, made their peace, or took sanctuary. Amongst the latter was Edward's heavily pregnant Queen and her daughters. For six months she was protected from molestation by the privileges of Westminster Abbey, 'in right great trouble, sorrow and heaviness . . . with all manner patience, and as constantly as hath been seen at any time [for] any of such high estate to endure'. On 2 November, with great mistiming, she at last bore a son, the future Edward V. His godfathers were Thomas Milling and John Eastney, respectively abbot and prior of Westminster; his godmother was Elizabeth Lady Scope. 'Those faithful to King Edward drew some consolation from the event', writes the Continuator, 'while King Henry's supporters, much the more numerous at this stage, thought the birth of the child of no importance'. The infant was heir to nothing, his parents exiled or in sanctuary, his future uncertain in the extreme.

But the new regime lasted only six months. King Edward was back in London on 11 April 1471. From St Paul's he went by water to Westminster, where he gave thanks and was crowned again by Cardinal Bourchier. For 'a long time he abode and sojourned there', comforting

> The Queen and the other ladies also.
> His sweet babes full tenderly he did kiss.
> The young Prince he beheld and in his arms did bear.

What she presented to him was 'a fair son, a Prince, to the King's greatest joy, to his heart's singular comfort and gladness, and to all them that truly loved and served him'.

> Thus his bale was turned to bliss.
> After sorrow, joy, the course of the world is.[76]

Edward's battles were yet to be won. Next Edward turned on his enemies, destroying Warwick at Barnet and Henry VI in the same month. Now he was more secure on his throne than ever. And Prince Edward was heir to it all.

3

HEIR PRESUMPTIVE

The Prince as a Symbol

The seal was set on Edward IV's triumphs by the birth of a son to continue his dynasty. It was 'the great bounty of our lord God', he declared, that 'has pleased to send unto us our first begotten son, whole and furnished in nature, to succeed us in our realms of England, of France and lordship of Ireland. For the which we thank most humbly his infinite magnificence'. The Prince was God's 'precious visitation and gift and our most desired treasure'.¹ The victories that ushered in his father's second reign, moreover, abruptly transformed the future of the six-month-old infant born in, and restricted to, the sanctuary of Westminster. Prince Edward was the King's first begotten son, as the King's own grants and petitions to the Prince himself constantly stated. His own letters patent (and the inscription on his great seal) were in the name of 'Edward, first begotten (*primogenitus*) son of the illustrious King of England and France Edward IV, Prince of Wales, Duke of Cornwall and Earl of Chester' and were dated by the regnal years of 'his dread lord and father'. 'By the Prince', which headed his signet letters, clearly aped his father's 'By the King'. Henceforth it was the Prince's soul that was coupled with those of his parents in licences in mortmain and replaced that of his sister Elizabeth, over whom he now took precedence. Henceforth Edward was to be regarded as a prince, indeed *the* Prince, Prince of Wales, heir to the crown of England, and the potential king that he so briefly became. Although doubtless initially oblivious, Prince Edward was a central part of the King's celebrations. God had given his verdict on the Yorkist cause in battle, had unexpectedly confounded the much stronger (but divided) forces of their foes, and placed their principal opponents at their mercy, which his father did not fail to exploit. The King gave thanks in church. The official histories and verses that commemorated his triumph celebrated also the birth of his heir.

Complete though the victory appeared, some dissidents remained at large and the events of 1469-70 had taught how the most solidly established regime could divide against itself. Determination not to risk any repetition made King Edward extremely cautious about popular unrest. His second reign was also finite, lasting only to his death. Up to now his heir presumptive was the Princess Elizabeth, whom he had promised in marriage to Montagu's son George Neville in 1469, but daughters offered no stability or continuity. They could not reign, so contemporaries supposed, nor could they rule, govern or command obedience, wage war or fight. For a king to leave only daughters promised, at the very least, the conveyance of the crown to a husband, if not to the scion of a faction like George Neville, then most probably a foreign potentate, and, at worst, division and civil war. The birth of a son, in contrast, foretold an undisputed and indisputable succession. Prince Edward's birth prolonged the House of York well beyond his father's lifetime, promised continuity to the Yorkist dynasty and all it stood for, and eased any fears and doubts about what would happen when King Edward died. Moreover the Prince survived infancy and was well on the way to adulthood when his known history ended. The births of a second son, Richard of Shrewsbury, Duke of York, in 1473, and of a third, George of Windsor, Duke of Bedford, in 1477, emphasised the point. York was the permanent ruling house.

From the moment of his return, the King had regarded Prince Edward as his heir: the traditional titles and endowments were bound to follow. 'With the assent of the lords of our blood', King Edward formally created his son Prince of Wales and Earl of Chester at the palace of Westminster on 11 June 1471. Creation as Duke of Cornwall followed. The lands and estates attached to the titles were added in further charters dated 17 July. By the time he was eight months old, the Prince already possessed a chancellor, a chamberlain and steward of his household, probably a subset of that of the King or Queen, and his own council to administer his estates up to the age of fourteen. This was more than a fiction, since the council was authorised to appoint to offices on the Prince's estates during the Prince's pleasure until he was fourteen.[2] The earldom of Chester had been borne by all eldest sons of kings since the Lord Edward, Edward I. All eldest sons of kings since Edward of Caernarvon, later King Edward II, had been princes of Wales. In 1337 the Black Prince was the first heir apparent to be duke of Cornwall. Similarly all since Edward III had been knights of the order of the Garter, to which the future Edward V was to be briefly sovereign. The next Garter chapter was held on 24 April 1472, the King presiding at Windsor in person, at which seven vacancies – the stalls of Warwick and his brother among others – were filled. First on the list of those elected was 'my lord the Prince'; the King of Portugal came next. The others included those longstanding and stalwart Yorkists Barons Ferrers of Chartley, Mountjoy and Dynham.[3] Any royal grants to the Prince came free of fee and fine and he was routinely allowed tuns of red wine by the chief butler of England. Yet other titles, as Earl of March and Earl of Pembroke, were added in 1479, and also the possessions appurtenant to them.[4]

On 3 July 1471 a great council of the Lords spiritual and temporal and some selected knights met with the King in the parliament chamber at Westminster. The King's uncle Cardinal Bourchier acknowledged his great-nephew as the future Edward V and swore allegiance to him on the gospels:

I Thomas, Cardinal Archbishop of Canterbury, acknowledge, take and repute you Edward, Prince of Wales, Duke of Cornwall, and Earl of Chester, first begotten son of our sovereign lord Edward IV King of England and of France and Lord of Ireland, to be the true and undoubted heir to our said sovereign lord, as to the crowns and realms of England and of France and the lordship of Ireland. And I promise and swear, that if in case hereafter it happen to you, by God's disposition, to outlive our said sovereign lord, I shall then take and accept you for true, very and righteous King of England etc. And faith and trouth to you shall bear, and in all things truly and faithfully behave me towards you and your heirs, as a true and faithful subject ought to behave to his sovereign lord and righteous King of England etc. So help me God and his saints, and these holy gospels.

In corroboration, the cardinal also signed the act with his own hand. The oath was sworn and the act signed by the other forty-six people present: Archbishop Neville and eight bishops, including Chancellor Stillington of Bath; the five English dukes, including the King's brothers Clarence and Gloucester and brother-in-law Suffolk and young Buckingham; five earls including the Prince's great-uncle Essex, sixteen barons and eleven knights. Besides the Prince's three uncles and two great-uncles on his father's side, the oath was taken by his maternal uncles Anthony, now 2nd Earl Rivers, Buckingham, Maltravers, Grey of Ruthin, Strange and Bourchier, the last five of whom were married to sisters of the Queen. Lords Hastings, Berners, Ferrers of Chartley, Howard, Mountjoy and Dynham were longstanding Yorkist partisans, all of whom owed their titles to the King.[5] It was an impressive and representative display of loyalty. Fourteen of the forty-six had died when the anticipated event ensued twelve years later and the Prince became Edward V: Gloucester, Buckingham and perhaps Stillington then failed to keep their oaths. Taken twelve years before the eventuality arose and witnessed by their peers, there was no question of duress.

Nor indeed was there any duress after dinner on 9 November 1477 when, in the presence of the great council, Gloucester led the dukes of Buckingham and Suffolk, Dorset, Rivers and their peers in rendering homage to the seven-year-old Prince. Unbelted and 'on both his knees, putting his hands between the Prince's hands, [Gloucester] did him homage for such lands as he had of him and so kissed him'. In response, in one of the few speeches recorded of him, the Prince thanked 'his said uncle that it liked him to do it so humbly'.[6] Rather than making a formality of what was by this date an almost meaningless gesture, Gloucester went much further than was necessary and, from the King's youngest brother, his conduct carried particular weight just ahead of the trial of the middle brother Clarence. Not only did it signal his consent to what was happening, but it surely stiffened any waverers. Gloucester was well-rewarded for it. Almost everybody who was anybody in 1483 had witnessed the duke's oath in 1471 and/or his homage in 1477.

Edward held no immediate parliament in 1471, but it was obvious that one would be required in due course to confirm his dynastic revolution, to attaint the vanquished and to reward those who had returned to their allegiance. Plenty of negotiation was to precede the formal legislation. Prince Edward's own promotion was an important part of the consolidation necessitated by the upheavals of 1469-71. Once the worst culprits had been slain or executed after Tewkesbury, Edward was willing to make peace with the rest. Diehard Lancastrians, now bereft of a cause, like Sir John Fortescue, Queen Margaret's chancellor in exile and prime propagandist, and Dr John Morton, were allowed to make their peace and even to recover their forfeited possessions. If Fortescue was too old for further employment, Morton was earmarked for promotion – he was soon keeper of the rolls of chancery and Bishop of Ely en route for the chancellorship, archbishopric of Canterbury and cardinalate under Henry VII. Warwick and Montagu, Henry VI and his son were dead and Margaret of Anjou a captive, but one foe lay beyond Edward's reach – King Louis XI of France, the mediator between Warwick and Margaret and key instigator of the

Readeption. Understandably Edward wanted revenge on him and had allies in the dukes of Burgundy and Brittany. Treaties with them made an invasion like that of Henry V look feasible. Edward might recover the lost English possessions in France and could make good his 'right' – the otherwise empty title of king of France that he still bore. There were also advantageous by-products: foreign war was good for law and order at home, since unruly and troublesome elements were diverted abroad; the expenses of the navy could be cut if Edward ruled both shores of the Channel; and war offered advancement to militaristic 'younger brothers'. So declared John Alcock, Bishop of Rochester, standing in for the sick Bishop Stillington, to King Edward, the Lords and Commons in the parliament chamber on 6 October 1472. The first week of the parliamentary session was spent in formal business, such as the choice and presentation of William Allington as speaker.[7]

Contracting the necessary alliances was no problem for Edward, although it proved difficult to hold his new allies to his agreement. Much more difficult was persuading the Commons to vote the necessary funds for what was bound to be an extremely expensive venture. Late-fifteenth-century taxpayers and their representatives were reluctant to vote taxes and, even when persuaded, invariably voted too little. They remembered that Edward had requested and secured funding once before for a war that had not happened. If parliament was therefore primarily forward looking, in anticipation of foreign triumphs and glories, the opportunity was also taken by the regime to celebrate past successes, which indeed it was hoped, through a paean of ceremonial self-congratulation, might induce the Commons to loosen their purse-strings. The central figure for both was Louis of Bruges, Lord Gruthuyse, who had received Edward IV in exile and had helped him prepare his return, whom the King now created Earl of Winchester (with an annuity of £200) in grateful thanks.

Lord Gruthuyse arrived on embassy from Burgundy with the proposals of his master Charles the Bold in September 1472 and concluded agreements with the King for an aggressive alliance against France. He was met and feasted by the Calais garrison, the corporations of Dover, Canterbury and Rochester, and recuperated briefly at Westminster in St Stephen's College deanery, before he was escorted by Thomas Vaughan to Windsor Castle for another round of festivities. Two chambers were provided for him richly hung with arras and equipped with beds of estate, an attempt to match the splendour of the court of Burgundy, to which Gruthuyse was accustomed. The King took him to the Queen, who entertained him with music played by her ladies and herself: the King danced with his eldest daughter, the six-year-old Elizabeth of York. Next day, after Gruthuyse had attended divine service and taken breakfast with the King and had been given a bejewelled gold cup containing a fragment of a unicorn's horn, the even younger Prince Edward appeared. He was carried by his chamberlain Thomas Vaughan, who bade Gruthuyse welcome in the Prince's name. Presumably the Prince had not yet learnt to talk. Hunting, dinner, a visit to the castle garden and vineyard of pleasure, filled the hours until a great banquet given by the Queen in her chamber. Again Princess Elizabeth was deemed old enough to attend and to dance, this time with Henry Duke of Buckingham. King and Queen took Gruthuyse to three specially equipped chambers of pleasure, where he took a bath with Lord Chamberlain Hastings, and afterwards took dessert of 'green ginger, divers syrops, comfits and hippocras (spiced wine)' before turning in. On the morrow, Gruthuyse returned to Westminster for a week.

The King, as we have seen, was at the opening of parliament on Tuesday 6 October. A week later, on Tuesday 13 October, the feast of St Edward the Confessor, who of course lay buried at Westminster,

> our most dread and liege lord kept his royal estate in his palace at Westminster. And about 10a.m. the King came into the parliament chamber in his parliament robes, wearing on his head a cap of maintenance, having before him the Lords spiritual and temporal and also the speaker of the parliament,

William Allington, the which declared before the King's good grace and his noble and sad (sober) council the intent and desire of the Commons.

Allington, of course, was the King's servant, selected as was customary by the King and salaried by him. His address consisted principally of commendation of all those involved in the victories for their 'knightly demeanings' (the royal dukes), the 'constant faith' of those, like Rivers and Hastings, who had shared the King's exile, and of those obliged to take sanctuary. 'Our sovereign lady' Queen Elizabeth was praised for her 'womanly behaviour and great constancy' and the birth of the young Prince was to 'the great joy and security of this land'. Last but not least, Allington commended 'the great humanity and kindness' of Gruthuyse to the King in exile, 'the foresaid Lord Gruthuyse being present'. After giving thanks through Bishop Alcock, the King withdrew to his chamber and Gruthuyse to the royal closet, where he hastily dressed up as an earl, before the King returned to the parliament chamber 'in his most royal majesty'. Wearing his crown and with the grandest ceremonial, Edward invested Gruthuyse as Earl of Winchester, the King's secretary reading out the patent of creation. The King then proceeded to the White Hall, where he was joined by the Queen, also crowned, and 'my lord the Prince in his robes of estate' – difficult to imagine of a year-old infant! – 'who was carried after the King by his chamberlain Master [Thomas] Vaughan'. They processed together into Westminster Abbey to the shrine of St Edward, where they made their offering. After sitting for a while in state on his throne in the choir, the King held a splendid banquet in the White Hall in the honour of the new earl, who sat on the King's left, and created a new king of arms. Gruthuyse bestowed the expected largesse on the heralds. Next day the new earl returned to Burgundy:[8] Edward's invasion was to be repeatedly postponed until 1475.

Doubtless Prince Edward missed Lord Gruthuyse's banquet in the White Hall, having returned to his cradle, but he must have been the most splendidly attired of babes in arms. No rompers and babygros for him! A surviving account records clothing delivered for his use not later than November 1472: five doublets price 6s 8d, two of velvet – purple or black – and three of satin, two being green or black; five long gowns, price 6s 8d, three being satin – purple, black, and green – and the others of black velvet; two bonnets, price 2s, one of purple velvet lined with green satin and the other of black velvet lined with black satin; and a sixth, even more splendid, long gown – perhaps what he wore for his audience with Lord Gruthuyse – cloth of gold on damask, priced £1.[9] Regrettably this is the only such account.

Meantime his father acknowledged him in parliament as 'his most entirely beloved first begotten son and heir apparent', and had the Lords and Commons ratify his charters of creation as Prince of Wales, Duke of Cornwall, and Earl of Chester. They also conceded the revenues from the estates attached to these titles with effect from Michaelmas 1472. That this transfer of possession was a reality is indicated by the protracted negotiations that Winchester College had to undertake to render homage to the new lord for their manor of Allington (Hants.). After preliminary discussions with the feodary of the Prince's honour of Wallingford and St Valery, Warden Baker and Bursar White and others unnamed had to spend ten days in London in October 1472, putting up at the Cardinal's Hat in Southwark, and a further brief visit in November for the actual homage, for which they needed their best clothes. Altogether it cost over £20. Albeit adorned with a splendid red seal, the resultant writ of 24 November is unimpressively brief. It ordered only that the college should not be distrained or molested; however, the college's endorsement to the writ – that they were exonerated from suit to the honorial court – explains why they thought it worthwhile.[10] Presumably other tenants were in the same position. About this time several gentry bound themselves in large sums to Vaughan as Prince's chamberlain. The earldom of Chester proffered £2,000 and the lordship of Haverford £80 in recognition.[11]

The Gruthuyse celebrations are the Prince's first recorded appearances – not exactly activities – on the public scene. It demonstrates the young Prince's symbolic significance. Simply to exist, to represent continuity and to be displayed, served royal and political ends. Edward's eldest sister Elizabeth, although aged only six, attended Gruthuyse's banquet and danced with her father and cousin. Tiny though he was, Prince Edward's involvement in the Gruthuyse celebrations was seen as essential. No doubt there were other ceremonial occasions, such as Christmas and Easter, for which we lack details of the celebrations penned by heralds, at which he was also on display. On all such occasions, the infant Prince had a public, if rather passive, role to play. He was the visible sign of the succession and that the House of York was to endure.

A last celebration of family solidarity before Edward's invasion of France took place at Westminster on 18 April 1475. The Prince was knighted. So were his next brother Richard Duke of York, his two older step-brothers 'the Lord Thomas [Grey] the Queen's son and his brother the Lord Richard [Grey]', and twenty others. They included some adults, headed by the Queen's youngest brother Edward (who took precedence over the barons and sons of earls), Lords Neville and St Amand, Vaughan the Prince's chamberlain, judges and courtiers. More prominent were children of the Prince's own age and adolescents, such as the earls of Shrewsbury and Wiltshire and the heirs of lords Berkeley, Audley, Stanley, Stourton and Hastings. Later the same day, before dinner, Sir Thomas Grey was created marquis of Dorset.[12]

How others regarded the Prince emerges on 28 April 1474 on his first visit to Coventry. Such princes were one of the lords of the city in their capacity as earls of Chester and enjoyed a special relationship with it. Coventry was the Prince's chamber, just as London was the King's. The city raised £80 as a gift, spending 100 marks (£66 13s 4d) on a 15-ounce gilt cup and the balance on a 'kerchief of pleasance' and associated expenses. He was greeted at New Cross by a supposed King Richard:

Welcome, full high and noble Prince, to us right

To this your chamber, so called of antiquity!

The presence of your noble person rejoices all our hearts

We all must bless the time of your nativity.

The right line of the royal line is now as it should be

Wherefore God of his goodness preserve you in bodily
    health,

To us and all your tenants here, perpetual joy, and wealth
    to all the land.

A patriarch, King Edward (the Confessor) and St George then made their speeches to the Prince 'being of the age of 4 years in a chair'. The speeches were blessedly short. Afterwards the mayor and corporation were received by the Prince, to whom they swore allegiance. Allegedly he also stood godfather to the mayor's son.

The Prince had come to Coventry from Wales,[13] where from 1473 he normally resided, principally at Ludlow in the marches. This explains his absence from some of the principal formal occasions at court, such as the funeral of his elder sister Mary in 1482 and the christening of his youngest sister Bridget in 1480. Most surprisingly, because more easily predicted, he missed the greatest celebration of his dynasty in July 1476, when his grandfather Richard Duke of York and uncle Edmund Earl of Rutland were re-interred at Fotheringhay College in the presence of the King and Queen, the royal dukes, and two of his sisters. Apart from Vaughan's house at Westminster Abbey,[14] where Abbot John Eastney (1474-98) was his godfather, the Prince does not seem to have lived much in his own residences away from Ludlow. It was there that his estate officers delivered their revenues and in 1481-2 that a royal fish (a sturgeon) was despatched from Chester. He does occur elsewhere, apparently at Haverfordwest in 1473, at Warwick with his uncle Clarence and at Coventry in 1474, at Chester in 1476, at Shrewsbury in 1478-9 and 1480, at Worcester and Wigmore Castle in 1479 and at Bewdley (Worcs.) in 1482,[15] but his signet warrants were normally dated at Ludlow from 1474. Given that we have no household accounts with which to plot his itinerary precisely, he appears quite frequently with his parents and in some years for much of the time. He was with the King at Windsor in May 1474, in April and at midsummer; in company with his mother and Cardinal Bourchier at Windsor on 18 August 1477; at Westminster for the great council from 9 November 1477 and thereafter at the parliament of January/February 1478; at The More in Rickmansworth (Herts.) on 19 May and with the King in November 1478; with him in May 1479, with both his parents from November at Woking, for Christmas, and at Greenwich on 30 December 1479; at Greenwich with the King on 16 July 1480; with the King in February, May, August and in the winter of 1481; and with both parents for Christmas 1481 at Windsor, Christmas 1482 at Eltham and for Christmas 1483 at Westminster. Although apparently always sharing the royal Christmas, the Prince normally missed the New Year festivities, at which his largesse of £3 to the heralds was usually presented *in absentia*.[16] Given the distance from the Thames Valley to Ludlow, he must have been frequently on the road.

Two examples of his symbolic significance deserve more attention, marriage and regency. The marriages of the royal family were important political opportunities for the ruler, whether contracted to subjects or to members of other royal families. Edward IV might have been more readily accepted abroad had he not squandered his own hand in marriage on Elizabeth Wydeville. He had plans for his brothers, plans primarily to his own benefit and by extension the national interest, but Clarence and Gloucester had insisted on their own choices to their own personal advantages. Only his sister Margaret of York, Duchess of Burgundy, made an advantageous diplomatic match. The King's own offspring now offered more scope. Against the alliances that might be forged, however, had to be set the dowries to be paid, for which the King's distaste was so strong as to be diplomatically counter-productive. It was a factor in his failure: none of his children were married at his death and only five did marry, none of them to foreign princes or princesses. Elizabeth herself had been betrothed as heiress presumptive in 1469 and was to be contracted, or at least considered, twice more, before ending up aged twenty as Henry VII's Queen. In 1473 her sister Cecily was engaged to the future James IV of Scotland, in preparation for Edward's campaign against France in 1475, the principal fruit of which was the betrothal of Elizabeth to the dauphin, the future Charles VIII of France. A list of nativities of the King's children of 1476-7 names Elizabeth and Cecily respectively as 'dauphiness of France and princess of Scots'.[17] Poor Mary, the short-lived middle sister, was reserve to both. Edward, however, particularly valued his French pension, which made him reluctant to exploit fully new opportunities, which threatened it, Elizabeth's marriage and war with France. These commenced with Charles the Bold's death in 1477, leaving his daughter Mary desperate for allies against France. If Clarence was a serious candidate for her hand, which Edward scotched, and Rivers less so, she actually married Archduke Maximilian, the emperor's son, and quickly bore him a son Philip, to whom Edward's fifth daughter Anne (b.1475) was proposed in 1479 and contracted next year. Less contentious was the match proposed in 1479 and again agreed in 1482 of his sixth daughter Katherine to John, the infant son of the Spanish monarchs Ferdinand of Aragon and Isabella of Castile. The French and Scottish matches had foundered before Edward's death, as he engaged in war with Scotland, and his alliance became dispensable to Louis on the treaty of Arras (1482). The other child matches lapsed with the King's death.[18]

Prince Edward had a role in such negotiations. He was five years Elizabeth's junior, but he was male and his claim to be heir apparent could not be superseded as her's had been. His hand in marriage was the most valuable of all. His consort could expect to be Queen. King Edward realised this. First of all, it was proposed in 1476 that he should marry Ferdinand and Isabella's eldest daughter and heiress presumptive, the Infanta Isabella. Negotiations dragged on till 1478, but the birth to them of a son made Princess Katherine's marriage look a more attractive Spanish match. Soundings were taken for other matches, with a daughter of the emperor – never very attractive to the English – or to a well-dowered Milanese princess. Neither proceeded very far. Much more attractive – and much more serious for both sides – was a match that would have kept Brittany out of Louis' hands. As yet Duke Francis II had only daughters. The proposal, formally ratified by the duke on 22 June 1481, was for the Prince to marry Anne, the elder daughter, who was to bring a dowry of 100,000 crowns, half payable on the day of the wedding. Younger siblings, his brother Richard and her sister Isabella, were to be substituted if either party died; if Francis had a son, the latter would marry an unnamed English daughter and the dowry would be doubled.[19] None of these contingencies arose, Anne ending up as Francis' sole heiress. She was to be queen in turn to Charles VIII and Louis XII of France. Scheduled for about 1489, any such marriage would surely have brought war with France and the loss of the pension that Edward IV so valued, but should have added Brittany to Edward V's possessions. It was surely what Edward V expected at his accession in 1483.

The second instance was the Prince's role as figurehead in 1475. This was when the King embarked, at last, on his invasion of France. King Edward took command in person. He could not rule England effectively from abroad and he was accompanied by both the royal dukes. It was not customary in England, in contrast to France, for queens to act as regents. What was customary – and there were many precedents, such as Edward III's young sons – was for a royal prince, even under age, to be left as keeper of the realm, titular head of government. On 20 June 1475 Prince Edward was appointed keeper of the realm and lieutenant in the King's absence. He had already travelled up from Ludlow to Westminster. All government acts from 7 July to 22 September 1475 were witnessed in his name. The toddler's role was, of course, titular, nominal and conventional. Others ruled for him. The influence of the Queen was especially strong: she was granted an extra £2,200 to cover the additional costs of the Prince's household. The King's ministers remained in place and a council of twenty was appointed, nine being also the Prince's councillors, Alcock (again acting chancellor), Dacre, Vaughan and Allington amongst them. Moreover Edward IV, we may presume, continued to exert his will from afar as much as he could. Supposedly all ministers and officers acted on behalf of the Prince: actually, of course, they acted instead of him.

The keeper's role was limited. The four patents of 20 June allowed him only to issue licences for cathedrals and monasteries to elect superiors (*congés d'élire*), to approve the elections, restore the temporalities, and receive the fealty of minor prelates, to present to church livings valued between 20 marks (£13 6s 8d) and 40 marks (£26 13s 4d), the chancellor presenting to those of lesser and the King to those of greater value, and to arrange for pleas of marshalsea to be held.[20] These powers were of little political importance. Moreover the Prince held them only briefly. It was so late in the campaigning season that the King can only have expected to be away for a few months. Actually the campaign fizzled out. Finding his chief ally Charles the Bold engaged elsewhere and that he was facing the formidable French alone, King Edward was quick to accept the generous terms that King Louis offered him. The betrothal of his daughter to the dauphin and a French pension offered an honourable escape, even if subjects enough were unhappy about the taxes he had wasted. Peace was made in fifty-six days and the King was back in England in thirteen weeks. But it could have been different. The war might have turned violent and the King could have been captured or even killed. It was 'remembering inwardly that we, as other creatures of the world, be transitory' and 'considering also that we be now upon our campaign and in taking our passage' to France, therefore, that he drew up his will. It was sealed at Sandwich on 20 June 1475, a fortnight before his departure (4 July) and the same day of the Prince's patent as keeper. Obviously it was 'our son the Prince' that he expected to succeed.[21] The arrangements for the Prince's keepership, therefore, could well have become those for the reign of Edward V.

Such symbolism was only one aspect of the Prince's role. In 1471-2 Prince Edward very young and very small, probably still unable to walk and talk and certainly not an independent political actor, but he was destined to grow bigger and to take a progressively larger role in the management of his own, his father's and national affairs. Even in 1483 he was still a child, not even a teenager. Four aspects of his life and career during these years deserve consideration. His function as national symbol has already been considered. His upbringing and his role as a young nobleman are considered next. Finally the Prince was the figurehead to Edward's management of Wales, which deserves more elaborate treatment in the next chapter. These four strands are not readily separable and never were; inevitably they intertwine.

The Prince at School

Adults do not happen. They are shaped through infancy, childhood and adolescence by the way in which they are brought up. The future Edward V was genetically fortunate: 'whole and furnished in nature',[22] he was physically and mentally complete. Like all the eldest sons of all aristocrats in late medieval England, the Prince Edward V had his future mapped out for him. The point of education was clearly defined in his teacher's patent of appointment.

> And how be it that every child in his young age ought to be brought up in virtue and cunning [knowledge] to the intent that he might delight in and continue in the same and so consequently deserve the merits of everlasting salvation and in this world to be therefore the more happy and fortunate.

Education was the foundation for life-long learning, salvation and the child's career. It was well-known what the Prince was going to become, what he would have to do and what capacities, skills and accomplishments he would require, and therefore what objectives his upbringing had to attain. His father was clear about what he wanted. We 'purpose by God's grace to purvey that he shall be so virtuously, cunningly and knightly brought up to serve Almighty God, christianly and devoutly, as accords to his duty and to live and proceed in the world honourably after his estate and dignity'. What that meant is explained by his tutor's patent. 'Such persons, as God hath called to the pre-eminent state of princes and to succeed their progenitors in the estate of royalty, ought the more diligently to be informed and instructed in cunning and virtue'.[23] Moreover there was less time than for lesser men. The young Prince had to be prepared for adult society and political responsibility by his middle teens. The aristocratic education of the nobility was accelerated, enhanced and intensified for a king-to-be. Doubtless there were plenty of academics, churchmen and other experts to advise the King what to do. That the Prince's household ordinances and even the patents for his chief officers were in English,[24] which King Edward could readily understand, and were so emphatic suggests that the King had a big role in shaping the upbringing of his son undertaken in his name.

In the meantime, of course, Edward was a mere baby, a babe in arms, the youngest of the King's four children. He had three elder sisters, a family to which his parents were to make numerous further additions and subtractions. Margaret was born in 1472 (and died next year), Richard in 1473, Anne in 1475, George (d.1479) in 1477, Katherine in 1479 and Bridget in 1480. It can only have been rarely, at great feasts and on special occasions, if then, that they were together and they cannot therefore have known one another particularly well. Allowing for the premature deaths of Mary, Katherine and George, Edward had six siblings at his accession in 1483. Prince, duke and earl, he needed first of all the care that any infant requires adapted, of course, to the expectations of aristocracy and royalty.

His first need was a wet-nurse, since Queen Elizabeth was probably like other aristocratic ladies in not suckling her own children: Edward's nurse was Mrs Avice Welles, who was granted on 12 November 1472 a tun of red Gascon wine yearly from the port of London. Since Edward had just turned two years of age, this may well have been a reward marking the end of her special service as the young Prince was weaned and turned to solid food. Perhaps, not certainly, he resided together with his elder sisters Elizabeth, Mary and Cecily in the royal nursery run by its mistress, perhaps already Elizabeth Lady Darcy, and other unidentified servants and rockers. Some such provision was essential. He was certainly with his mother at Windsor on 5 March 1472.[25]

His second need, apparently, was his chamberlain, for which the King deputed the treasurer of his own chamber, his trusted and intimate servant Thomas Vaughan. A substantial landholder in the Home Counties, Vaughan had been in royal service since at least 1446, a squire of the body to both Henry VI and Edward IV, and had held a string of responsible offices, as master of the ordnance, keeper of the great wardrobe, and ambassador, J.P., M.P. and sheriff, and had committed himself to the Yorkist cause in 1460. Vaughan, still in office at Edward V's accession, was already his chamberlain by 8 July 1471. It was in the house that Vaughan had erected on the monastic chamberlain's garden within the precincts of Westminster Abbey that the Prince was expected to stay when at court, quit of all obligations to entertain magnates, officers or others. The Prince was so 'young and tender [in] age that he cannot yet guide nor direct himself as it appertains to his high estate and dignity', runs the formal patent of 12 January 1474 that gave Vaughan all the power that former chamberlains of princes had possessed. The Prince needed

> to have about him a true, witty, expert, loving and diligent chamberlain, as well for the surety and safeguard of his person as for hourly attendance and assistance in counsel and other matters that concern his honour and profit.

Not only did 'our right trusty and well-beloved Thomas Vaughan' meet these criteria, but the King also knew 'the faith and love that he bore to us and to our issue'. The chamberlain rationed access to the Prince. It was Vaughan who certified to the Prince's chancellor

Winchester College's homage in 1472 – was the baby really involved in person, one wonders? – and to whom the college paid 6s 8d.[26] The relationship of Prince and chamberlain must have been very close: too close for the Prince's enemies to overlook. No wonder Vaughan was arrested alongside Rivers and Grey at Stony Stratford in 1483 and died with them at Pontefract.

Also by 8 July 1471 the Prince's godfather Abbot Milling was the Prince's chancellor and Richard Fiennes, Lord Dacre of the South, erstwhile controller of the King's household and 'greatest about the King's person', was his steward. It was presumably to Milling that Winchester College paid 43s 4d in November 1472 for sealing their discharge with the Prince's great seal. The keeper of his privy seal sealed the warrant to the Prince's chancellor and received 10s.[27] We know the identity neither of the keeper nor of the Prince's secretary, custodian of his signet – for the Prince's small establishment, like the government of the King, had a hierarchy of three seals – great, privy and signet. Dacre, like Vaughan, was destined to perish in 1483 at the hands of Edward V's usurper. Milling had already been superseded.

Nowadays husbands and wives customarily sleep together and share their households (and sometimes their beds and bedrooms) with their children. Older aristocratic practice was different. Our current British royal family conform to such past conventions. Late medieval English nobles and their ladies slept together by arrangement, when at the same addresses, and possessed their own separate households, often large, elaborate and expensive, and frequently apart. This was always the case with King Edward IV and Queen Elizabeth. She had her own residences, her own Queen's apartments in the King's own castles, palaces and hunting lodges, and her own well-staffed and ceremonial household that mirrored that of the King, admittedly on a smaller, but still substantial, scale. The revenues of £4,500 that she derived from her Queen's lands exceeded those of many a duke. So did her expenditure on her household. Similarly, too, with the children of the aristocracy. Once past infancy, they might not live with either parent. It was normal for them to be boarded out with other aristocrats, where they learnt the discipline and proper behaviour appropriate to their rank and inherited careers. The future Richard III, for instance, resided with Warwick in the mid-1460s. Contact between parents and children was likely to be irregular and hence somewhat formal: love there may have been, interest and concern there certainly was, but intimate first-hand acquaintance there could seldom be. Royal princes were often dignified with their own establishments – separate households, premises, staff and revenues. The future Edward IV and his next brother Edmund were living separately from both parents from at least 1454, whilst their younger siblings Margaret, George and Richard remained with their mother, the Duchess Cecily, until 1460. Following King Edward's accession, the younger three were relocated in a tower at Greenwich palace in the early 1460s before their ways also parted. Queen Elizabeth was granted the substantial sum of £400 a year extra for looking after her eldest two daughters in 1468. Separate provision for Edward Prince of Wales was thus entirely to be anticipated. It could be expected to be elaborate. He had the income. What perhaps is unexpected is his youth: a separate household, as opposed to a subsection of a parent's, was provided for the young Prince on 28 September 1473, when he was not quite two. At that point formal job descriptions became necessary for his governor and teacher (10 November) and chamberlain (12 January 1474). How much the Prince was aware of all this, of course, is questionable.

It is safe to presume that what was intended for him was the conventional education of the aristocracy like that provided for the henxmen of the royal household which trained them in virtue and prepared them for 'after they be of honour'. 'Schools of urbanity and nurture' taught them what they needed to know, from riding, jousting and book-learning to the correct behaviour in courtly society. Daily worship was prescribed. The master taught languages, 'harping, to pipe, sing, dance', and whatever else his pupils had aptitude for. He taught patience, self-restraint and 'courtesy in words, deeds and degrees', precedence and etiquette: at table he oversaw and corrected 'their demeanings, how mannerly they eat and drink'.[28] Aristocrats could not afford intemperance or bad manners or lack the accomplishments expected of their social echelon. Still less could a prince destined to be a king.

Edward V, however, was not brought up in the royal household by the master of the henxmen, but separately in his own self-contained and all sufficient establishment. Hence his upbringing had to be planned, was planned, and was indeed projected for many years ahead in considerable detail to shape him into an acceptable aristocrat, a Christian, and a future king. The King his father had written ordinances drawn up for him in 1473 and updated them ten years later, when he was twelve. The Prince was aged almost three in 1473: the ordinances aimed to cover all eventualities until he was fourteen. Certain aspects are amplified in the patents of appointment dated 10 November 1473 of his governor and teacher. The Queen's brother, his uncle Anthony Earl Rivers, was to be his governor and ruler – the Prince's master, as he was sometimes called. To him was committed 'the guiding of our said son's person' with the same powers as any predecessor with any previous prince in the past.[29] He was well-suited for the role. Maternal uncle to the Prince, he had shown himself devoted to the House of York. Rivers was pious, a good warrior, veteran of all campaigns since 1459, a model of chivalry – his tournament with the Grand Bastard of Burgundy in 1467 had been a chivalric high-point of the fifteenth century – and an aspirant crusader. He had pronounced literary interests and aptitudes. The earl could guide the Prince in 'truth, honour, cunning, virtue and knightly demeaning'. Moreover, he was meticulous, predatory and ruthless, well able to induct his charge to the realities of politics. To him was assigned not only the governance and rule of the Prince, but all his affairs. He was 'to guide and oversee that all [the Prince's] servants now being and hereafter do duly and truly their service and office' and they were all ordered to 'assist, aid, and obey' the earl. Rivers rated his service to the Prince highly. He entitled himself 'Anthony

Wydeville, Earl Rivers, Protector and Defender of the rights of the Papacy in England, Governor of the Lord Edward Prince of England, first-born of the most illustrious Prince Edward IV King of England, Lord of Scales, Nucelles and the Isle of Wight'.[30] He also proved willing to devote an inordinate amount of time to the task. It took him far away from his own estates and country, but in the short-term it brought him high standing, great authority and lucrative rewards. On the boy's accession to the throne, even greater advancement beckoned.

Such a commitment in time may not have been part of the original plan, as the earl spent much of the early to mid-1470s abroad, in Brittany, Santiago de Compostela in Spain (1472), Rome and Naples (1473-4), Portugal, northern France (1475) and at Morat (1477) on embassies, pilgrimage and campaigns. He even planned a crusade. Into the 1480s he was contemplating marriage to a foreign princess.[31] That may partly explain Dr John Alcock's role. One of the Prince's councillors from the beginning, Alcock's role was defined at the same time as Rivers'. Whereas Rivers was the Prince's governor and ruler, Alcock was deputed 'to teach and inform our said son in all spiritual cunning and virtue' which, as a bishop and doctor of civil law, a man of 'wit, virtue, and cunning', he was well able to do. His commitment to education emerges in his subsequent foundation of Jesus College, Cambridge. His devotion to the House of York, the 'love and affection ... to us and our issue' that was expected of him, as well as Rivers and Vaughan, is demonstrated by the suite of glass that he commissioned at Little Malvern Priory of the King, Queen, princes and princesses that stimulated prayers for their souls. Alcock had a big role in the Prince's day-to-day upbringing. Additionally, of course, he was keeper of the rolls and a master of chancery and an ex-acting chancellor, well-suited for his other role as president of the Prince's council, for the handling of suits before it and auditing accounts, and better qualified indeed to be the Prince's chancellor than Milling, whom he had succeeded by 1483.[32]

The ordinances of 20 September 1473 set down a strict timetable for the Prince that was designed to fill every hour of his day constructively. Only bedtime was fixed. Maybe the day commenced – as in sixteenth-century schools – at 6 a.m. or dawn:

The Prince arises from his bed

Matins in his chamber (his private oratory?)

Breakfast

Mass (with his household in the chapel?)

School – 'such virtuous learning as his age shall now
  suffice to receive'

Dinner ('Meat'), 'then to be read before him noble stories'

More school

Recreation – 'disports and exercises'

Supper

Evensong in his chamber (his private oratory?)

Recreation to make him 'joyous and merry'
  about going to bed

8 p.m. Bed

The ordinances recognised that the precise hours would vary with Edward's age and the seasons, also with the religious calendar (Church festivals were different), his itinerary, important engagements, the inevitable childhood ailments and doubtless other activities. A schedule that appears gruelling may not have been so in practice or had perhaps been alleviated by 1483, when he had broken the back of Latin. His bedtime was put back to 9 p.m. and lessons lasted only three hours, one hour in the morning and two in the afternoon.[33]

As we can see, religion loomed large, with matins in his chamber, mass in his private chapel, presumably sung (as he had his own choristers' grace at meals), and evensong in his chamber. Saints' days were special, determining the day and diet of everyone in the household. Offerings and sermons were prescribed. Prince Edward had his own almoner, who was Dr John Davison, Dean of Salisbury and Windsor, in 1477; his own confessor; and his own chaplains. The brass of Adam Grafton, vicar of St Alkmund's, Shrewsbury and then master of Battlefield College on the site of the battle of Shrewsbury (1403), proudly claimed him as one; Thomas Bold MA, an absentee rector, was another.[34] As the Prince was taught Latin, his religious role was not restricted to that normal for a layman, the reading of an English book of hours whilst professional clergy did the Latin services: almost certainly he possessed his own Latin breviary, as his father had done in 1454.

Alcock may have been designated his teacher, but Edward was actually taught Latin by a professional schoolmaster John Giles, who by 1476 was tutoring the three-year-old Prince Richard,[35] and also French, no longer the language of the English aristocracy, but that of his international counterparts and diplomacy and hence essential for a future King. As an aristocrat, destined to become both a warrior and a general, the Prince needed to develop the required physical and martial tastes, skills and accomplishments, such as riding, handling weapons, hawking, hunting, singing and dancing: what the ordinance described as 'such convenient disports and exercises as behoveth his estate to have experience in' and the association with horses, dogs, and the 'youthful exercises to invigorate his body' that Mancini writes about. We know he learnt archery: probably also to wear armour and to tourney. As eminent jousters, who competed at Westminster in 1474, his uncles Rivers and Sir Edward Wydeville and his half-brother Dorset could have inducted and instructed him themselves.

Prince Edward also needed to be able to speak, read and write in English, and to imbibe the literary culture of his class. No doubt his reading included the *Mirrors* – books of instruction for princes – and contemporary manuals of warfare and of hunting. Edward was to read or to have read to him such 'noble stories as behoveth a Prince to understand' – tales of great warriors like Alexander, Roland and Arthur, whose courage and renown he would wish to emulate – and moral tales to make him wise. We know that he possessed a French copy of the *Testament of the Sultan*, an account of current Turkish divisions that was reassuring to Christian readers. Indeed special reading was prepared for him: the printer Caxton published two English translations of such works, *The History of Jason* that he dedicated to the Prince and the *Dictes and Sayings of the Philosophers* translated by his mentor Earl Rivers. An illumination proudly depicts the earl's presentation of his handiwork to his King and Prince in 1477. It was not essential that the Prince read such instructive texts in the original – it was the message that mattered, rather than the pure classical style that the humanists of contemporary Italy and their few English counterparts sought to emulate. That said, his literary education was highly developed by late medieval standards and went beyond the normal grammar school education prescribed for the clergy and so commonly unfulfilled. The Prince had read widely by the age of twelve: he could already pronounce and fully comprehend any prose or verse 'unless it were from among the more abstruse authors'.[36] So wrote Mancini, the Italian humanist and author, whose own attainments were high. It would be nice to know whether Mancini's praise was absolute, up to the highest standards that he expected at home, or relative, in the sense that Edward's education was superior to that of other English aristocrats. We have no inventory of the Prince's books: Earl Rivers may have possessed the skills, but not the time, to teach him and, so far as we know, his entourage included no recognised Renaissance teacher.

Edward's upbringing was much more than merely a matter of content. It was designed to equip him as a member of society, of polite society, in which he was destined forever to command, and to train him in virtue. It was 'for the virtuous guiding of the person of our dearest first begotten son Edward, Prince of Wales, Duke of Cornwall and Earl of Chester'. Whilst his world was almost exclusively male – there were no women other than laundresses on his staff and none whom he encountered socially – he must not be seen as a solitary figure. Prince Edward was never unattended, at first, hourly, by his chamberlain, latterly by servants, mentors, adults and companions around his own age, although these were carefully selected to ensure that they were good influences. Earl Rivers' criteria, we may presume, included rank, conduct and character. He was to be accompanied all day everywhere by two 'discreet and convenient persons'. The worship, honour and prestige of the Prince, like any other aristocrat, was enhanced when his attendants were worshipful men and when his affairs were worshipfully conducted. Dinner and supper, for instance, were highly ceremonial, whereat he was 'to be honourably served and his dishes borne by worshipful folks and esquires bearing our livery'. His was a great household at least fifty strong: it was a statement of his rank, eminence, and wealth to local dignitaries, who probably benefited from his open-handed, yet calculated, generosity.

The household also contained the Prince's henxmen, other young aristocrats, the 'sons of nobles, lords and gentlemen', who shared his schooling and recreations. They were allowed no idleness or meals in their chambers, and sat with him at meals, like the unfortunate Edmund Audley, the son of Lord Audley, who died about 1478. Another was apparently the Prince's considerably older half-brother Richard Grey – the Lord Richard as he was known – who came of age about 1476 and was in his late twenties in 1483. Placements in the household of the Prince and future King were intended by their parents as the first stage of an honourable career in royal service, but they also carried with them functions, duties and responsibilities, of which these lordlings were kept fully aware. They were to keep the Prince happy, but had also to ensure that their 'communication at all times in his presence was of virtue, honour, cunning, wisdom, and deeds of worship, and nothing that should move and stir him to vices'. He needed to learn aristocratic, princely and chivalric virtues and conventions, such as courtesy, mercy, justice, honour and generosity, to talk, eat, drink and do everything else politely, and to avoid the obvious temptations, to which princes were especially prone and to which his father had generally succumbed, of lust, gluttony, sloth, avarice, malice and cruelty. Fellow children, who were bad examples or bad influences, could be as readily excluded from his company and even dismissed from his household as any other servants. Care was to be taken to protect the Prince from vicious and malign influences. What these were we can perhaps guess, though our notions differ from those of Edward's protectors and perhaps also of those suspected of preying on him. Child abuse, abduction and ransom demands were certainly not in his father's mind when prescribing that nobody should enter the Prince's apartments before breakfast and that he should be guarded at night.

Preparation for rule involved subjection to adults, masters and conventions. If kings were at risk from courtiers and evil councillors, who served their masters only to advance themselves, who lured them into self-indulgence and tyranny by pandering to their self-esteem and preferences rather than telling them the truth, how much more exposed and potentially permanently deforming to the character of a young child were such flatterers and those whose examples – perhaps older children or more natural sportsmen – whom he admired. Might they not attract him into dangerous or unworthy activities, into ribaldry, persuade him to reward them, or develop in him undesirable characteristics? What servant or mentor would not be chary of thwarting his employer, the source of future advancement and one day able to dismiss him, ultimately his King? If not really relevant to a toddler, such considerations were for the twelve-year-old Prince of 1483, two years from his minority. It was presumably because he had been giving commands and had been tempted – like any lively youth - that it was then ordained that none of his orders should be obeyed, unless ratified by his governor, the president of his council, or his elder half-brother, that his servants were not to encourage him to do anything unprincely, and that, if he did act unworthily, he was to be warned. Three warnings meant that he would be reported to his father the King – a threat that was intended as a deterrent and which the Prince presumably wished to avoid. If even the young Henry VI proved too much of a handful for his governor, who sought the backing of the royal council for his disciplinary regimen, it is not surprising that the intelligent and apparently normal Edward V was already outgrowing by 1483 the upbringing instituted for him as a toddler.

Rivers, as we have seen, was responsible for the Prince. His teaching, subcontracted to specialist schoolmasters, his household and his council were consigned to John Alcock, bishop in turn of Rochester and Worcester, and president of his council. Edward's household had to cater for all his needs – food, drink, clothing, religion, service at meals, travel and recreation. It mirrored the King's formal organisation, just as the households of the Queen and nobility did. There were the equivalents of the upper household (*domus magnificencie*) in attendance on the Prince and the lower household (*domus providencie*) of the menial service departments. All Edward's life Vaughan was chamberlain in charge of the private apartments and staff of his upper household. The lower household was regulated as strictly as that of the King, for 'the politic, sad, and good rule of his following', with regard to ceremonial, value for money, accountancy, personal conduct on and off duty. All staff were to be adults, everyone was to live in, the porter was to open and shut the gates at fixed hours, there was to be no violence, extortion, or embezzlement. Richard Fiennes, Lord Dacre of the South, progressed from the controllership of the King's household via the stewardship of the Prince's to the chamberlainship of the Queen; by at least 1481, and perhaps in 1478 or earlier, he was succeeded by Sir William Stanley, brother of the King's own steward. Sir Richard Croft was treasurer by 1480 and the Wydeville kinsman Richard Haute was controller by 1476. We know also of Richard Minors, usher of his chamber by 1474, Nicholas Shere, his yeoman porter in 1477, Thomas Crub, marshal of the hall in 1482, John Argentine, his final physician, and of *Ich Dien*, the pursuivant named after the Prince's motto.[37] Initially smaller than that of the King, as befitted the household of an infant, it almost certainly grew, perhaps towards the hundreds. However we cannot tell. Other than the ordinances for his upbringing, there are no statutes for its internal organisation and operation, no household accounts and scarcely anything else other than references to its principal officers.

Young aristocrats were normally supported by their parents or guardians, who paid their bills or assigned annuities to cover them. Even if heirs, they had no access to the revenues of their estates until they were certified of age. This also applied to royal princes, such as the King's brothers, whose grants of titles and lands whilst under age meant little as they could not be enjoyed. Their royal brother felt free to take back, exchange and revise his grants at will. It was only in 1466, in the case of Clarence, and in 1468-9, for Gloucester, when they were sixteen and were declared of age – five years ahead of ordinary mortals – that they were able to receive their rents and spend them as they chose. Young Edward, even more favoured, was scheduled to come of age at fourteen, a landmark that he never attained. Until October 1472 his expenses were probably absorbed by his parents. At that point, however, in parliament, the King granted him the revenues of his possessions with effect from the previous Michaelmas, 29 September 1472. This did not mean that the Prince himself controlled them. 'For the ignorance' to be expected 'in every young and tender age', he could not: 'the same our son suffices not as yet to rule and direct himself to his honour and profit'. Although the King would have liked to oversee the Prince and his affairs, so he said, actually he could not, and had therefore to delegate all the Prince's resources and responsibilities to the management of those who ran his household, and to the council that the King appointed the following year.[38] The King surrendered thereby direct control of substantial revenues that one would have thought he himself needed. Apart from supporting the Prince's household, the greatest item of expenditure of any aristocrat, we do not know how this income was spent. The coffer with three keys, to be held respectively by the Queen, Rivers and Alcock, was designed to prevent it being diverted to private purposes. No doubt the King remained free to dip in when he chose. He certainly interfered with the wardships.

Young Edward was the greatest of aristocrats, whose estates rivalled and probably exceeded in extent and value those of any of his contemporaries. They were the traditional possessions of the King's eldest son. Since kings did not always have such sons and it was rare for them to be of age, these extensive possessions were normally managed on the King's behalf by officers that he had inherited or appointed. It was to this existing administration and to existing officers, many appointed for life, to whom Edward now acceded. There were three principal components: the principality of Wales, the earldom of Chester and the duchy of Cornwall.

The principality of Wales was confined to west and north-western Wales. In origin it consisted of the resources confiscated from the Welsh princes. It comprised the five shires of Carmarthen and Cardigan in south Wales and Merioneth, Caernarvon, and Anglesey in the north. Parts were held by the principality directly, such as the numerous castles and towns – for instance, Beaumaris, Conway and Aberystwyth – and manors, each with their own constables, stewards and other ministers, but much else was held by Welshmen, gentry and peasants, who however were subject to the Prince's jurisdiction. There were sheriffs for each shire and, at a senior level, chief justices and chamberlains for both north and south Wales. Gross revenues of £1,800 were burdened with fees, some for duties performed and others not, so the Prince could probably count on liveries of only about £500 net a year to his coffers.

The earldom of Chester consisted principally of the two counties of Cheshire and Flint. As in the principality, the Prince as earl held some possessions –castles, towns, manors, rents – directly, but much else was held by lesser men. Cheshire and Flint were counties palatine, in which the Prince had regalian rights – he stood in the position of the King. The King's writ did not run there. The Prince had therefore to substitute his own administration – his own chancery, his own exchequer and his own law courts. It appears to have been an efficient system of devolved central government. The Prince as earl possessed a hierarchy of officers, headed again by a chief justice and chamberlain. Chester and Flint rendered £2,000 at the Prince's first entry: instalments were still being collected in 1475. In 1481-2 the palatinates yielded £1,200 gross, £1,000 net.[39]

The duchy of Cornwall, thirdly, was somewhat different. It lay entirely in England. Whilst the Prince as duke inherited many franchises, none of w   equalled the regalian rights that he possessed in Wales and Cheshire. The earls of Cornwall, to which he succeeded, had important properties in Cornwall and Devon – the castles of Tintagel and Restormel, the towns of Liskeard and Lostwithiel, manors, parks, fisheries, rents and the important stannaries of tin. They had the right to appoint the sheriff of Cornwall, who in 1478 secured the return of M.P.s from the Cornish boroughs very much to the liking of the King. Additionally, however, the Prince as duke had possessions of all kinds in eleven other counties, from Byfleet and Kennington in Surrey – the duchy is still landlord to the Oval cricket ground – to Wallingford (Berks.), and Castle Rising (Norfolk). Thirteen Gournay manors in Somerset and Dorset were other assets. Many knights fees were held of the duchy. Altogether the duchy was worth about £3,000 to the Prince:[40] much more than his other possessions.

Total revenues of £4,500 were very substantial. They compare with, for instance, Clarence in 1467 and are thrice the statutory minimum for a duke. If the Prince brought a household of fifty to stay with the King, so his father's *Black Book* calculated, the Prince's daily allowances of 30s would amount to £547 15s and his fifty attendants at 12d each to £912 10s, total £1,460 5s. This was more than the revenues of a duke, but a mere third of his own.[41] It could be done more cheaply. Others kept households this size at a third of the price, but fifty servants was meagre for a Prince and was surely subsequently exceeded. Anyway, the Prince's riding household would have been smaller: he cannot have taken everyone when staying with the King, especially if charged at this rate. He could afford such expenditure on his income. Moreover his revenues increased. King Edward granted his other possessions in Wales to the Prince as well. In 1476 he assigned his son all his Mortimer lordships in Wales: however it is not quite clear which were held by York's feoffees and they were probably worth much less than the £1,900 of thirty years before. The duchy of Lancaster, lordships of Monmouth, three castles of

Grosmont, Skenfrith and White Castle, and also Elvell followed in 1477-8.[42] In 1481-82 the Lancaster lands produced liveries of only £140, not apparently for the Prince. In 1479 Edward was created Earl of March and also Earl of Pembroke, acquiring at that point the marcher lordships such as Pembroke that Earl William Herbert (henceforth Earl of Huntingdon) had surrendered in exchange for the Gournay lands. Usk and Caerleon followed in 1483.[43] Taking all into consideration, the Prince eventually had revenues of at least £6,000 a year and probably much more, approximately a twelfth of the King's own income if Professor Ross' estimate of £65,000–£70,000 is correct.[44] The Prince's total revenues should have greatly exceeded his living costs. Perhaps it was the Prince, not the King, who had built up a treasure by 1483.

Every adult magnate had his great seal, usually controlled by his chancellor, and a more personal seal, handled by his secretary. We do not know who the Prince's secretary was, although we know of a considerable number of his signet letters and warrants. He possessed a confusing number of great seals, chanceries and chancellors. It was a privilege of every marcher lord to have his own chancery (and hence seal) for each marcher lordship. Prince Edward could have possessed a score of them about which we know absolutely nothing. Probably most were superfluous by this date and had been super-seded by the chancellor of the earldom of March, currently Dr Richard Martin, who presumably sealed its acts and enrolled them like the duchy of Lancaster chancellor whose records survive. In 1483, after Martin's death, the Prince as earl had a separate keeper for the seal of the earldom: possibly a temporary locum, but perhaps because it had been decided that a separate chancellor was superflu-ous.[45] There were chanceries or exchequers at Chester, at Carmarthen and Caernarvon for both north and south Wales, each with its own seal, and William Allington was chancellor of the duchy of Cornwall.[46] Enrolments for Chester and some originals for the principality survive. Each chancery evidently had its own way of dating and warranting its acts. Thomas Milling, first as abbot of Westminster and then as Bishop of Hereford, was the Prince's first chancellor – presumably his chancellor in chief with his great seal. We have witnessed his role in Winchester College's homage in 1472. Quite what else Milling sealed is unclear. However we know he had a chancery roll, now lost, on which the Winchester College certificate was enrolled. There was also a privy seal. The prime movers, in the Prince's administration, were Rivers and Alcock. It was they who controlled the key instrument, the Prince's signet, with which out-letters were sealed and which presumably moved the seals of the duchy, the earldom of March and his other chanceries, by which his commands were expressed directly to his officers and outsiders. Sometimes, Rivers' own signet or oral commands sufficed.[47]

The Prince is well-known to have possessed a council. All lords possessed them. Made up principally of estate officials and retained lawyers, they often had authority to undertake many minor actions, such as leases and litigation, without recourse to the lord. The councils that King Edward appointed for his son in 1471 and 1473 had a prescribed membership, prescribed procedures – Alcock as president was authorised to summon and close meetings as he chose – and also fixed duties, broadly to act on behalf of a lord who was actually incapable, which were quite restricted. The first council was allowed to make appointments to the Prince's offices temporarily, during his pleasure and thus open to review, certainly when he came of age. The 1473 council was additionally empowered to remove all the Prince's officers and to make new ones during the Prince's pleasure, to present to all ecclesiastical livings in his gift, to license and approve ecclesiastical elections, to receive fealties, to administer all his feudal rights including the disposal of the custody of the lands and bodies of heirs and to present to churches, to dispose of custodies of heirs and marriages and to grant pardons.[48] We know of some presentations to churches and some appointments to estate offices. Any adult lord exercised these powers himself. It is therefore best to regard these powers as restricted to this council and these councillors. The King's patent did not confer any other unusual powers or confine anything else done on the Prince's behalf to this particular group of councillors.

This point is worth making for at least five reasons. Neither patent established a council with authority over Wales. Other people acted as the Prince's councillors, he apparently possessed several councils, his councils are to be found acting in unusual ways, and there is no clear-cut division between the different groups of councillors. In 1472 Winchester College hosted two expensive breakfasts to five of the Prince's legal counsel – John Catesby, the judge, William Danvers and Richard Jay, future serjeants-at-law, Thomas Well and Thomas Windsor, none of whom were on the formal council that the King appointed in 1471 or 1473.[49] Judge Catesby does occur handling suits before the Prince's council, an area of judicial activity for which there is a relative wealth of material relating to eighty-two cases. The majority relate to the duchy of Cornwall and to Cornish affairs, particularly to the Prince's stannaries and the oppressions of Sir Henry Bodrugan.[50] Whilst there is no concrete evidence for his involvement, this judicial role may have been stimulated by Alcock, a master in chancery, briefly head of the court of chancery, a councillor of the Prince from 1471 and from 1473 president of his council, to which, also in 1473, two judges and two other common lawyers were added. It was surely quite exceptional for any council other than the King's to immerse itself in cases of equity. The Prince's council, of course, was actually a royal council, run by royal councillors and legal counsel, and operated principally at royal palaces. Somewhat confusingly, the Prince seems to have possessed several such councils. Councillors for the duchy of Cornwall handled dozens of complaints from aggrieved tenants both at Westminster and on commission in Cornwall itself in 1475. One of those most involved was William Allington (d.1479), the Prince's attorney-general and chancellor of his duchy of Cornwall and later chancellor also of the Prince's brother Richard.[51]

David Lowe drew a contrast between the Prince's council in the marches and 'the Prince's council learned' at Westminster. We cannot tell if Milling was often with his godson at Ludlow, since it was within his diocese: only once, on a trip to Chester, did he have to appoint a vicar-general explicitly to cover their absences.[52] Once bishop of Worcester, Alcock seems to have remained nearby. He presided over the councillors with the Prince, visiting Coventry and Chester on his behalf. Whilst petitions were presented to the Prince and councillors at Ludlow, from the marches and Coventry alike, some were rebuffed – the Prince's councillors had no desire to supersede the jurisdiction of town councils or the courts of the principality, counties palatine and marcher lordships, which for most purposes should have sufficed. Others were referred to arbitration and yet others to the councillors at Westminster, who were also handling duchy matters. The Prince's councils met at the same time in different places. It is not altogether clear to which council belonged the councillors recorded officiating who were not on the 1473 list – such as the current and future judges John Catesby and William Nottingham (1475) and John Fyneux (1481) – or to which council the book(s) of acts mentioned with reference to Castle Rising, part of the duchy, and in the 1483 household ordinance appertained.[53] The book was an effort to keep track of potentially confusing and counterproductive conflicts of jurisdiction. Whilst the Prince's council in the marches could operate judicially, its prime functions were administrative and governmental – again a distinction that may have seemed anachronistic in the fifteenth century.

The Prince's possessions thus comprised an enormous range of assets that were managed for him. There were very substantial revenues to spend, rights of all kinds to dispose of, offices and livings to be filled. The route to preferment was through the Prince's patronage as exercised by his councils and officers. Not surprisingly, many of the beneficiaries were those already in the employment of the King, his councillors, his officers, and their dependants. Their advancement actually contributed to the Prince's own authority. Moreover, service to the Prince was the route to promotion that remained in the gift of the King. Thus the three bishoprics of Hereford (1474), Worcester (1476) and St David's (1482) fell to three of the Prince's principal councillors, two of his chancellors and the president of his council.

There is actually no reason to suppose that the Prince visited most of his estates: Castle Rising in Norfolk, for example, West Wales, or the West Country. The area that he surely did come to know well was the central Welsh marches and the adjoining shires, since it was there, principally at Ludlow, that he was to spend most of his short life.

4

THE PRINCE OF WALES

From Westminster to Ludlow

Prince Edward was born at Westminster Abbey. He spent the first
two years of his life in or around Westminster, where the King and
Queen had a range of residences – Greenwich, Eltham, Windsor,
Woodstock, the Tower and Westminster – and where several of his
key officers had other roles that demanded their attention and
presence. This was true of the Prince's chancellor Thomas Milling,
still abbot of Westminster, his chamberlain Thomas Vaughan, still
treasurer of the King's chamber, and, not least, John Alcock, first as
master of chancery and then acting chancellor, dean of St Stephen's
Westminster until 1472 and thereafter bishop of Rochester. Whilst
it is logical to suppose that the Prince resided with his mother, she
received no financial allowance for him, and several of his officers
and councillors were seconded from the King's household. The
personnel of the council appointed for him in 1471 and even that
of the enlarged council of 1473 seem to imply continued residence.
His household ordinance of September 1473 gave one of the three
keys to the coffer containing his cash and signet to the Queen and
implied therefore her continued availability.[1] Though in the
marches briefly in 1473, where Edward's brother was born, Queen
Elizabeth certainly never intended permanent residence there. It
was a sacrifice to the King when servants as trusted and useful as
Alcock and Vaughan moved to Wales.

The Prince himself visited the marches in the spring and summer of 1473 in the company of his parents. Unlike them, however, he remained. A stay, that may initially have been intended to be short, became permanent. Ludlow, now in Shropshire but then in the Welsh marches, became his home, from which on occasion he visited his parents, siblings, court and capital. This was obviously an important development, which decisively changed the Prince's life in many ways and may also have predetermined his death. Historians have also attached great significance to it, as a phase in the evolution of Welsh government that anticipated the Act of Union of 1536 and the tighter grip of the Tudors and their successors on the provinces. The Prince's council *in* the marches is commonly seen as the precursor of the Tudor council *of* the marches. Historians from Thomas More on have credited this to Edward IV,[2] whose plan it was and who saw it through to fruition. Yet it is not by any means clear that the Prince's council had so much in common with its Tudor successor, and it seems unlikely that King Edward saw the future so clearly or reached all the conclusions in one leap. That Ludlow was not even part of the Prince's own domains is one reason for scepticism. The sequence of events and the wording of the relevant documents is another. If the Prince was granted access to his estate revenues from Michaelmas 1472, the council to administer his Welsh possessions was appointed only on 20 February following, and the ordinances for his household, dated almost a year later on 27 September 1473, included provisions (as we have seen) that were surely unattainable and very inconvenient if he resided in Ludlow. Moreover it was the King himself, who remained Earl of March, it was as Earl of March in June 1473 that he contracted agreements with other marcher lords, and it was only in 1477, 1479 and 1483 that Edward IV handed over the rest of the crown's very substantial possessions in Wales. There was also a political significance to these developments. The Prince's estates and authority over Wales greatly enhanced the regional power and authority of his Wydeville kin. The power they accrued in Wales after 1473 was deliberately demolished in 1483, its figurehead – Edward V – included.

Certain historians have argued that the membership of the council appointed for the Prince on 20 February 1473 to handle his affairs foreshadowed what was to follow. It enlarged that council of 8 July 1471 and possessed more powers. Both were to last until the Prince was fourteen. The earlier council could only grant offices during the Prince's pleasure. A list of its fourteen members follows:

Queen Elizabeth, the Prince's mother

Thomas Cardinal Bourchier, Archbishop of Canterbury,
    the Prince's great-uncle

George Duke of Clarence, royal duke, the Prince's elder
    paternal uncle

Richard Duke of Gloucester, royal duke, the Prince's
    younger paternal uncle

Robert Stillington, Bishop of Bath, Chancellor of
    England

Laurence Bothe, Bishop of Durham

Anthony Earl Rivers, the Prince's eldest maternal uncle;
    from 1473 his tutor and governor

William Lord Hastings, the chamberlain of the King's
    household

Richard Fiennes, Lord Dacre of the South, steward of
    the Prince's household

Sir John Fogge, treasurer of the King's household

Sir John Scott, controller of the King's household

Sir Thomas Vaughan, the Prince's chamberlain and
    treasurer of the King's chamber

Master John Alcock, dean of St Stephen's Chapel, Westminster;
    later Bishop of Rochester and Worcester
    and from 1473 the Prince's teacher and president of
    his council

Richard Fowler esquire, chancellor of the duchy
    of Lancaster

It included the principal members of the royal family and royal household, from which the Prince's attendants were carved, and the administrative expertise to run his estate.[3]

In 1473 all components were enlarged and a legal element was added. The extra members were:

> *Edward Storey, Bishop of Carlisle*, the Queen's chancellor
> *John Earl of Shrewsbury*, a distant cousin
> *Walter Devereux*, Lord Ferrers of Chartley, a distant
>   in-law of the Prince
> *Sir John Needham*, justice of king's bench
> *Sir Richard Chok*, justice of common pleas
> *Dr Richard Martin*, chancellor of the earldom of March
> *William Allington esquire*, royal councillor, perhaps
>   already chancellor of the duchy of Cornwall
> *Richard Haute esquire*, maternal cousin of the Prince
> *John Sulyard*, serjeant-at-law
> *Geoffrey Cottesmore*, lawyer [4]

The membership has often been analysed, somewhat anachronistically. Whilst the new council was responsible for Prince's possessions in Wales and Chester, so too were they for the duchy in West Country and elsewhere. All the original nominees were the King's choice: all were loyal – for who could not be, when he no longer had any rival? – and all were devoted to his service. Most had long track records. They offered a range of expertise. If twenty-five members is a substantial number, when consideration is given to single-figures normally present at royal council meetings and actual subsequent attendances known for the Prince's own council, it was small by comparison with the Lords in parliament or great council and omitted such obvious members as the Lord Treasurer (Essex), Lord Privy Seal (Bishop Rotherham) and the steward of the King's own household. That several local figures apparently excluded, such as Buckingham, Maltravers and Stanley, were almost simultaneously (1 February 1473) commissioned within the Lancaster lordships of Kidwelly, Monmouth and Ogmore suggests that their omission from the council was not initially significant.[5] As contemporaries expected, it was a balanced council of the three estates ranging from the royal family through select peers (spiritual and temporal) to knights, doctors of law and common lawyers.

There were five overlapping categories: the national elite; the Prince's own officers; the King's household; experts; and peers. The national elite of the King *ex officio*, the Queen, her eldest brother (Rivers), the King's two brothers (Clarence and Gloucester), the primate (Cardinal Bourchier) and the chancellor (Stillington) were surely automatic. Bishop Alcock of Rochester had recently deputised for his mentor Stillington as chancellor, Bishop Bothe of Durham was shortly to succeed him, and Bishop Storey of Carlisle was chancellor to the Queen.[6] Second come the Prince's own officers – Rivers his tutor, Milling his chancellor, Vaughan his chamberlain, Alcock his teacher and his steward Dacre. Third were the King's own household dignitaries – his chamberlain (Hastings), his treasurer and controller (Fogge, Scott), his former controller (Dacre), and Vaughan, the treasurer of his chamber. The fourth category comprises the experts: Richard Fowler, William Allington, and Master Richard Martin, chancellors of the three greatest royal estate complexes, the duchies of Lancaster, Cornwall and the earldom of March.[7] (Vaughan also possessed complementary expertise as treasurer of the King's chamber.) There were two judges, John Nedeham and Richard Choke; two common lawyers, John Sulyard and Geoffrey Cottesmore; and in Stillington, Storey, Alcock and Martin, four doctors of law. Finally, as Lords, there were six peers spiritual – Cardinal Bourchier, Abbot Milling, and four diocesan bishops – and seven peers temporal – the two royal dukes (Clarence, Gloucester), two earls (Rivers, Shrewsbury) and three barons (Dacre, Hastings, Ferrers of Chartley).

A lot has been made of the representation here, intentionally and 'from the very beginning', of connections of the Wydevilles, especially amongst those who were to act in Wales, and the absence of marcher lords.[8] The interests of the Queen and her family were certainly represented. Haute's sole qualification, admittedly, was as a Wydeville connection and perhaps Bishop Storey's too, but most of the Wydeville adherents, such as Ferrers, Fogge, Scott and Dacre, were the King's men before the King ever married a Wydeville. Shrewsbury was Clarence's satellite, Martin had risen in the service of the earl of Worcester, and the East Anglian Sulyard, a future judge, was Howard's client. Alcock, a Yorkshireman, was the protégé of Lord Chancellor Stillington, another Yorkshireman.[9] Actually Clarence or Gloucester, Shrewsbury and Ferrers were the most important magnates currently of age and active in Wales: in 1474 the Prince visited Clarence at Warwick.[10]

There is no evidence that the council was selected with the Prince's residence in Wales primarily in mind and much to contest it. Most of the members were peers, bishops, courtiers or officers fixed at Westminster or in other provinces, in Kent, Hertfordshire, or East Anglia, and lacked Welsh connections, as David Lowe observed. He deduced thereby that they were to be passive, silent, or honorific councillors, even though he found evidence of some acting as councillors at Westminster and elsewhere. If the council met at Ludlow, a maximum of six councillors, he argued, could be active: the Queen, Rivers, Alcock, Milling, Dacre and Vaughan.[11] The alternative and preferable deduction, however, is that the Prince and his council were not originally destined for transfer to Wales. It is striking that even in September 1473 it was ordained that the Prince's money and signet be consigned to a coffer that required the Queen's key to open it and was not therefore to be located in Wales. It was not just the honorific councillors, such as the royal dukes, who cannot have expected to leave court and may indeed have been busy with the Prince's affairs there, but also such working members as Chancellor Milling, Chamberlain Vaughan, the estate experts, judges and lawyers. It is surely evidence of a change that Milling was promoted at the next vacancy in 1474 from Westminster to the see of Hereford. Were Alcock's increased responsibilities in the household in September 1473, his appointment as the Prince's tutor (November), and his translation to the see of Worcester (1476) all indications of some changes? That the patents of himself and Rivers bear the same date suggests that Rivers was not initially expected to sideline himself in Wales and that Alcock was to deputise. Did the earl choose to reside there more continually only when the potential of his role – its real power – became more apparent? By 1483 Rivers, Alcock and Richard Grey rather than the Queen authorised disbursements.[12] It is perhaps more likely that the Prince's council was appointed before it was decided to send the Prince in person to Wales, that his household was regulated ahead of the decision to make his sojourn there permanent and that it was only gradually that the King realised the advantage of delegating royal authority there to the Prince's resident council. We know that membership changed without knowing who was added or how much it changed: we cannot tell for sure whether marcher lords such as Buckingham, Strange and Stanley became councillors once its role in governing Wales evolved.

Previous princes had taken regional responsibility in Wales. They were always princes of Wales and Earls of Chester: e.g. the future Henry V. At first the Prince's affairs were handled like those of previous princes in the past. To settle his heir in Wales, moreover, was to treat him as King Edward himself had been treated. It was Edward IV's own Mortimer patrimony, where he was most at home. Prince Edward did not find it strange or consider himself to have been sidelined by his father. However the King may have been pushed into such action by complaints about the state of Wales. Perhaps, as historians have often suggested, the 2nd Earl of Pembroke was not the man that his father had been and not so suitable a royal instrument, and certainly he and Buckingham, as members of a younger generation, lacked the 1st earl's longstanding and intimate relationship with the King. There was no crisis that required again the wholesale offloading of royal power on some great nobleman. Given such considerations, given also that he could not spare the time to act himself, given the value of royal authority and the regional prestige of Mortimer and York, and given finally that he had surrendered so many of his possessions and powers to his son, it was logical for Edward to despatch his son thither as figurehead for others devoted to law and order. In essence, after all, it repeated the King's own experience.

We must never forget that Edward knew the marches at first hand. If he had a home county, it was the marches. The two earliest surviving letters of 1454 that he and his next brother Edmund wrote to their 'most greatly redoubted lord and father' Lord Protector York were dated at York's castle of Ludlow, where they were already living in their own separate household on a permanent basis, since education had been laid on for them there.[13] No doubt they ventured out to hunt and hawk, to visit their neighbours and to show their faces on York's estates. Most probably they also knew the rest of York's Welsh castles, such as Wigmore, Radnor, Montgomery and Denbigh, each with a diminutive town beyond its gates, all of which Duke Richard can be shown to have visited from time to time, local towns like Shrewsbury and Wenlock, and the cathedrals of Hereford and Worcester. Wigmore, the mausoleum of their Mortimer ancestors, celebrated the Mortimer line in its chronicle and genealogy. Their two letters record some contacts with local aristocratic society, such as Walter Devereux of Weobley (Herefs.), the future Lord Ferrers of Chartley and the Crofts of nearby Croft Castle (Herefs.), of whose 'odious demeaning' the boys childishly complained.[14] By extension they also knew York's trusted retainers to be Edward's as King, William Herbert, the future Earl of Pembroke, John Donne, later a knight of Edward IV's body, and all those marcher men who fought for him in 1461 at Mortimer's Cross, close both to Wigmore and Ludlow. Edward had a 'feel' for the marches, the men of the marches and marcher problems, which influenced what he did for his son.

Although his father Richard Duke of York held lands in London and many English counties, in Ireland, and in France until 1449, he was also the greatest of Welsh marcher lords through his Mortimer earldom of March. It was from there that his wealth and military power principally derived. Even after the mid-fifteenth century collapse of seigniorial revenues in Wales the duke's marcher lordships brought in £1,958 net.[15] The great lordship of Denbigh lay on the north Welsh coast, Caerleon and Usk in the south-east, with Blaenlyffni, Ewyas Lacy and Clifford a little further north, and Cleobury Mortimer to the east. But these were outliers. In the central marches, from west to east, lay a great swathe of territory: Builth, Cwmd Deuddwr, Gwerthynion, Malienydd, Cydewain, Ceri, Montgomery and Radnor, Wigmore and Ludlow. Each of these was a separate lordship, in which York, as lord, possessed most of the powers of a king. After the Act of Union (1536) they comprised much of the counties of Denbigh, Montgomery, Radnor, Brecon, Monmouth and western parts of Hereford and Shropshire. York looked for support for his enterprises to his marcher tenants and neighbours in 1450, in 1452 – 'to my right worshipful friends the bailiffs, burgesses, and commons of the good town of Shrewsbury'[16] – and in 1455, in 1459 and 1460. Edward IV had been heir to all these possessions, loyalties and friendships, bore the courtesy title of Earl of March during York's lifetime and retained the earldom in his own hands after he was King, neither allocating it to his mother in dower nor granting it out to others. Unlike the duchy of Lancaster, the earldom required no separate act of annexation and incorporation from parliament, but was kept as a separate entity with its own seal, chancellor, receiver and records, which regrettably have disappeared.

Evidently King Edward felt a sentimental attraction to it as his patrimony: he felt similarly about Shropshire and perhaps Herefordshire too. 'Afore this time by your letters patent', observed Sheriff Robert Charlton of Shropshire in 1472,

> your said noble grace … has granted so large liberties and franchises as well to the bailiffs and burgesses of your town of Ludlow, to the abbot and convent of Shrewsbury, and the bailiffs and burgesses of Wenlock as others within your said county, where through such issues and profits as might or

> ought to have grown to your said orator by reason of his office
> be greatly withdrawn and diminished.[17]

Charlton cited Ludlow as an example. 'The town of Ludlow stands on a hill', wrote Leland half a century later, 'so that from whichever direction you approach it you have to climb'.[18] It stands on a steep ridge by the confluence of the Rivers Corve and Teme. There was a five-span stone bridge across the Corve to the north of the town and a three-span stone bridge with a chapel dedicated to St Catherine just downstream at Ludford, where York had planned his last stand in 1459. Walled, with seven gates, it was a prosperous cloth centre and packed about 2,000 people into its square grid of streets. Ludlow had suffered 'rapines, depredations, oppressions, losses of goods and other grievances for our sake' following York's flight. The town's fortunes were closely tied to the House of York: just as it shared their sufferings, so too it flourished with their success. Ludlow Castle, towering over the River Teme, had been York's principal seat. He had confirmed earlier Mortimer charters in 1449 and Edward IV, when at Ludlow, had made it a royal borough of two bailiffs, 12 aldermen and 25 councillors and a parliamentary borough eligible to return two burgesses to parliament. Freed from the oversight of the lord's steward, the corporation secured most of the lord's rights in the town for an annual feefarm of 40 marks (£26 13s 4d) and the right to dye cloth. This was during a visit at which he gratefully acknowledged 'the laudable and gratuitous services which our beloved and faithful subjects the burgesses of the town of Ludlow had rendered unto us in the obtaining of our right to our crown of England'. Further privileges, such as the right to appoint their own aulnager to seal their cloth, followed in 1478.

Most prominent citizens and many outsiders, apparently including Duke Richard and Duchess Cecily, belonged to the palmer's gild, actually dating from the thirteenth century, but supposedly to Edward the Confessor. The gild was dedicated to the Virgin and St John the Evangelist, who allegedly sent a message via Ludlow men to the Confessor. It operated from St Lawrence's church and its warden perhaps was the most important figure in the town. So generously was it endowed, at least 150 Ludlow men endowing obits *c*.1300-1550, that the palmers employed ten priests in 1472-73, who by the 1530s lived communally alongside Hosyer's almshouse west of the churchyard. The rebuilding of what became one of the largest parish churches with its tall central bell-tower and its twenty chapels was completed only in 1471. The townsmen equipped it also with fine choir stalls with misericords, amongst them York's badge of the falcon and fetterlock, and fine stained-glass windows of the legends of St Lawrence. The King contributed both to the parish church and building at the Carmelite friary in 1465; there was also an Austin friary. At Ludford Bridge was a hospital of St John of Jerusalem, to which the round chapel of St Mary Magdalen, within the castle, had been appropriated by York in return for masses for the souls of himself and his family.

Ludlow Castle itself was large and impressive. There was a Norman keep, partly rebuilt about this time, two wards, the round Norman chapel in the inner ward, at which York, the future Kings Edward IV and V, and their households surely worshipped, and another chapel of St Peter in the outer bailey, at which St John's hospital was bound to celebrate mass daily in 1478 by Richard Duke of Gloucester. As York's son, Richard surely knew Ludlow well, and was indeed there during the Ludford debacle. There is still a thirteenth-century hall and chamber block where, with up-to-date furnishings, they resided. An aspirant for kingship and the three Yorkists kings surely used the garderobes (toilets) built into the western curtain wall. The Prince was not the lord at first – it was held in trust by Cardinal Bourchier and others for paying the debts of his grandfather Duke Richard – or, perhaps, at all.[19] Surviving estate accounts extraordinarily make no reference to him, the inevitable expenditure on construction and maintenance evidently being recorded elsewhere. The Prince's household and council were the largest local consumers and surely dominated the town. His officers leased castle meadows and other properties in the town. The Prince must have visited the parish church, perhaps frequently, where his councillor John Sulyard and servant Piers Beaupie, also receiver of the lordship and the corporation's recorder, chose to be buried.[20] Beaupie's widow founded a chantry at the altar of St Gabriel and St Mary.[21]

Shrewsbury town, in contrast, had long been a royal borough and fortress against the Welsh. It had been populous for much longer and contained not just one, but four churches, two of them collegiate, a Benedictine monastery, three friaries and two hospitals. It was a town that mattered. The Prince's councillors intervened several times in the corporation's affairs and in 1478 devised ordinances to guide its conduct. Shrewsbury stood on a hilly ridge almost encircled by the River Severn, which was crossed on each side by bridges, the western Welsh bridge being the more massively fortified. It bore the statue of an armoured man, now on the market hall, that was traditionally supposed to be the Prince's grandfather Richard Duke of York. Shrewsbury is a red town. The soil is red and red too is the stonework of the castle, church and abbey. The castle was at the highest, north-eastern point. The inner ward with its hall protected by curtain wall and round towers survives; so too, close by and within the vanished outer bailey, does the massive but now redundant collegiate church of St Mary, a royal free chapel, its lofty Norman tower topped by the spire completed in 1477. Edward IV knew it personally, since before his accession he had been a trustee of properties there for the Shrewsbury clothiers gild, which in 1462 he licensed to apply them to a chantry in St Mary's to celebrate for the souls of, amongst others, his father and his brother Edmund; he also made the gild corporate.

Perhaps it was at Shrewsbury Castle that parliament had met in 1398 or where Edward IV and his son stayed in 1473, when Prince Richard was born at the neighbouring Shrewsbury Blackfriars.[22] The castle was not garrisoned, nor probably maintained in good repair and it surely lacked the up-to-date facilities of King or court. Far more probably the King and Prince stayed across the Severn at the royal abbey of Shrewsbury, whose abbot was one of only twenty-six with a seat in the Lords and where Elizabeth Countess of

Shrewsbury, mother of the Prince's councillor, was buried in 1473. It was certainly there that the Prince stayed in 1478-9, when the town's gift, wine 'in honour of the town', and ale was delivered there by cart, and presumably also on his visit in 1480. It had been to the abbey, not the town, that Sheriff Charlton had been alluding. In 1466, supposedly in confirmation and clarification of earlier charters dating back to the twelfth century, the King had exempted the abbey and all its lands from the jurisdiction of sheriffs and much else. There remain the nave and the refectory pulpit, which stands incongruously in a car park. There are also fragments of the shrine of St Winifred at which the Prince surely offered. If the gild of St Winifred was only formally incorporated later in the 1480s, in 1474 the Prince granted £4 a year for a chaplain to celebrate mass several days each week at St Winifred's holy well in Denbighshire.[23] Much more survived (and was captured in prints) before the construction of Telford's Holyhead road across the precinct and the surrounding railway stations, now removed. Although the islets in the Severn and the wharves have disappeared, those approaching from the east are still confronted by the red-stone hall with stores beneath that the Yorkist royal family encountered.

There were many other modest towns in Shropshire and Herefordshire, each with its monastery or college, such as Leominster and Much Wenlock. At Hereford itself King Edward repeatedly allowed the corporation to levy murage towards the cost of the walls and in 1472 authorised the cathedral's college of vicars-choral to establish themselves in a prebendal house.[24] Charlton referred to Much Wenlock, a small unprotected town built around a few streets and with an ancient parish church. Where Ludlow is greystone and Shrewsbury red, Much Wenlock is black-and-white. Doubtless it was dominated by the Anglo-Saxon priory of St Milburga, whose shattered, but imposing, church contrasts with the half-timbered domestic comfort of the (regrettably somewhat later) prior's house. Perhaps Edward IV had visited and his son would pray at the shrine of St Milburga, although it was actually at the insistence of John Lord Wenlock that in 1468 he made it a free borough, granted it an annual fair at midsummer, and even the right to return one burgess to parliament.[25]

Ruling Wales

Modern standards of law, order and justice are not those of the fifteenth century. Late medieval England was perceived as law-abiding by its own inhabitants. Casual violence, which we would find intolerable, may have been endemic and routine, and perversion of justice – the maintenance of cases, the pressurising, suborning and even bribing of jurors, judges and law-enforcers – was inescapably part of the system and indeed an acceptable facet of it. Perhaps the mediation and arbitration of kindred, neighbours and lords was more effective in keeping the peace, restoring order, and settling differences than the course of law through the courts. Society itself, every local community, had an interest in order and its own mechanisms for attaining it. That said, every region witnessed crimes that affronted even contemporaries, and there appear to have been areas that were particularly disorderly. If the northern borders were especially chaotic, if the west too was wild, the state of public order in the marches of Wales towards England was often also deplored and had indeed become proverbial. So much is justice subverted, wrote the Northumbrian John Hardyng, that 'the law is like a Welshman's hose, which stretches and adapts to each man's leg'. 'Which country', wrote the decidedly metropolitan Thomas More, 'being far off from the law and recourse to justice, was begun to be far out of good will and waxed wild, robbers and reivers walking at liberty uncorrected'.[26] Such complaints are difficult to substantiate. Wales itself was a mosaic of different jurisdictions, few of which we know anything about, not least because the great sessions of the marcher lordships were so often cancelled on payment of a fine. To the residents, it appears, the cure for disorder – the great sessions – was frequently worse than the ills that were to be corrected. Moreover, legal conventions differed in Wales – the blood feud flourished into the seventeenth century – and any depredations by Welshmen on Welshmen or from one lordship on another were of little interest to parliament and have left little imprint on our records. All complaints need handling with caution, since England was an extremely law-minded country, in which litigation burgeoned apace, and was increasingly regulated, as parliament legislated against ills which had long existed, but were no longer to be tolerated. More complaints might signify higher standards rather than worse crime. Promises of better public order, however, were always popular. King Edward, as we have seen, offered it as a by-product of his invasion of France. The Commons responded more prosaically and practically. 'Yet sovereign lord', they lamented,

> it is so that in divers parts of this realm, great abominable murders, robberies, extortions, oppressions, and other manifold maintenances, mis-governances, forcible entries, as well upon them being in judgement as otherwise, affrays [and] assaults are committed and done by such persons as either are of great might or else favoured by persons of great power, in such wise that their outrageous demerits remain unpunished.

They cited recent outrages in Southwark and Westminster, even whilst parliament was sitting and sometimes in the King's household. If Edward III had been able to curb his domestic servants, why could not Edward IV? Was this gibe another factor in Edward IV's thoroughgoing regulation next year of his household? Please consider 'the intolerable extortions, oppressions and wrongs, that to your subjects daily been put', they begged.

> And in especial in the parties of this your land adjoining to the country of Wales, which by the outrageous demeaning of Welshmen, favoured under such persons as have the keeping of castles and other walled places of strength there, as it is supposed, are wasted and likely utterly to be destroyed.[27]

This too was rather close to home: was not Edward IV, as Earl of March and Duke of Lancaster, by far the greatest marcher lord? Had he not also for a whole decade held additionally the principality, Chester and Flint? Admittedly no names were cited. It was not Edward's tenants, on whom Sheriff Charlton simultaneously blamed 'the great murders, robberies, rebellions, and mischievous rule daily committed and done in your said county' of Shropshire, but particularly 'the evil disposed people of Powis and Oswestry hundred as other places of the marches adjoining', who broke the law, disobeyed the King's officers, rendered whole districts 'waste and desolate and depopulated', so that neither the sheriff's tourns nor the courts could be held. If Charlton's pleas were self-interested and designed to excuse him from collecting certain liabilities as sheriff, they carried at least *some* conviction since, on 6 October, the day parliament opened, he was allowed the £100 a year that his predecessors had received.[28] Was it from Charlton that the Commons obtained their information? Complaining was more widespread than this, the King reported next summer, emanated from Gloucestershire and Herefordshire as well as Shropshire, related to misconduct within the marches as well as the shires adjacent, and included additionally the ravishing of women.[29] The King could act directly in these shires, but only indirectly within the marches, where the Commons cautiously proposed 'that such direction may be taken by the advice of the lords marchers, that your true subjects their inhabitants may in like wise live out of the fear and danger of Welshmen'.[30] It was this course of action that Edward opted to pursue.

Edward IV had a crowded schedule in the summer of 1473. He proceeded to Nottingham on 12 May, where he imposed order on Gloucester and Northumberland, through the north midlands, cowing his brother Clarence in his dispute with Gloucester, and on to the marches to settle the affairs of Wales. Signet warrants indicate his presence at Ludlow from 23 May to 7 June. He was accompanied by his Queen, who gave birth on 17 August at the Shrewsbury Dominicans to his second son Richard, the younger of the two Princes in the Tower. King, Queen, and Prince, 'accompanied with many great lords spiritual and temporal', visited Hereford and held judicial sessions there.[31] There survives an indenture between the King himself and Henry Duke of Buckingham, as Lord of Brecon, Hay, Huntington and Newport one of the principal marcher lords, which records agreements between all the lords marcher for 'reformation and punishment' and 'for the guiding and good governance as well of the said counties as of the said marches'. If it was presented as a contract between equals that did not infringe the autonomy and regality of the marcher lordships – Edward sealing his part as Earl of March – he was nevertheless flexing his muscles as a King with authority over what the marcher lords held outside Wales, for none of them were merely marcher lords. We may presume that Sir William Stanley and Lord Abergavenny, coparceners of Powis, the Earl of Arundel as Lord of Oswestry and Clun, the King's brothers as contenders for Glamorgan, Abergavenny and Elvell, the Duke of Norfolk for Bromfield and Yale, Lord Stanley for Hawarden, and the Earl of Pembroke, for a whole string of lordships, attended in person or were represented. Altogether they agreed on twelve clauses. 'First it is ordained that the most principal and expedient remedy, as it hath at all times by experience been proved', was for officers of good disposition to be appointed. Stewards must officiate in person – and indeed must give sureties to do so – and constables (or their sufficient deputies) must be resident, if their fees were not to be discontinued. There were to be no more letters of the marches – licences to pursue private wars – and no more safe-conducts, except on the authority of the marcher lord himself. Criminals that took refuge in other lordships were to be extradited, on pain of a 100-mark fine for the steward responsible. Notorious felons were to be denied bail, which too often led to acquittal, and were to be imprisoned in their lord's castle. 'And for lack of execution there', in the castles of individual Mortimer lordships, that then 'such felons of the earldom of March to be brought to the castle of Wigmore as of old time it hath been used heretofore'. There were to be no raids on other districts, grievances being settled in the courts, no unlicensed livery and no idlers and vagabonds, all being set to work. If none of this was original, for there had been earlier agreements about the management of the marches, there were significant innovations in the formal contracts sealed by the lords, the enforceability of the sureties of all officers in England and the reference of any variances to such councillors as the King assigned. With the arrival at Ludlow of the Prince, enforcement was at hand.

The lords marcher sitting in parliament had heard the laments of the Commons and were now dealing in person with one of their own. It was because the lords marcher were not all members of the royal council or on that of the Prince that the King had to contract individually with them as Earl of March. The indenture specified that it was the King's council that was to handle disputes – it was probably the King's council at Westminster that was meant and that the marcher lords understood. Even after the governmental authority of the Prince's own council came to be recognised, suppliants and litigants in the marches were referred for settlement to his councillors at Westminster: a recognition that legal expertise at least remained there and perhaps that there was insufficient business to justify the permanent residence of lawyers at Ludlow. That the Prince's councillors were simultaneously appointed justices of the peace in the marches in March 1473 indicates that their powers to act as local governors in the marcher shires arose from these commissions, not from their membership of the council, nor from the Prince's position as marcher lord. Inclusion in commissions was permissive, however, enabling the Prince's councillors to officiate if they wished. Very few seem to have done so.[32] Remember that in 1473 Prince Edward was not yet lord even of Ludlow where he resided. Only six of the surviving suits before his council relate to Wales. Even if initiated locally, lawsuits were often referred to councillors at Westminster. What was new was not that the King's power and jurisdiction were devolved locally. Welshmen had still to traipse to Westminster for their remedies. They may indeed have been more likely to do so than hitherto because of the proximity of the Prince. Their cases were not handled locally. What did not exist initially was the Tudor council for the marches, a fully-fledged judicial institution, sitting *in* the marches with authority *over* the marches. Perhaps it evolved: the evidence we possess is insufficient to tell.

From 1473 the Prince had councillors in the marches, who certainly moved around his estates and beyond and made decisions. Lowe discovered them operating at Hereford in 1473, at Monmouth, Chester and Coventry in 1474, at Wigmore and Haverford in 1478, at Chester and Worcester in 1481, and at Chester again in 1482. 'The reality of the control exercised by his council over the Prince's affairs', he wrote, 'is clear enough from these occasional glimpses of its activity'. [33] If the King had always wanted his own men on the spot as his eyes, ears, and agents, three years on he had apparently realised the potential value of the Prince's council. On 20 February 1476 he deputed the Prince and his councillors to meet the lords marcher at Ludlow on 24 March following. The King himself was still to be involved, but as back-up a fortnight later.[34] He may not have come. Perhaps it was at that point that Prince Edward succeeded his father as contractor in renegotiated indentures of the marches with the lords marcher rather than in 1479, when he formally became Earl of March. It was Rivers who raised and led the regional contingent several thousand strong to the siege of Berwick in the Scottish war of 1482-3. Most of the references to the council date from the period after 1476.

This applies also to its well-known interventions in Shrewsbury and Coventry. Shrewbury's accounts record two visits by the Prince in person and many by his messengers and other dealings with his council. Most important, on 10 April 1481, Bishop Alcock, president of his council, Earl Rivers, his governor, 'and other of his honourable council' were at Shrewsbury town hall where, with the citizens' consent, they imposed a set of ordinances 'for the weal, rest and tranquillity of the same town and for good rule to be kept by the officers, mysteries [guilds] and inhabitants thereof'.[35] The Coventry leet book records more regular contact by King, Queen and Prince with what was the largest town in the midlands and the Prince's chamber, with which he had a special relationship. Coventry had several internal disputes with dissident patricians (Lawrence Sanders and William Briscoe) and with the cathedral priory that embroiled the Prince and his council. Whilst inclined to back the corporation, referring one dispute back, another time ordering the commons to obey the mayor and even imprisoning two dissidents in Ludlow Castle, the Prince's council held the corporation to account and its very presence, by offering an alternative to the established authority, may have encouraged disobedience. Its authority was limited. All its efforts to impose 'a good and restful rule' on the Briscoes failed, because the latter preferred the courts, to the Prince's displeasure. Perhaps they were wise, since he favoured 'our said tenants' the citizens: if the Briscoes caused any more trouble and hence enabled him to intervene, as evidently he hoped, 'you may be sure of our good lordship', runs his signet letter, 'and to have our lawful favour and assistance therein'. His promise of good lordship came to fruition in 1482, when the Briscoes accepted his arbitration and bound themselves to accept his verdict at the city from Bishop Alcock himself. The Prince's authority derived largely from the King, but Edward IV reserved his own rights: they had not punished evil-disposed people enough, he complained in 1481, and ordered the city to do so.[36] That the Prince could so far exceed his formal jurisdiction in Shropshire and Warwickshire, so Lowe argued, implied even greater control, where he had formal powers, than the available evidence indicates.[37]

Originally Edward had conceived the Prince's establishment as a sub-set of his own. The 1473 ordinances had ordained that the Prince be 'honourably served and his dishes born by worshipful folks and esquires bearing *our* livery'. He had no livery of his own. His men were the King's men and wore the King's livery. One can imagine the problems that may have ensued: on the one hand royal livery bestowed by the Prince did not indicate or impose obligations of service to the Prince; on the other, people could misbehave in the King's livery – indeed use it as a cloak for misconduct and to escape retribution – without the King being party at all. How could either Prince or King control their men? 'The King our sovereign lord, considering that princes first begotten sons to kings of England have been at their liberties to give their liveries and signs at their pleasures', persuaded parliament to exempt the Prince from the 1468 statute of livery and to allow him to bestow his own livery. The Prince had an exemplification (registered copy) of the act made on 6 July 1474.[38] Whilst no concrete examples either of indentures of retainer by the Prince or casual distributions of livery are known to us, this act marks a symbolic stage in the independence of the Prince's regime from the King's and in its capacity to operate in the same way as other lords.

The second conference of the marches in 1476 indicates that the first one in 1473 had failed to do the trick. Wales had not been reduced to order. Nor had the adjoining shires. The King's success in 1473 in extracting indictments from fearful jurors regardless of persons, Allington (acting as J.P. for Hereford) conveying the returns to king's bench, had been followed on 28 October 1473 by acquittals at Ross-on-Wye 'to the emboldening of all the misgoverned persons in those parts and to the great discomfort of all the well-governed people of the same'. Like Henry V in the same region before him, King Edward found that it was only when personally present – and then temporarily – that national standards could be imposed. It seems unlikely whether annulling the acquittals faraway in parliament in 1474 was any more effective.[39] It is doubtful, of course, that any set of measures by a mid-fifteenth-century government could bring law and order anywhere, least of all to Wales, with its myriad jurisdictions. We cannot tell whether the indentures or council had any impact, whether officers resided, entered sureties for good behaviour, held great sessions, or extradited offenders, even within the King's own lordships, still less whether the depredations of the men of Oswestry and Powis had been curbed. What few indications of the council's activities we have relate to disputes among the Welsh gentry, notably *Vaughan v.*

Croft in Dinas. Perhaps the local populace followed their leaders and their officers. It is questionable whether Welsh offices really 'carried far more prestige and power than their equivalents in England' and that 'office-holding, not landownership, determined local power'.[40] We cannot show whether any of the provisions of the 1473 indentures were enforced or neglected. An Anglophone council applying English procedure and English law may not have reached down to the Welsh-speaking population below the gentry operating traditional Welsh custom.

It is true that the Welsh marches were particularly destitute of resident lords in 1473-4. The King, Gloucester, Norfolk, Arundel, Abergavenny and Strange were non-resident from preference and Buckingham, Pembroke and, from 1473, Shrewsbury were minors. There was exceptional scope for a new broom. Yet the new regime did not fill a vacuum, but supplanted what was already there. During the 1460s south Wales had been run in the traditional way by a great magnate. William Herbert, Lord Herbert (1461) and Earl of Pembroke (1468), a member of the old Mortimer connection and King Edward's most trusted friend and ablest lieutenant. Originating from amongst the Welsh gentry, he was granted marcher lordships of his own – Caldicot, Crickhowell, Haverford, Pembroke and Raglan, which Edward carved out of Usk into a separate lordship – and both chief offices of the southern principality were granted him in tail. In 1468 he had also acquired by exchange the Duke of Norfolk's lordships of Chepstow and Gower. After he had captured Harlech in 1468, his authority extended to north Wales also. He counted nationally. He married his son to Mary Wydeville, the Queen's sister, and projected an ambitious (and potentially explosive) network of marriages for his daughters. When he died in 1469, King Edward at first honoured the entails on behalf of his under-age son William, 2nd Earl, whose offices were exercised for him only nominally by his own brother Gloucester and temporarily by the earl's uncle Lord Ferrers. On May 1472 Edward appointed Pembroke a justice itinerant within the Lancaster lordships in Wales.[41]

In Chester and Flint, it had been Thomas Lord Stanley – head of the leading regional family, marcher lord of Hawarden, and Warwick's brother-in-law – who had monopolised local power and office. Parliament's confirmation in 1472 of Prince Edward's estates effectively revoked all previous grants, as the Stanleys complained: now in royal favour, Thomas Lord Stanley being steward of the King's household, they secured a second act that confirmed their rights.[42] Their authority waxed thereafter.

If the 2nd Earl of Pembroke also secured confirmation of the rights that had been abrogated for the Prince, there is no evidence of it; possibly the 1473 Act of Resumption also cancelled those other grants of crown and Lancaster lands and offices entailed on his father in the 1460s. His lordship of Haverfordwest and also Newcastle Emlyn had been included in 1471 in the grant of the principality of Wales, but the Prince compensated him and his heirs male with an annuity of 80 marks – most of the issues – in 1472 and sent warrants pursuant to the receiver and auditors next year.[43] These apart, Pembroke retained his offices and lordships at first, but in due course he was eased out of these too. The Prince made new appointments in Pembroke in April 1479 and was created Earl of Pembroke and March on 8 July, the same date as Herbert was obliged to accept the earldom of Huntingdon instead. For his royal grants of marcher lordships and offices in Wales, he took the Prince's Gournay lands – part of the duchy of Cornwall and of lesser value - in Somerset and Dorset. The exchange of Gower and Chepstow was reversed.[44] These setbacks were preceded by a power struggle, since the Prince's men chose not to rule through Pembroke or apparently to include him on the council, but to supplant him. Since he could not be wholly excluded, Raglan and other family properties remaining, the earl and his brother Sir Walter were bound on recognisances in chancery 'not by space of a whole year then next ensuing nor after without our licence, pass west of the River Severn into Wales or the Marches of the same'; another William Herbert esquire, also so bound, was released from his bonds in 27 November 1479 and was allowed to enter Wales on sureties of 300 marks 'for his good behaviour'. The earl's two-year-old bonds were cancelled by the King at the Tower of London on 12 April 1481.[45] Two of the six cases from Wales before the Prince's council involved Herbert clients. In the winter of 1474 two of the Herbert bastards were being pursued by the King's council, there was apparently a Herbert-Vaughan feud, and in 1479 Grey and Croft headed eight commissioners to take action within the Lancaster lordship of Newport against yet another Herbert, John *alias* the bastard of Pembroke, formerly Pembroke's deputy as justicier of south Wales. It was Pembroke's man, Gruffydd Vaughan ap Einion, in the heart of Pembroke country, who complained unavailingly of the tyranny about the treasurer of Prince Edward's household, Sir Richard Croft of Croft. His complaint, so Lowe considered, indicated the total collapse of the Herbert connection where it had been strong.[46] Force always was needed to achieve and maintain dominance in Wales. If the Herbert connection appears through the Prince's archive to be the main source of disorder, with which the Prince's councillors had to contend, their decision to oust it surely contributed to instability until it was decisively defeated.

If ever it was. Ties of loyalty and service were not so easily dissolved. Ironically the Prince's authority was asserted by demolishing his father's creation of the previous decade and over some of the key leaders of the Mortimer connection in Wales. What was erected in their place, moreover, was bound to be short-lived. The Prince's regime was limited to his father's lifetime, after which – like Edward IV himself – his attention would pass elsewhere. A self-perpetuating, self-sustaining, and enduring institution had not yet been created. When the particular combination of absenteeism and minorities of the mid-1470s passed, marcher lords like Buckingham and Strange were bound to revive, to confront the new regime, or be allowed to share in it. Richard III reverted, twice, to the magnate model, on the second occasion turning to Herbert. It was the latter's son-in-law and grandson, the Somerset barons Herbert and earls of Worcester, who revived their traditional hegemony under the early Tudors.

The Prince followed in the footsteps of his father, grandfather and Mortimer forbears during his ten-year sojourn at Ludlow. He lived in a Mortimer castle, on the Mortimer estates, amongst those who had served his family in person or through their own ancestors. He visited Wigmore Abbey, the mausoleum of his Mortimer forebears, who were celebrated in the abbey's chronicle and genealogies. Whilst direct evidence is lacking, he surely developed a feel for the locality, came to share in the family's achievements and renown, and drew on enduring loyalties to his dynasty. He may have been much less conscious of those of the House of York preserved by Clare Priory (Suffolk) and celebrated at his father's re-interment at Fotheringhay (Northants.), particularly as his own father was establishing superior traditions at Windsor at his new chapel of St George. A further three aspects of his regime in Wales deserve emphasis. It extended its authority, it operated in the private interests of its members and it came to be dominated by the family of the Queen.

First of all, as we have seen, the Prince's powers were repeatedly extended during his decade in Wales, both formally and informally. His possessions took in Lancaster, March and Herbert lordships and were consolidated. Most of the Mortimer lordships were granted on 1 December 1476: the exchange of the Lancaster lordship of Ogmore for Elvell in 1477-8 rounded off both Gloucester's dominance of Glamorgan and the Prince's rule in mid-Wales. Caerleon and Usk followed eventually in 1483. The replacement of Herbert and the appointment to local bishoprics of Alcock, Martin and Milling facilitated local co-operation. So too did the Wydevilles' control over the Mowbray inheritance, notably Gower with Swansea and Bromfield and Yale. The Prince himself secured the custody of the Hakluyt lands around Leominster in 1480 on the surety of Sir Richard Croft and Sir Richard Delabere. The Prince's officers and councillors were appointed to local commissions of the peace, of array (2 January 1476), and of oyer and terminer (29

December 1476).[47] Indeed the Prince was deputed to appoint to the latter two: he appears never to have used the second. Also, as we have seen, his council operated informally beyond these powers.

The Prince's officers and councillors sought not only to extend his grasp, but also, secondly, to advance themselves in the process. This was true of all medieval regimes. They served the interests of their members. It was natural, sensible and obviously advantageous for the Prince and King alike to fill vacancies as they arose or to install replacements from amongst those men, who were already their devoted and trusted servants. They were great pluralists. Already the holder of many other offices elsewhere, in 1473 Rivers had replaced Hastings as receiver-general of the duchy of Cornwall and also later became sheriff of Caernarvonshire and master forester of Snowdon. He was steward of the duchy from 1476 and receiver of Chester in 1482. The Prince's men shared the spoils of Herbert's fall so greatly that one wonders if this was why he fell. Haute benefited particularly from the takeover of Pembrokeshire, becoming steward, butler and constable of Haverfordwest, armourer of Pembroke, butler and customer of Tenby, and farmer of mills at Pembroke, Castle Martin and Coedreth. In 1478 he was also appointed steward of Gower and constable of Swansea on Prince Richard's Mowbray estates. Richard Mynors esquire, an usher of the Prince's chamber in 1474, was deputy-chamberlain of south Wales in 1476-7, steward of Cantrefmawr, substantive chamberlain of south Wales and treasurer of Pembroke in 1479. He was not the only deputy drawn from the Welsh gentry to rise to substantive office. The Prince's uterine brother Richard Grey became constable of Chester in 1479 and in 1482 was granted the Lancaster lordship of Kidwelly to himself and his male heirs.[48] The Prince's men were English, haling mostly from the Home Counties and East Anglia, cannot have spoken Welsh and rarely exercised their offices in person. Individuals often combined all the principal offices in a particular lordship and operated principally through deputies, who acted, for instance, for the receivers and the stewards of both Radnor and Malienydd.[49] Generally local men, such deputies belonged to local factions. They owed any loyalty first to themselves, their family and faction, secondly perhaps to the substantive officer who had appointed them, and only afterwards to the Prince, just like the officers which the 1473 indentures of the marches had striven to root out.

The Prince's officers also exerted their authority locally – they were as liable to tyrannical abuse as anyone else. Gruffydd Vaughan ap Einion complained that Sir Richard Croft was falsely claiming their property in the Prince's lordship of Dinas (Blaenllyffni). He could have no justice because of Croft's great might. Not only was Croft 'one of your great officers', but all the Prince's other men 'owe [him] right great and special favour and some of them [were] of fee and counsel of the said Richard', against whom no local lawyers dared act. Vaughan had already appealed to the Prince, who had referred the matter to his councillors at Westminster, without effect, whilst Croft pursued his claims locally, immune and untouchable. It is only from a second bill that we even know of the case.[50] It is unlikely that Gruffydd secured justice. Were the Herberts defeated only by promoting their rivals and taking sides in the endless factional disputes? Were such self-interested tyrannies accepted as the inescapable price for effective service? Just as bad, so later petitions allege, was the Prince's half-brother Lord Richard Grey.[51] It is doubtful whether the Prince's regime was any improvement on whatever it replaced.

Thirdly, the regime came to be dominated by the Wydevilles. The standard warranty for the Prince's charters and patents was 'by the advice and assent of the Queen and his council'.[52] Elizabeth, however, was far off and can rarely have been consulted on such issues. Actually the original council had consisted of much more than her and her partisans, whom Lowe somewhat exaggerated: it was not true that even 'from the very beginning of its residence at Ludlow the Prince's council must have been securely under the control of the Queen and her family'.[53] As time went on, however, changes occurred. Vacancies arose from death, of Shrewsbury (1473), Clarence (1478), Allington (1479), Bothe (1480) and Martin

(1483), and from advancement: Dacre was the Queen's chamberlain by 20 February 1478.[54] There were internal promotions, newcomers became officers and councillors, and the original balance subtly changed. Alcock occurs frequently as president of his council. He was chancellor by 1483 and perhaps some years earlier.[55] Rivers held great sessions in person (south Wales 1474 and 1478, deputising for Pembroke, and Denbigh, 1477), presented to a chantry in the Prince's name, used his own signet as sufficient warrant to move the seal of the Carmarthen chancery, rewarded his own men from the Prince's offices, and exploited the electoral influence of both princes to return his men to parliament.[56]

The Queen's in-law Sir Richard Haute, controller of the Prince's household, was active in 1481-2 in undertaking repairs to both castle and mills at Pembroke, where he was the new steward. It was John Isham, servant of the Queen and a longstanding Wydeville client, who twice communicated for the Prince with Coventry corporation.[57]

In 1483 the new household ordinances coupled the Prince's second stepbrother, Lord Richard Grey, in control alongside Rivers and Alcock. Grey is a neglected figure. Probably somewhat older than is usually supposed, he was knighted with all his brothers in 1475 and appointed to local commissions of the peace. He accompanied his brother Dorset through Shrewsbury to Oswestry in 1474[58] – perhaps to sort out crime? – and actually officiated at quarter sessions, unlike most of the Prince's councillors, at Ludlow and Hereford in 1476 and at Shrewsbury next year. It was he and Lord Stanley, not Rivers or the Prince, who were guests of honour at Alcock's enthronement feast in the priory refectory at Worcester in 1476. Grey, not Rivers, was the most visible Wydeville in Wales in the mid-1470s.[59]

We do not know more than a fraction of the newcomers by name nor how they were selected, but we may guess that Rivers, Alcock and Vaughan filled junior vacancies and that the Queen, Rivers and the Prince's own councillors had an important say in the senior appointments. They were not by any means all obvious

Wydeville clients. Sir William Stanley of Holt and Sir Richard Croft of Croft, now respectively steward and treasurer of the Prince's household, were men of substance in their own right. Stanley was lord marcher of Chirk from 1475, husband of the dowager-countess of Worcester and hence co-lord of Powis, constable of Holt and steward of Bromfield and Yale to Norfolk, from 1478-9 steward of Denbigh, and was brother of Lord Stanley and uncle of his son George, from 1479 Lord Strange of Knockin. Croft was Edward IV's playmate, brother to the receiver of the earldom of March, and head of an important Shropshire family.[60] Each had his own important connections at court, was undoubtedly loyal and possessed interests of his own to further.

Whatever their backgrounds, the King's men who served the Prince remained the King's servants, but they had also become the Prince's committed retainers. There was no incompatibility. On a day-to-day basis it was service to the Prince that came first – Vaughan, for example, was the Prince's chamberlain first and treasurer of Edward IV's chamber when time and location permitted. Since the Prince's affairs were run by the Wydevilles, these men had become the Wydevilles' allies. They were regarded as such and patronised accordingly. Allington and Sulyard, for instance, were appointed by Chief Butler Rivers as his deputy-butlers at Ipswich. Wydeville control over Prince Richard's estates brought two offices to Vaughan.[61] The Prince's men were bound to support the Prince's interests – or what the Wydevilles identified as the Prince's interests – in any factional struggle and were committed in particular to his accession, to the inevitable reversion of power to him on Edward IV's death, from which they all hoped to benefit. They expected their proximity to him as Prince to continue when he was King. After all, they knew him personally and he knew them. Who else was he to trust and advance, but those he knew and valued? Such considerations had no impact on their allegiance. They were as loyal to Edward IV as ever they had been. Lowe is correct that the Wydeville-dominated regime of the Prince in Wales was a stable element within the King's own rule – 'an affinity in which ties of loyalty were channelled towards the crown through the King's close relatives by blood and marriage'.[62] Within the ranks of those loyal to King Edward, however, the servants of the Prince were now led by Rivers and Grey and aligned therefore with the Queen and the other Wydevilles. Potentially they were foes to opposing factions – Hastings and Gloucester – and certainly to any attempt to deny Edward V his crown. Edward IV was unconcerned by such factions – they were all his men, loyal to him, whom he could control – but his death removed his restraining hand. At that point, they ceased to be a stable element, and threatened disruption.

During Edward IV's life, his son's regime came to be an important extension of Wydeville power – their most important area of authority – and indeed the principal sphere within which Earl Rivers operated. It was not the only one. Through the Prince, Rivers exercised a regional dominance throughout Wales and the adjoining English counties. This could have involved little more than the oversight and co-ordination of existing authorities. One might have expected the Prince's regime to have become a different kind of family concern, his council an assembly of brothers-in-law, of those uncles of the Prince, who were also marcher lords themselves or heirs to them: his paternal uncle Gloucester, as Lord of Glamorgan, Abergavenny, and Ogmore; his maternal uncles Buckingham, Lord of Brecon, Newport, Hay and Huntington; Pembroke; Strange Lord of Knockin; Maltravers of Clun and Oswestry; and Grey of Ruthin. Only Gloucester is known to have belonged to the Prince's council and he surely, as lord of the North, was eternally absent. As we have seen, the council came to be more than this, certainly intrusive and perhaps also effective. At least some of the brothers-in-law were not partners in a shared enterprise. Herbert and Ferrers, as we have seen, were ousted and Buckingham, on the basis of 1483, had aspirations that were thwarted – admittedly excessively extravagant ambitions to rule the whole of Wales. What the others experienced and thought we cannot tell. The creation of a Wydeville hegemony in Wales, however, had its victims: Buckingham and Herbert in turn sought to manage Wales for Richard III.

For most of his short life, Prince Edward's acts were surely the deeds of other people in his name. Few of the letters patent under his great seal survive even as copies. They were commonly authorised by others. Even the signet warrants that moved all his other seals and authenticated his letters to the corporations of Coventry, King's Lynn, Shrewsbury and York cannot have required his personal involvement. He was merely a cipher in his own affairs, so his uncle Gloucester indicated at Stony Stratford in 1483. However, he probably became more than that. It was important that his upbringing should prepare him early for command and the management of his affairs. A lease of 1481 dated at Caernarvon under the seal of the chief justice of north Wales was warranted by a signet that the Prince had also signed.[63] He initialled others as King. Whatever the formal distribution of powers, it was because the Prince's wishes had to be considered that disciplinary provisions were added to the 1483 ordinances. No longer needing to be carried or continually attended, the Prince had less call for his chamberlain, who was away more frequently, and consorted more with his uncle Rivers and his half-brother. To their own eyes, to the Queen and the King, it was appropriate that such close kin should shape the future monarch. To their opponents, certainly to Gloucester in 1483, their influence was of the undue kind that the Prince's household ordinances had originally warned against.

1 *Edward as Prince of Wales. Fifteenth-century glass, Canterbury Cathedral*

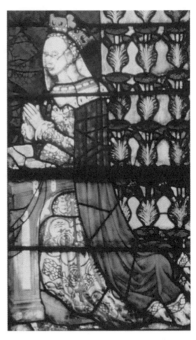

2 *Edward V's mother, Elizabeth Wydeville, from the Royal Window, Canterbury Cathedral*

3 Above: *Signatures of Elizabeth Wydeville (top) and Edward IV: 'Edward R' (bottom)*

4 Left: *Edward IV in middle age showing the corpulence described by Commynes. (Engraving of Windsor portrait)*

5 Far left: *Brass of Margaret Lucy, possible mistress of Edward IV*

6 Left: *Figure of Elizabeth (Jane) Shore, Edward IV's mistress, from her parent's brass at Hinxworth. Margaret could have been betrothed to Edward IV, thus illegitimising his later marriage to Elizabeth Wydeville*

7 *St Mary's Chapel, Sudeley Castle, built by Ralph Lord Butler. Lady Eleanor's father c.1460. Lady Eleanor Butler was also one of Edward IV's alleged conquests*

8–11 *Memorial brasses to some of Edward V's councillors.* Clockwise from top left: *Inscription and fragment to Sir John Fogge (d.1499), Ashford Kent; John Eastney, Abbot of Westminster, Edward V's godfather; Brass to John Argentine, the prince's doctor who accompanied Edward V and his brother to the Tower; the prince's chaplain, Adam Grafton*

12 *Prince Edward's schooling, under the tutelage of Dr John Giles would have been similar to this scene in a contemporary woodcut of a schoolmaster and pupils*

13, 14 *In addition to 'such virtuous learning' the 'disports and exercises' laid down by Edward IV's ordinances for his education included such martial accomplishments as jousting or titling at the quintain (13 right) and archery. The last recorded appearance of the princes has them 'shooting at Butts' in the Tower Gardens (14 below)*

15 *Reconstruction of the Abbey and Palace of Westminster as it appeared in the early sixteenth century.* A *indicates the sanctuary, Queen Elizabeth's refuge and* B *the site of Sir Thomas Vaughan's house where Prince Edward stayed when at court*

Ere endeth the book named the dictes or sayngis of the philosophers enprynted/by me Wyllm Caxton at Westmestre the yere of our lord. M.cccc. Lxxvij/ Whiche book is late translated out of/frensse into englyssh. By þ noble & puissant lord Antoine Erle of Rpuyers lord of Scales & of the/Isle of Wyght. Sefendour and directour of the siege Apstolique.for our holy Fader the Pope in this Royame of englond and gouernour of my lord prince of Wales. and It is so that at suche tyme as he had accomplisshid this said Werke it liked hym to sende it to me in certayn quayers to ouisee/Whiche forthwyth I sawe & fonde theryn many grete notable. and Wyse sayengys of/the philozophies. Accoz:

16 *One of the 'noble stories' recommended reading for Prince Edward. The* Dictes des Philosophes *translated by his mentor, Earl Rivers, and printed by Caxton at Westminster, 1477*

18 Detail of the statue of
Richard Duke of York as it
appeared on the bridge. Hence, the
quality of the image

17 The Old Welsh Bridge, Shrewsbury, now destroyed, showing
the statue of Richard Duke of York in the centre, above the arch

19 Engraving of the remains of Roger de Montgomery's Castle at Shrewsbury, where Prince Richard (later
Duke of York), Edward's brother, was born in the neighbouring Blackfriars

20 *The circular nave, all that survives, of the chapel of St Mary Magdalen, Ludlow Castle*

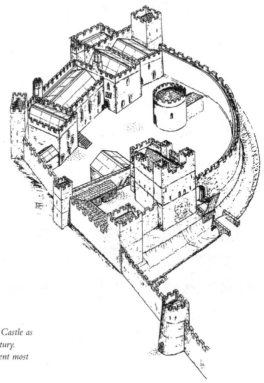

21 *Reconstruction of Ludlow Castle as it appeared in the fifteenth century. Ludlow was where Edward spent most of his short life*

22-25 *'Brothers in Arms': paintings of heraldic arms above their stalls as Knights of the Order of the Golden Fleece. Clockwise from top left: King Edward IV; Charles the Bold, Duke of Burgundy; Louis de Gruthuyse; Anthony, bastard of Burgundy, celebrated for his joust with Earl Rivers*

26 *Examples of Edward V's sign manual 'RE' (for* Rex Edwardus) *from grants dated back May 1483. The first is countersigned by 'our dearest oncle' protector and defender of the realm 'during our yonge age'*

27 *Seal of Edward V as Prince of Wales for the Principality of North Wales*

28 Left: *Engraving of Babulake gate, Coventry, where the City Corporation welcomed Prince Edward with a figure of 'King Richard' on his visit in 1474*

29 Below: *Radnor from John Speed's 'Atlas' of 1610. The vignettes that decorate the county maps of the Atlas illustrate a number of York's Welsh Castles, such as Denbigh, Radnor and Montgomery, 'each with a diminutive town beyond its gates'*

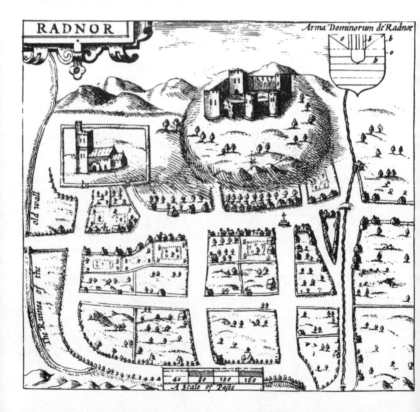

30, 31 Top left: *Monmouth Castle*. Top right: *Skenfrith Castle. Both castles were part of the duchy of Lancaster lordships which belonged to Edward*

32 Below: *The Anglo-Saxon priory at Much Wenlock, where Edward IV and probably Prince Edward, prayed at the shrine of St Milburga*

33 *Beaumaris Castle, Isle of Anglesey*

34 *Impression in white wax of the great seal of King Edward IV*

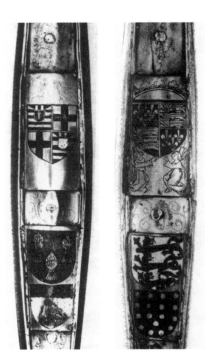

35 Right: *Hilt of a fifteenth-century royal sword of German manufacture, carried before the Prince of Wales. The shields on the left include the arms of Mortimer and Burgh with Chester below. Those on the right show the differenced royal arms and Cornwall below. They were probably made for Edward before his accession*

36, 37 Below: *Artists over the centuries have created these, largely imaginary, portraits of Edward V. Left: John Rastell (c.1529). Right: Francis Sandford (1677)*

Eduardus de. b.

Edward the. v.

The picture of Edward the 5. who at the age of 13 yeares was deposed, and cruelly murdered. by the procurement of Richard Duke of Gloucester his vnnaturall vnkle, when he had raigned 2 moneths and 11 dayes. and obscurely buried in the Tower.

38–40 Top left: *Antwerp (1534)*. Top right: G. *Godet (1560-2)*. Left: *R. Elstrack* (1617)

41-43 Top left: *P. Vanderbanck (1647)*. Top right: *G. Vertue (1736), credibly based on the Lambeth Palace MS, but adding Shakespeare's 'tender lambs'. Existing oil portraits in long gallery sets such as at Longleat (right; c.1595-1605) are probably derived from ill. 39 or portraits of Edward VI*

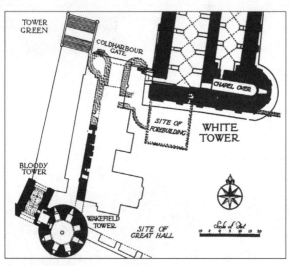

44 Diagram showing the site of the destroyed forebuildings, under the stairs of which were discovered the bones now interred in Westminster Abbey, as those of the murdered princes

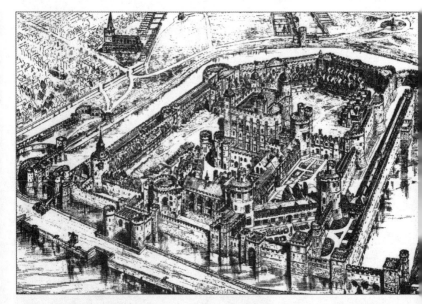

45 Reconstruction of the Tower of London, as it appeared in the fifteenth/sixteenth centuries. Engraving by H.W. Brewer

46 Top left: *Edward IV: detail from Canterbury Cathedral Royal Window*

47 Top right: *Portrait of Elizabeth Wydeville with later inscription to 1464, the date of her marriage to Edward IV*

48 Right: *Centre panel of sixteenth-century triptych said to show marriage of Edward IV and Elizabeth Wydeville.*

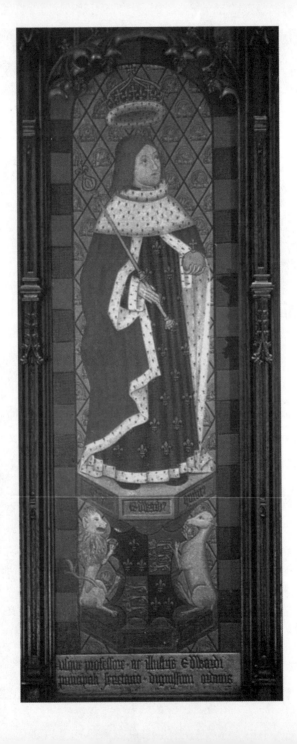

... atque professore · ac illustris Edwardi
principali secretario · dignissimo quondam

49 Opposite: *Painting of Edward V on the Bishop Oliver King Chantry Screen, St George's Chapel, Windsor. The artist here has placed the crown hovering above Edward's head, once again reminding us of 'the King who was never crowned'*

50 Above: *Miniature in the 'Dictes des Philosophes' showing Earl Rivers kneeling before Edward IV and family including Prince Edward, to whom he became tutor and governor in 1483*

51 Right: *A Knight in the Gruthyse Arms with signature and motto of Louis de Gruthuyse*

52,53 Left: *Richard Duke of York and Edward IV.* Right: *Edward Prince of Wales (Edward V) and Prince Arthur, by Thomas Willement Glass (1786-1871), St Lawrence's Church, Ludlow*

54,55 Left: *John Morton, Bishop of Ely and later cardinal. Panels from the Archbishops of Canterbury Window, Sevenoaks Church, Kent.* Right: *Thomas, Cardinal Bourchier, the Prince's great-uncle and council member from 1471. He officiated at the coronations of Edward IV and Richard III and also Queen Elizabeth Wydeville, from whom he obtained the surrender of the Duke of York to join Edward in the Tower*

56 *Fifteenth-century stained-glass portrait of Edward V, St Matthews's Church, Coldridge, Devon. This village was once the property of Thomas Grey, Marquis of Dorset. His park-keeper, Sir John Evans, whose effigy is in the North Chapel, may have installed this memorial*

57–60 *St George's Chapel, Windsor. Stall plates of the Knights of the Order of the Garter, of which Edward was briefly sovereign.* Top left: *As 'my Lord the Prince' Edward V's name heads the list of those elected in 1472. It is followed by* bottom right: *the King of Portugal and others, including longstanding and stalwart Yorkists,* top right: *Baron Ferrers of Chartley and* bottom left: *Mountjoy*

61, 62 *Two further stall plates from Windsor: (left) stalwart Yorkist John Lord Dynham and (right) Edward's brother, Richard Duke of York*

63 *Edward IV's Grant of Arms as Earl of Winchester to Louis of Bruges, Lord Gruthuyse (1472). Records of the festivities on this occasion include an early appearance of the baby Prince Edward, carried by his chamberlain, Thomas Vaughan*

64 *Edward V and The Duke of York in the Tower* (les enfants d'Edouard), *Paul Delaroche, 1830. On a four-poster bed decorated with appropriate heraldry, as well as the graffito 'King Edward V' carved on its frame, the artist creates a psychologically sobering study of the minutes before the princes' execution, evoked in an anxious and suspenseful mood. Alerted by the spaniel, the Duke of York turns towards the shadow glimpsed at the bottom of the door. Probably the most theatrical of his works, the painting would have had a particular resonance in France, with echoes of the guillotine and mysterious death of Louis XVII. A copy of the original is situated in the Louvre, Paris: this version was sold in New York in 1990*

5

THE POLITICS
OF THE FAMILY
1475-83

The Royal Family

Edward IV rated his family exceptionally highly. His 1483 sumptu-
ary act distinguished between royalty and the nobility, even dukes.
Whereas Henry IV long left his younger sons untitled and Henry
VI raised his half-brothers only to earldoms, King Edward made his
younger brothers and sons into dukes. Why this was he explained
in 1478, with reference to his younger son Richard:

> For so much as the great security, honour, defence, and the
> politic governance of this realm, stands and ought to be in those
> noble persons born of high blood and exalted in high estate
> and power. And the more high they be in the King's blood, the
> more they ought of right to be honoured and enhanced of
> right and power . . . And since it is so that such a high estate
> may not ordinately nor honourably be sustained, without [that]
> a sufficient livelihood be therefore purveyed and ordained.[1]

Hence his brothers George and Richard were created Dukes of
Clarence and Gloucester and knights of the Garter whilst they
were still children, were advanced to their majorities at the age of
sixteen and, in 1467, a target of £4,400 was set for Clarence's
income, more than three times that of an ordinary duke and six

times that of an earl. King Edward raised his father-in-law to an earldom and all the Queen's unmarried sisters were contracted to earls or the heirs of earls, two of which he now created. He bought a duke's daughter for his elder stepson and provided the endowments necessary to persuade two of the fathers-in-law.[2] In 1467 his first nephew John de la Pole, son of his sister Elizabeth, was created Earl of Lincoln. When his eldest daughter was engaged in 1469, her child bridegroom became a duke and his father a marquis. The £6,600 he thought appropriate for each daughter in 1475 doubled the largest known dowry paid by any English aristocrat.[3] We have seen how rapidly his eldest son secured not just his traditional titles and patrimony, but also, still an infant, the Garter. The first Yorkist king, like the first Lancastrian and Tudor, sought spouses for his children among the royalty of Europe.

The royal family evolved. Most of Edward's children were born after 1471. His siblings had children of their own, another two whom he created earls: his godsons Edward, son of Clarence, Earl of Warwick; and Edward, son of Gloucester, Earl of Salisbury. His sister Anne Duchess of Exeter remarried and then died. On his Queen's side, he had lost both his parents-in-law, and his step-daughter-in-law and niece Anne of Exeter. Two of the Queen's sisters died (Jacquetta Lady Strange and Mary Countess of Pembroke) and another two were widowed (Anne Lady Bourchier and Joan Lady Grey of Ruthin), Anne remarrying to a brother-in-law George, the new Lord Grey of Ruthin. The Queen's son Thomas remarried and made her a grandmother. Her grandchildren entered the marriage market. Elizabeth had nephews and nieces a-plenty. The royal family of 1464, much inflated by the sheer numbers of siblings, had multiplied. All were his kin or her kin, their kin, the royal family. All attended court and featured at family christenings, marriages, elevations, funerals and re-interments. Amongst them, however, there were already gradations. If King and Queen celebrated on 2 July 1480 as a royal wedding the espousing of Anne Bourchier (née Wydeville) to George Grey, already both the King's existing kinsfolk, and supplied them with gear,[4] the bride was nevertheless *her* sister and the ceremonial was much less grand than when the King's own sister and son were wed. Similarly George Lord Strange, husband of the King's niece by marriage, was less royal than he became when (half-) brother to King Henry VII, and much less so than the actual progeny of either monarch.

Royal ties mattered more to such relatives (*consanguinei*) than they did to the King and Queen themselves. With the single exception of the victim, who was executed, the wider royal family united in 1478 for the destruction of the King's brother George Duke of Clarence. They were all involved, actively or symbolically. The King, who led the prosecution; the Queen, who may have been the inspiration; his other brother, who did not oppose; his sons, symbolically; her brothers, sons, and brother-in-law; and all their connections. The most scandalous of family rifts, moreover, was presented in the guise of a family reunion – the marriage of the King's second son Richard to Anne Mowbray – accompanied with all the ceremonial, banquets and jousting to be expected of such a state occasion. Clearly Clarence's interests no longer coincided with the rest of his family. Neither did those of the minor royals, Suffolk and Buckingham, the latter of whom was appointed steward of England to pronounce the sentence: the rewards that both secured to assure their compliance had no sequels.[5]

It was a matter of priorities. All families evolve. The nuclear family of the marital couple and children dissolves, as parents die, children marry, beget, and set up their own nuclear families, as the vertical ties of parents to children take precedence over horizontal connections with collaterals – siblings, uncles, aunts and cousins. So it has always been. The Nevilles and Hungerfords are striking instances. Although royal families remember collateral ties to an exceptional extent, they nevertheless give precedence to the closest ties – not merely in terms of sixteenth in line to the throne – and distinguish between them. Witness the stress on Prince Edward as the King's first begotten son. Moreover, everyone has a different nuclear family. King, Queen, their brothers and sisters, and even her sons each had different nuclear families. Siblings and their families grow apart, have less in common, develop their own interests and even come into conflict. On many issues, the royal family ceased to feel and act as one, even if on fundamentals – that they were royal – they agreed. Even there, however, they disagreed in 1483-5 who should be the next king.

Edward could not advance them all. Indeed he had already provided adequately for most. He could not be as generous after 1471 as he had been before. Endowments had been settled on the Queen, Prince and his brothers, which he was repeatedly persuaded to enhance. The great pool of forfeitures of 1461 had been dispersed amongst his devoted servants or retrieved by the original possessors. There were no significant new confiscations, partly because his brothers made sure of Warwick's possessions for themselves. Competitors for royal favour, royal or otherwise, must be satisfied from the existing pool, perhaps wresting away what others had received. Amongst the royal family, it was Edward's own children, who now took precedence over his Queen's siblings, his own sons over hers. Queen Elizabeth also had choices to make: her sons, by whatever husband, were her priority. Some lesser royals, as they are called today, did less well than others: her younger son Lord Richard Grey and her younger brothers Sir Richard and Sir Edward Wydeville. Her priorities were not identical to the King's. Her eldest son now had his own children to think about. Her childless brother, Earl Rivers, fraudulently entailed property on his next brother Sir Richard Wydeville and remembered his nephew Lord Richard Grey in his will.[6] Her sisters were still her sisters, their husbands still (in contemporary parlance) her brothers, they and their offspring were all the King's kin, but consanguinity was a less potent force than before they were provided for. Moreover, just as the King aspired to place his daughters without cost to himself, without dowries, so he kept in his own hands what he had resumed and had confiscated from Clarence, so that his younger son and stepsons had to be endowed with what rightfully belonged to others.

Edward had provided for his Queen, brothers and sisters-in-law by 1470. His stepson Thomas married his niece Anne Holland, the Exeter heiress, and became Earl of Huntingdon, a Holland title. The division of Warwick's inheritance removed the King's need to provide further for his brothers – it enabled him to retrieve the Lancaster honours of Clitheroe, Duffield, Halton and Tutbury that he had given them – though Gloucester was successful several times in persuading him that their interests coincided. We have already seen what he bestowed on his heir, in both name and reality, and how he repeatedly extended his heir's titles, lands and authority. The French expedition of 1475 required him to take stock and to make a will, which provides an insight to his strategic thinking at that time.

As befitted his last will, Edward's priority was his immortal soul, for which he had settled most of the duchy of Lancaster in the midlands and north-east for twenty years to complete his mausoleum at St George's Chapel, Windsor, and to pay his debts. He had already decided that Windsor would supersede the unfinished mausoleum of the House of York at Fotheringhay. The duchy lands in Lancaster and south Wales were earmarked for other obligations, raising the £20,000 required in dowries for Elizabeth, Mary and the unborn Anne: £12,000 still due for Cecily's marriage had been approved by parliament and was therefore, so Edward considered, properly a public charge. When he reached discretion, Prince Edward could join his mother in shaping his sisters' marriages. The Queen received the south parts of the duchy for life. Their second son Richard of Shrewsbury, whom he had created Duke of York on 28 May 1475 and who was due to come of age when sixteen in 1489, was to receive three great estates: firstly, in tail male, on the death of his mother Cecily, those parts of the duchy of York in Northamptonshire, Lincolnshire, and Rutland – principally Fotheringhay, Grantham and Stamford; secondly, after the twenty-year term, the honour of Bolingbroke and other Lancaster lands in Northamptonshire; and, thirdly, the very substantial Lancaster lands in Norfolk on his mother's death. His future was to be as a royal duke and great magnate in the East Midlands and East Anglia. He may have been endowed as lavishly as the King's own brothers. Admittedly he would have to wait for it: if his mother died in 1492, his grandmother survived until 1495, when the trust was due to end. Evidently Edward regarded the duchy as private wealth at his command, much like his Lancastrian predecessors, and so too much of the crown lands, which he had acquired himself. Some of the latter he left to his son Edward in compensation for those York estates which, as male heir, he could have expected to inherit. Prince Edward, indeed, scarcely features, since his future was assured: he would be king, albeit bereft for his first twenty years of almost the entire duchy of Lancaster available to his father.[7] The will never took effect. Its provisions were modified, for instance in the allocation of the Lancaster marcher lordships to the Prince. That the final will was equally extravagant, however – testators tended to develop their plans in successive wills and, by the time of his death, King Edward had acquired other daughters to endow – is suggested by the refusal of the King's executors to act.[8] Their decision probably revoked the long-term trusts. Perhaps, therefore, Edward V actually acceded no worse off than his father, albeit burdened with moral obligations.

One major change, by 1483, was that Prince Richard was provided for, at least in part, from another source. Probably his share of the Lancaster lands was forgotten, but the reversion of the York estates retained. In 1476 John Mowbray, Duke of Norfolk, died and left as sole heiress his infant daughter Anne. She was a royal ward, whom Edward at once grabbed for his son Richard, whom he created additionally Earl of Nottingham on 20 October 1476 and Duke of Norfolk and Earl of Warenne on 7 February 1477. The wedding of the pair, both under five, was celebrated with the utmost splendour at St Stephen's Chapel, Westminster on 15 January 1478.[9] The Mowbrays were one of the wealthiest families in late medieval England with extensive estates in East Anglia, the East Midlands, Sussex and Surrey, and elsewhere.

Although all this would eventually devolve on Prince Richard, much of it was held by dowagers: Katherine Neville, widow of the duke who died in 1432, and Elizabeth, widow of the latest earl. The Duchess Elizabeth naturally wanted the best for her daughter and was induced to surrender much of her own entitlement. The deal that Edward struck gave immediate possession of the Warenne lands in Surrey – such as Guildford, Gatton and Reigate – and the marcher lordship of Gower with Swansea in Wales. This prince also received a seal, a chancellor – initially Allington – and a council appointed by the King. His acts also specified the assent and advice of the Queen,[10] with whom he lived, and it was Wydeville connections that profited most from his patronage. And if the infant Anne Mowbray were to die prematurely, as indeed she did, even though she was never of age, her 'husband' was to be allowed a life estate in most of her estates, both actual and prospective.

As descendants of Duke Thomas (d.1399), William Lord Berkeley and John Lord Howard should have been heirs and should have divided the Mowbray inheritance had Anne never been born. Unfortunately she had been. In November 1481, however, she died and again they should have inherited. Such a misfortune could not be allowed to upset their King's careful plans. Nor could their good service, which in Howard's case had been outstanding. The two lords were stopped from inheriting. The King revived debts of £22,666 13s 4d arising from the Berkeley-Lisle dispute due from Berkeley and his trustees, which, it appears, they had left unpaid for decades and had no intention of repaying. Potentially, however, they were ruinous and the King now released Berkeley from them in return for surrendering his rights to the Mowbray inheritance to Prince Richard and his male offspring. Berkeley, who was the King's cousin via his grandmother, was raised to a viscountcy at Greenwich on 10 June 1481. The agreement was confirmed in the 1483 parliament,[11] after which an indenture was drawn up to surrender Berkeley's reversionary rights to the King: perhaps it was never executed, the King's death intervening.[12] Duke Richard had a life estate in Howard's share.

Whatever Berkeley's sentiments, Howard evidently felt aggrieved. Amongst Richard III's first acts – certainly before the deaths of the princes – was the restoration of both heirs, Berkeley becoming Earl of Nottingham and Howard Duke of Norfolk.

The Wydeville Perspective

The principal asset of the Wydevilles was the Queen. Her influence, her household, and her estates provided many openings for her relatives and their dependants. However they were temporary: to last, like her mother's dower, only for her lifetime. It might all have ended with her first childbirth or in 1469. The enduring Wydeville asset was the modest Rivers estate, principally Grafton Regis (Northants.) and the Mote at Maidstone (Kent), held by Anthony Earl Rivers and to which his brothers were next heirs. He was already Lord Scales, in right of his first wife Elizabeth (d. 1473), who was persuaded before her death to resettle her modest Norfolk estates away from the rightful heirs on Rivers and her brothers. It is questionable whether Rivers or his brothers looked much beyond themselves to the future of their line, since all four were unmarried for eight years from 1473. Rivers' best route to personal fortune and the permanent establishment of his dynasty lay in marriage to some heiress: Mary Lewis, whom he married about 1481, was a modest heiress with potential to be more. However Rivers certainly aspired to chivalric and international fame and at least considered marrying two princesses, Mary of Burgundy and Margaret of Scotland. He accumulated a range of offices in many parts of the country. He was chief butler of England, held most of the offices at Castle Rising in Norfolk, added Clarence's lands in the Isle of Wight to his own and, as we have seen, acquired a varied clutch of offices from the Prince. He aspired to the constableship of England, which went to Gloucester, and the captaincy of Calais, which Hastings secured. If Rivers prospered from his royal connections, as he deserved, and if his brother Lionel secured the livings and eventually the bishopric that cost his brother-in-law Edward IV very little, neither Sir Edward Wydeville K.G., still less Sir Richard, benefited much at all. Richard, presumably, was a nonentity, but Edward was a soldier, a notable jouster and an intimate of the King.

The Perspective of the Greys

The Queen had two sons by her first marriage – *her* two eldest sons – that she wished to promote. Eventually, of course, Thomas Grey, the eldest, would succeed to the Ferrers of Groby barony, but that was long-delayed, until the death of his grandmother (1483) and her second husband Sir John Bourchier (1495), and might not materialise at all. Dowager-Lady Elizabeth had resettled as much of her inheritance as she could in 1462 and their influential feoffees, the cardinal archbishop and the Lord Treasurer, confirmed her second husband's title in 1474.[13] The second son, Richard Grey, had no such hereditary expectations. Unfortunately the King viewed his stepsons rather differently from the Queen and did not treat them as generously as might have been expected.

Admittedly Edward had provided £2,500 and the requisite pressure to persuade his sister Anne to engage her daughter Anne Holland, heiress of her husband Henry Duke of Exeter, to his stepson Thomas Grey.[14] The mother held the inheritance for life, which anyway was less grand than the ducal title suggests – Henry had been under-resourced – and comprised principally the three Devonshire lordships of Dartington, Torrington and Barnstaple. It may have been worth little more than £1,000 a year, less than the normal endowment of a duke.[15] Early in 1473 the young couple secured Rochford, Foulness and two other Essex manors. Altogether it justified his earldom of Huntingdon on 14 August 1472, perhaps when he came of age. His countess died soon after without bearing any children: the contract had allowed for this contingency and he secured lands worth 500 marks (£333 6s 8d), those in Essex, and in 1476 Thorpe Waterville and others in Northamptonshire for life.[16] He had promptly remarried in 1474-5 to Cecily, the daughter of William Bonville, Lord Harrington, and great-grand-daughter of William Lord Bonville, both slain at the second battle of St Albans in 1461. Whilst her mother retained her jointure and dower worth £400 a year, Thomas and Cecily had livery of the rest on 23 April 1474, and next year Thomas was created Marquis of Dorset. Whether two modest baronies, one centred on the north-west and other in the south-west, and neither of which materialised before 1476,[17] really justified a marquisate, Dorset thereby indicated where he saw his future as lying. Clarence's fall enabled him to become master of game and steward on the duke's Courtenay and Butler estates in Cornwall, Devon, and Wiltshire. When his consort produced a son, Dorset made another bid for the Exeter inheritance by betrothing his heir, another Thomas, to Anne, daughter of Anne Duchess of Exeter (d. 1476) by her second husband Thomas St Leger. His son, if not he himself, would be a leading West Country magnate. For £2,000, Dorset also secured a grant of the wardship and marriage of a truly great heir, Clarence's son Edward Earl of Warwick, whom he doubtless intended for an infant daughter, and secured the custody of Tewkesbury and some of the Salisbury lands towards the young earl's keep. [18]

Dorset's Bonville marriage deserves more careful attention also, both because it too gave rise to a separate act of parliament and because Cecily's parents and custodians from infancy were her mother Katherine Neville and her second husband William Lord Hastings. Although her mother was living, she was a royal ward, but her wardship and marriage had been granted to Katherine in 1462. Cecily was still unmarried, when the Queen opened negotiations, and was thirteen in 1474 when they were concluded. Her parents agreed on a dowry to be paid by the Queen for her hand. Apart from any down payment, however, this proved fictitious, since the 2,500 marks (£1,667) still due in 1477 was set off against debts owed by Hastings to the crown: her parents did not really benefit at all. The act occurred, not because there was anything legally complicated about the deal, but because Lord and Lady Hastings wanted parliamentary re-assurance – and they commissioned a registered copy (exemplification) too – that Katherine could keep the jointure which, they pointed out, her father had 'for great and notable sums.' Even so, they did have to give up the remaining issues of her estates, of which they were custodians, not initially to Cecily, who would be fourteen (and of age) very shortly, but to the Queen for two years. Another clause allowed for Cecily's marriage to Richard, if Dorset died first.[19] If Dorset was to be the long-term beneficiary, he was not the Queen's sole concern, and Hastings had good grounds for his qualms. When Dorset was a child in 1464, Hastings had designated him as spouse for one of his own daughters, but since then the balance of power had shifted decisively. The fact of the marriage does not indicate any interruption in the bad relations between Hastings and the Queen's family, including his new son-in-law. Lord and Lady Hastings had little choice in the match. Neither can have been pleased that their son-in-law became a competitor for the favours of Elizabeth Shore.

The Exeter inheritance, of course, had been neither the Duchess Anne's to give nor her second daughter's to inherit, for neither was a Holland and it belonged properly to Duke Henry and his heirs. After the duke had been attainted in 1461, the duchess, with parliamentary assistance, was allowed to hold it herself and to secure it on her new daughter. After both their deaths, St Leger held it, but only for life. He was party to a complex treaty now agreed between the King, Queen and her sons. Dorset, of course, wanted the marriage for his son, as cheaply as possible; the Queen saw the opportunity to provide for both sons; and, if Edward was happy enough with that, he wanted cash too. In the event the marriage occurred, most of the estate being settled on the younger Thomas and Anne and their heirs. Dorset had, however, to give up those Exeter lands he already held from his first marriage, originally valued at £333 6s 8d, which were passed instead to his brother Richard Grey, and received nothing immediate in return. It is likely that the King was reserving custody of the lands in any gap between St Leger's death and his daughter's majority. Five thousand marks was paid to the King, 3,000 (£2,000) by Dorset and 2,000 (£1,333 13s 4d) by his mother the Queen. Another act of parliament in 1483 legitimised a rather shady deal. [19] Again, however, it secured property to which the Wydevilles were not entitled and cut out a rightful heir, the son of Duke Henry's aunt, Ralph Lord Neville of Raby, from 1484 3rd Earl of Westmorland. [20]

The King recognised that Richard Grey would have to be provided for, but did not wish to do it himself. One contribution was 500 marks taken from the Exeter inheritance; the marcher lordship of Kidwelly, granted to him in 1483, with revenues of £172 gross and £59 net of expenses in 1481-2, [21] brought him status and raised him nearer to the comital income that Edward seems to have thought appropriate. The Lord Richard also held a number of offices and had still his marriage to negotiate. How might he have risen during his brother's reign?

The Prince's Perspective

The future Edward V's position appears clearly defined. He was the Prince and destined to be King Edward V. Since children often died prematurely, it was not certain that Edward would succeed. If he did not, his brother Richard was also in the Wydevilles' pockets. *When* Edward would succeed was unknown. Ideally the Wydevilles would have preferred his accession to be delayed, until he was of age, so there was no minority. Nobody expected Edward IV, in his early forties, to die. The event could have been long postponed. The Wydevilles prepared for it, enhancing their influence on the Prince and their hold on his estates, advancing themselves even as they worked for him. The interests of the Prince, at first, were compatible with other marcher lords and with his in-laws. Their very success changed this. His authority was asserted over others, who were viewed as potential rivals rather than partners.

The Prince's regime did not try to work with Mary Wydeville's Herbert husband, but to defeat and oust him: when they clashed, the nuclear family was to be preferred to the collaterals. The new Wydeville faction was preferred to that of Herbert, both subdivisions of the old Mortimer connection.

Edward V's entourage expected to gravitate effortlessly from service to the Prince to that of a king, which offered much more power and better rewards. For the Wydevilles this was the opportunity to move from the life estates of the Duchess Jacquetta and the Queen and their own modest estates to the permanence of a Wydeville king. It was at this point that his uterine brothers surely expected to become great magnates and his uncles, his in-laws, intimates and domestics to accrue the benefits for which they had worked. They were committed to the reversion. Edward V had no subjects more devoted. So others feared.

Perspectives at Court

Edward IV really ruled. He was an autocrat, strong-willed and determined, well able when he chose to confront and browbeat the greatest magnate. His execution of his own brother set new standards of rigour and ruthlessness. Edward was a good administrator, carrying a mass of faces, names and circumstances in his own head, and undertook on occasion the most gruelling sets of personal interviews. He was on excellent terms with his nobles. Brought up as one himself, with no expectation of the crown, he shared their values and their recreations – country sports, conspicuous consumption, munificent patronage, ostentatious piety and even sexual peccadilloes. He was, moreover, what his nobility most admired – a chivalric King, who was also a great warrior, proficient at the least at arms, the most successful general of the Wars of the Roses, interested in the latest fashions in ordnance and fortifications, above all bold, aggressive, and decisive. His title was unquestionable and he looked in control.

Yet he was not a great King. He was too inconsistent, too inclined to free-wheel and he made mistakes. He allowed factions to develop at court and in the provinces. These were little concern to him, because he was in control and could assert himself when he wished. If he planned the regional dominances of Warwick and Herbert in the 1460s, those in his second reign developed: Gloucester and the Wydevilles persuaded him that they were in his interests and secured from him more than he originally intended. He did not realise how he was being manipulated. He regretted the fall of Clarence, which was so much more to the Wydevilles' advantage than his own. As always, there were factions of court, led by those intimate with the King – his chamberlain Hastings, his step-son Dorset, and his brother-in-law Edward Wydeville – whose rivalries and petty squabbles did not alarm him even when, as it appears, they resorted to dirty tricks to discredit one another. Nobody could win during Edward's lifetime. The Queen could not oust Hastings, whose conduct in 1464 perhaps still rankled and whose preferment over Rivers and encouragement of Edward's self-indulgence was resented. Ostensibly supreme at court and at Calais, Hastings could not convert his eminence into real power or make it permanent.

Edward IV's death changed the situation, as it was bound to do. The inevitable advancement of the Prince's men, the Queen, the Greys and the Wydevilles threatened to supersede the servants of Edward IV. Hastings (and indeed all the King's men) faced demotion or worse. They had ominous examples in earlier victims of their self-advancement – in Wales and the heirs to the Norfolk and Exeter inheritances – and they could look to such victims for allies. If Rivers did not perceive the dukes as enemies and if the Queen could be statesmanlike, Dorset was triumphalist and Gloucester did not wait to see.

6

KING AT LAST

The Accession of Edward V

Edward Prince of Wales was a very good-looking boy. Evidently lively, perhaps even assertive and resistant to authority, and certainly pious, he was developing satisfactorily. Not only had he acquired the necessary dignity, the social and polite graces required of a king, but the scholarly attainments arising from classical literature and rhetoric were beyond his years. He could 'discourse elegantly, understand fully, and declaim most excellently'. So writes Mancini, who may have met him, who certainly talked about him with those who knew him well, and who felt obliged to testify to his promise.[1]

Edward was at Ludlow on Monday 14 April 1483, when news arrived of the death of his father Edward IV five days before. Prince Edward was now King Edward V. This was what he had been born for and for which all his life to date had been self-conscious preparation. The news did not come raw. It was contained in a formal letter from the royal council which also set the date for his coronation at Westminster for 4 May 1483, less than three weeks away. Edward's guardians were instructed to bring him to Westminster for that date with a noble escort limited in numbers to 2,000. Lamentations, requiem masses, and oaths of fealty to the new King must have followed next. On 16 April a letter was sent to King's Lynn (and doubtless many other towns and notables) urging them to attend the coronation.[2] In the new King's name, it was obviously drafted for him, most probably by his maternal uncle Earl Rivers. The shortest way to Westminster was south-westwards, via Worcester, Gloucester and Oxford, but instead the King took a more northerly route via Stratford-upon-Avon, Banbury and Buckingham to Grafton Regis, Earl Rivers' seat in Northampton-shire, where the Prince's parents had supposedly married. Still at Ludlow on Tuesday 22 April, they were at Grafton by 30 April. The diversion was made on the suggestion of Edward's surviving pater-nal uncle, Richard Duke of Gloucester, who had reported that he was proceeding from York via the Great North Road. Rivers, who must have had the ordering of the journey, had no quarrel with Gloucester and trusted him. He had just chosen the duke to arbi-trate a dispute in which he was involved. No doubt Rivers agreed 'that in their company Edward's entry into the city might be more magnificent'.[3] It would besides effectively quell any rumours of division between them and show how hopeless resistance to the Wydevilles was bound to be. This diversion proved a fatal error.

Although Edward IV was only forty years old, his death was not a complete surprise. Falling ill over Easter (28-30 March), he failed to overcome his ailment – perhaps a viral infection, not nor-mally fatal – and deteriorated so rapidly that already on 7 April his obsequies were being celebrated at York Minster. The alarm was only briefly false and the King did indeed die on 9 April. Edward had warning and time enough, however, to set at least some of his house in order. Only too aware of his sins, he sought to make amends in the most exemplary way. Divisions within his court, which he himself could tolerate and restrain, but which might escalate out of control when he was gone, were reconciled. In par-ticular his stepson Dorset and his chamberlain Hastings, respec-tively son-in-law and father-in-law, rivals in lust and much else, were obliged to make peace with one another. At the very least Edward saw roles in his son's regime for both parties. It was unfor-tunate that the King's uncle Essex, his long-serving Lord Treasurer and a crucial source of stability, had predeceased him by just a few days. Almost certainly Edward specified what form the government of his son should take both in his will and by word of mouth. His will does not survive and his intent is refracted through partisan media. We cannot be sure what form he intended it to take.

The royal council met immediately. There was no debate about the succession. The Prince was unquestionably heir and succeeded the day after his father's death (10 April 1483). The late King's body was exposed, to quell any suggestions of foul play or of a coup, and the new reign was proclaimed. Measures were taken in London to prevent any outbreak of disorder and an extra crew of 300 men from Derbyshire were thrust into Calais to ensure its security. Mourning was not allowed to interrupt the shaping of the new regime. Even Queen Elizabeth, the widow of the last King, attended in her capacity as mother of the new one. Once dead, her former husband's wishes were no longer decisive: no ruler could command from the grave. It was not the practice in England, unlike France, for queen mothers to be regents: a proposal along these lines by Queen Margaret in 1454 had received short shrift. Nor indeed was it normal to have a regency at all: the most immediate precedent, from 1422, had seen a protectorate, in which Henry VI's senior uncle had been appointed Lord Protector, an office that conferred the right to protect the person of the king and the realm only, and implied no right to rule. Richard Duke of York had been three times Lord Protector in 1454-5, 1455-6, and in 1460. The only possible candidate to be protector was Richard Duke of Gloucester, last surviving brother of the late King, paternal uncle of the new King, and senior prince of the blood royal. The King's four maternal uncles, Rivers, Sir Richard, Sir Edward and Bishop Lionel, and his half-brothers Dorset and Grey, though closely related to him, were not of the royal blood or the House of York and were therefore regarded as ineligible. But the royal council decided not to follow this precedent and not to appoint Richard as protector. That Richard himself was absent and unable to plead his case must have been a factor. To be fair, the council followed an alternative precedent, whereby the young Henry VI had been regarded as an adult from the age of seven in 1429 and the government had been conducted on his behalf by councillors. Instead they plumped for an immediate coronation. To crown the young King was to declare him of age. Aged twelve, he was still two years short of the expiry of his guardianship as Prince, four years ahead of the age of majority of his royal uncles, and nine years before that of ordinary mortals. He would nevertheless be responsible for his own rule. Mancini reports that Richard wrote to the council to put his case to be protector,[4] just as his counterpart John Duke of Bedford had done sixty years before. If true, Richard was too late. The decision was already taken.

Although obviously too young to rule alone, in need of others to guide him and govern him, constitutionally Edward would be of full age, with no need for a minority council or protectorate. Nobody was to dominate. His uncle Gloucester was to be merely one councillor among many. In his absence, unable to plead, it was Lord Hastings who argued for his protectorate, as much from self-interested motives as from altruism. His crucial role as chamberlain of the household ended with his master's death: its renewal and his equally key role as captain of Calais, coveted by Earl Rivers, depended on the new regime. The Wydevilles must surely have intended at least to control access to the new King and needed therefore to appoint a more sympathetic chamberlain. Hastings had good grounds therefore to fear that the change of King would decisively advantage his Wydeville rivals at his own expense. If the Queen and her family had no desire for Edward IV's death, nor indeed can have seriously anticipated it so soon, they had long invested in the Prince's future – the succession. When it arrived, mother, stepbrothers, uncles, aunts and cousins expected to accrue power, wealth and influence. Maybe they doubted what use Gloucester would make of the protectorate. If there was to be no protectorate, they were now free of Edward IV's restraining influence. Whether they intended to exploit their authority against former foes like Hastings, as he himself supposed, or whether they were content to share power, is uncertain. Their initial actions gave credence to Hastings' worst fears. Latent jealousies remained. Rivalries dating back to the 1460s, to King Edward's unworthy marriage and before and to the much resented aggrandisement of the Queen's family, now threatened the stability of the new regime.

In theory Edward V's majority should have prevented the dominance of any individual. In practice, however, still a child, he was bound to rely on those he knew and trusted. Who could these be other than his mother, elder step-brothers and the uncle who had been his guardian? Without any formal regency, they could expect to dominate him informally. Had Edward IV died suddenly, their chance might have passed, but Edward's last illness allowed time for the Queen, Dorset and their allies to prepare for the crucial council meeting and to seize the initiative. Professional administrators like Crowland, who considered themselves far-sighted, feared a revival of faction and opposed the domination of the new King's in-laws, but such mere functionaries were overridden by the higher rank and the ruthless power of the Wydevilles. 'We are so important', spake the marquis, 'that even without the King's uncle we can make and enforce our decisions'.[5] The council's decisions were transmitted at once to Edward V and Rivers at Ludlow, arriving as we have seen on 14 April. Queen, court and council proceeded to Windsor (16-20 April) for the late King's funeral and then returned to plan the coronation.

Edward V was sovereign. His authority was overriding and unquestionable. Everyone owed him allegiance and obedience. He should have been above party politics, especially at his accession and whilst under age. There is no reason to suppose that he was consulted about the politicking and manoeuvres undertaken in his name or was even aware of any of it. Yet he was denied the luxury of a honeymoon free of controversy and faction. Regrettably it was only to the people, admittedly the impotent majority, that he was truly the symbol of unity standing above faction. The Wydevilles saw him as their instrument, their means to domination; so did their foes. Anxious to prevent debate from becoming over-heated, Elizabeth agreed to limit the size of the young King's escort. Edward's arrival was timed to ensure that he was crowned before meeting his councillors. When the council met, an adult King would be in chair. In the meantime the Wydevilles strengthened their hands: supposedly Dorset seized the royal treasure; her youngest brother Sir Edward Wydeville secured the fleet; and Rivers would come to London in force.

Lord Hastings was well-aware that he had merely postponed the critical struggle for power. A mere 2,000 men, he apparently calculated, would be matched or outweighed by Gloucester's entourage. Others, like Lord Howard, reinforced their households. Yet the shape of the regime was to be decided not by force of numbers – who was best attended – but by political debate in a better-balanced council. Evidently Hastings anticipated Gloucester's support. So perhaps did Rivers, when he met him at Stony Stratford: perhaps he was unaware of the suspicions of his in-laws in London or indeed of the strength of factional divisions. Courted by both sides, Gloucester gave no overt sign of resentment at the summary rejection of his own claims to rule. He joined forces with Henry Duke of Buckingham, a great magnate who had also been denied his legitimate aspirations in Wale, most probably by his Wydeville in-laws. Gloucester exploited the information supplied by Hastings. United by their hostilities to the Wydevilles, Buckingham and Hastings thought that Richard was serving their purpose. What Richard himself intended, apparently a temporary protectorate and the management of the new regime, may really have been much more ominous. It appears most likely that he was already planning to usurp the throne when the time was right.

What Richard actually did, with the support of Buckingham, was to anticipate the impending crisis by a pre-emptive strike at the Wydevilles. This was his first *coup d'état*. Richard dallied on his southwards progress, reaching Nottingham (26 April) and on 29 April Northampton and Stony Stratford, where he racked up with Buckingham at an inn. They had passed by the King at Grafton Regis, whence Earl Rivers and Lord Richard Grey rode to join them. It was a pleasant evening spent in congenial company.' When first they arrived, they were greeted with particularly cheerful and merry face and, sitting at the duke's table for dinner, they passed the whole time in very pleasant conversation'.[6] Next morning, no doubt, the Wydevilles were to introduce the two dukes to their new King and all were to set off together for London. Instead, first thing, the dukes arrested Rivers and Grey, who were taken completely by surprise, proceeded in force to Grafton, where they seized Sir Thomas Vaughan, the King's chamberlain, and dismissed the royal entourage: almost all those particularly committed to Edward's interests, known and trusted to him.

Thus Edward V found himself bereft of his trusted attendants and councillors and already in the dukes' power when the dukes first met him. They placed the most reassuring light on their actions. Richard presented his actions to the new King as the purging of his evil councillors, not as a blow at him himself. He denied Edward none of 'the reverence required from a subject such as bared head, bent knee, or any other posture'. If Mancini is to be believed, he blamed King Edward's demise on his evil councillors and companions, whom he now intended to remove from the young King's side. Edward V, he apparently told, was too young to govern himself and the Queen's family were not appropriate councillors. He, Gloucester, would rule, for which he was well-suited by birth, experience and popularity. He pledged himself to be 'a loyal subject and diligent protector'.

This was almost the only known point in Edward's life in which his personal contribution is known. Bereft of his uncle, brother and chamberlain, he had nobody to speak for him. Nevertheless, 'possessing the likeness of his father's noble spirit', Mancini reports, he retorted that:

he merely had those ministers whom his father had given him; and relying on his father's prudence, he believed that good and faithful ones had been given him. He had seen nothing evil in them and wished to keep them unless otherwise proved evil. As for the government of the kingdom, he had complete confidence in the peers of the realm and the Queen, so that this care but little concerned his former ministers.

It was a good reply, but was abruptly brushed aside. Buckingham allegedly declared that rule was the business of men, not the Queen and that the King should rely instead on the Lords. Finally, the youth perceiving their intention, surrendered himself to the care of uncle, which was inevitable, for although the dukes cajoled him by moderation, yet they clearly showed that they were demanding rather than supplicating.[7]

Thirty years later More tells a rather more elaborate version of the same story. 'What my brother marquis has done I cannot say', young Edward is made to utter, but vouched for the innocence of Rivers and Grey. 'Yes, my liege', quoth the Duke of Buckingham, 'they have kept their dealing far from the knowledge of your good grace'. The King's attendants were dismissed and replaced by others who owed their loyalty primarily to the dukes, not to him. 'At which dealing he wept and was nothing content, but it booted not'. He was in the power of the two dukes and it was what they wanted, not his desires, that counted.[8]

Later that day King Edward was removed from Grafton to Stony Stratford, where he proceeded to London by slower stages than Rivers had intended. He therefore arrived on 4 May, the day originally designated for his coronation, but too late for it to proceed, had plans for it still been in train. There is slender evidence that the two dukes sought to secure his friendship and trust in a surviving slip of parchment on which each signed their names; the dukes added their mottoes.

King Edward V
Richard Gloucester   *Loyaulte me lie*
Harry Buckingham   *Souvente me souvenir* [9]

They may have succeeded. Edward must have already encountered the two dukes, both of whom were his uncles, Gloucester as his father's brother and Buckingham as husband to the Queen's sister Katherine. Both were young men, in their late twenties, amongst the youngest of the peerage.

When this news was announced in London, its unexpectedness horrified everyone. The coup came as a complete surprise. When news arrived next evening (1 May), Elizabeth and Dorset:

> began collecting an army, to defend themselves and to set free the young King from the clutches of the dukes. But when they had exhorted certain nobles who had comes to the city and others to take up arms, they perceived that men's minds were not only irresolute, but altogether hostile to themselves. Some even said openly that it was more just and profitable that the youthful sovereign should be with his paternal uncle rather than with his maternal uncles and uterine brothers.

The Crowland Continuator reports that supporters of the Queen gathered at Westminster and those of Hastings in London. By the following morning the Wydevilles knew that resistance was futile. Richard meanwhile wrote open letters to the City corporation, the royal council, and for publication that declared his loyalty to the new King and his intention merely to remove the Wydevilles from power. Many supported this action. On 2 May, Edward V wrote reassuringly to Cardinal Bourchier: obviously the words were those of his uncle.[10] The deposition of Edward V was not seen as a necessary sequel to Richard's coup: on many recent occasions blows had been struck at the evil councillors of kings who had retained their thrones. Understandably the Queen and her family thought differently. They recalled the unhappy precedent of 1469, when sidelining evil councillors had lethal consequences for several of their relatives. Elizabeth feared persistently for her son's throne: perversely to majority and informed opinion. They made no attempt to negotiate with Richard or to achieve the balanced council that had been the theoretical objective of the minority council the previous month. Once again the Queen took sanctuary at Westminster: following her last sojourn there, its privileges had been explicitly confirmed by her late husband. This time she was accompanied not just by her daughters, but also by her eldest and youngest sons

Dorset and Prince Richard, Duke of York and Norfolk. The latter was now heir apparent to the King. All were lodged in the house of Abbot Eastney. Initially the Lord Chancellor Archbishop Rotherham may have taken her side and handed her the great seal, which – realising the impropriety and breach of trust – he subsequently retrieved.[11] Certainly one of the first acts of the new regime was to appoint John Russell, Bishop of Lincoln, in his place.

Richard's letters and the manoeuvres of his supporters disarmed the Wydevilles and secured him admittance to London unopposed. The escort of 500 he brought was splendid enough for ceremonial purposes, but relatively modest in military terms, insufficient to overawe either the council or City. Hence it dispelled any fears amongst the uncommitted that he intended to use force to achieve his wishes. He had a track record of loyalty, repeatedly sealed by the oaths sworn to his nephew in 1471, 1477, and most recently at York and Stony Stratford, so his fidelity could hardly be doubted. Now he was careful to demonstrate anew and in public his respect as a loyal subject for his sovereign. All the Lords and the City council were obliged to swear allegiance to the new King, the dukes amongst them. King Edward V was lodged in the Bishop of London's palace, a relatively public venue in the City, where he was visible, accessible, but also secure. Just as capture of the King had placed power in Richard's hands, so his removal by others could have transferred it elsewhere. The coronation did not take place and hence Edward's majority was postponed until midsummer (22 June). Instead of deciding on government after the coronation, it could now be decided beforehand, with Richard's participation.

Edward IV's household became Edward V's: Edward IV's household chamberlain Lord Hastings and steward Lord Stanley retained their positions. The balance of the council was much changed by the coup. Whether Hastings knew of the coup in advance – Mancini claims that he did – he certainly applauded the results; like Buckingham he supported Richard. Minus the Queen, Dorset, Sir Edward Wydeville, Rivers, Grey and Vaughan, there was no effective Wydeville faction to overcome. Richard claimed that he had merely pre-empted a Wydeville coup and that they had planned to ambush him on his journey. He produced cartloads of weapons bearing the badges of the Wydevilles to demonstrate their intention to back their push for power, which everyone expected, with force. He also successfully slandered them with embezzling the late King's treasure, which in truth did not exist. By 8 May the council had approved Richard's appointment as Lord Protector. We lack details of his powers, presumably in accordance with precedent, and any financial provisions. For the next seven weeks of Edward's short reign uncle Richard was at the helm – the executive chairman of a ruling council.

The council was not partisan. Committed to the young King, it was also respectful to the Queen and anxious for reconciliation. The two dukes, as we have seen, rightly regarded the King as a child and not yet ready to rule, but they either could not move the council to change its decision to advance his majority or perhaps dared not. On the coronation rested everyone's hope for peace and prosperity, reports Crowland.[12]

The council did not cancel Edward V's coronation and majority, but merely postponed them, until 22 June 1483, at which point Richard's protectorate would cease. Parliament was summoned for 25 June. At that point a trial of strength was to be anticipated. The original dates indicate that parliament was to be opened by a King of full-age: his majority and the direction of his regime would not be in question. Subsequent unrecorded changes, to put parliament forward, would have changed the order, perhaps significantly, so that the form of government was not a *fait accompli*. The draft speeches of Bishop Russell for the opening of parliament seem to indicate a plan that would enable Richard to continue ruling beyond the coronation. Once declared of age, there was a risk that the young King would recall his mother, stepbrothers and maternal uncles, and might again allow them dominance. To avert that, Richard wanted Rivers, Grey and Vaughan not merely to be confined, but executed for treason. He knew, from the precedents of 1455, 1460 and 1469, that permanent exclusion from power was most decisively achieved by death. However friendly their previous relationships, his own actions had made the Wydevilles into his most implacable enemies. The royal council could afford a more considered, legalistic, and constitutional response. Whatever the Wydevilles had planned against Richard when he was not protector, it was not treason and did not merit death. Richard, reports Mancini,

> attempted to bring about the condemnation of those whom he had put in prison, by obtaining a decision of the council convicting them of preparing ambushes and of being guilty of treason itself. But this he was quite unable to achieve, because there appeared no certain case as regards the ambushes, and even had the crime been manifest, it would not have been treason, for at the time of the alleged ambushes he was neither regent nor did he hold any other public office. [13]

The council's respect for strict legality left Richard exposed to future revenge. He was able, however, to keep Rivers, Grey and Vaughan confined. There were objections even to that measure, surely necessary for Richard's peace of mind and personal security. Moreover it was 'a great cause of anxiety', writes Crowland, together with 'the fact that the protector did not show sufficient consideration for the dignity and peace of mind of the Queen'.[4] Overtures were made to her to come out of sanctuary as late as 23 May, which she rebuffed.

The Government of Edward V

Edward V's reign was not purely a struggle for power. A struggle there was or rather three struggles, separated by several weeks in each case, but in between routine administration continued and other issues were more pressing. Laws continued to be administered and money coined as normal, and 'all the things pertaining to the royal dignity were performed in the young King's name'. How the new regime would be run was very quickly decided, as we have seen. The old King's funeral followed and absorbed the attention of the political elite for a week or so. It cost £1,496: how to pay for it was a concern for much longer. More seriously, the foreign relations that Edward V had inherited were in a state of flux. For the past two years Edward IV had been at war with Scotland: victory, including the temporary capture of Edinburgh and the permanent recovery of Berwick, had not been accompanied by a peace treaty. The alliance with France, cemented by a marriage alliance and a French pension on which Edward IV had so prided himself, had collapsed: Elizabeth of York, the dauphin's intended bride, was abruptly jilted. If Edward considered war with France, it was only briefly. Relations were decidedly frosty and the French were amongst those engaged in serious piracy in the Channel. Their fleet was in the Solent. Might not the King's death be the occasion for a successful assault on Calais? Defence on more than one front was potentially costly. Whatever Edward IV had accrued in treasure earlier in his reign, most of it had been spent by his death, when his funeral costs alone exceeded the reserves in his exchequer (£490) and his chamber (£710). Whatever he planned in his will, it exceeded his assets, and on 7 May 1483 his executors refused to act.[15] How to match expenses against receipts was a pressing problem: a hand to mouth approach was inescapable. How to take effective defence measures was another. How to pay for the coronation was a third, although, on surviving evidence, the coronation scheduled for 4 May was to be a good deal less lavish than the coronation of King Richard that actually happened on 6 July.

We have already seen the Wydevilles asserting their dominance in the royal council. They were not merely a court or Westminster clique. Both the Queen's youngest brother Sir Edward Wydeville and his eldest stepson Dorset jousted and had military aspirations, but they had so far been denied much opportunity. Gloucester had commanded in the north, where he had made a banneret of Sir Edward in 1481, and their rival Hastings commanded at Calais. Now, however, their chance had arrived. Both were commissioned to raise naval forces for defence of the realm. The defences of Calais and the Isle of Wight were strengthened. Dorset agreed to take 1,000 men to sea until Michaelmas, priced £800, and Sir Edward a further 2,000 for two months. With wages, rewards for captains and lodesmen, jackets, and ordnance from the Tower his force cost £3,269 14s 4d, making a grand total of £4,069 13s 4d. If the Wydevilles abstracted much of the King's paltry treasure, as Gloucester skilfully smeared them, it was with the consent of the council and for the defence of the realm. Sir Edward indeed took to the sea and with doubtful legality confiscated a great carrack in Southampton Water containing £10,250 of English gold coin.[16] They certainly were not preoccupied with reinforcing their tenure on power at the centre at the expense of the public interest.

Moreover, they had little power. Ruling councils avoided as far as possible taking any actions that were not inescapable, making any permanent decisions, or in any way infringing the prerogative of the king. Henry VI's council, for instance, sought to hand over power at his majority unabridged. Much minor administrative business continued. Re-appointment of the royal judges was no doubt essential and their patents of 21 April were authorised by the King himself: one wonders quite what that meant, in the King's absence and without any surviving warrant.[17] That date also saw the mayor of the staple of Calais admitted, and sheriffs and escheators were appointed; coroners followed on 23 April. No authority is stated for three commissions of 26-27 April against piracy and to tax aliens. Their appointments apart, however, there are no grants or appointments under the great seal enrolled until 14 May and no surviving chancery warrants before that date. Probably the council took necessary administrative actions using the privy seal, for which no archive survives. Perhaps Edward V had no great seal as King. He retained those seals that he possessed as Prince. A signet letter from him to King's Lynn survives. As yet, a minor, he had no power to move the royal seals other than those that he had possessed as Prince. It is not therefore surprising that the first signet warrant recorded in his signet register – a stray dated 5 May at St Albans[18] –

ordered the presentation to a church living under the seal of the earldom of March that he had already been able to command when Prince. It is only from 9 May that instructions were regularly issued under his signet in his own name. The first surviving treasurer's bill dates from 18 May,[19] the day after Wood's appointment.

There is no sign that Edward V had any larger say during Gloucester's protectorate than he had during the previous month of conciliar rule. Only seven warrants for the great seal bear the King's sign manual, the initials RE in his own hand, two somewhat sketchy and experimental. One of 18 June, to distrain those refusing to take up knighthood, was countersigned. The boldest signature authorises the summons of parliament.[20] All acts of the government were still undertaken in the King's name and all correspondence was addressed on his behalf, only the actual instigator having changed. It was a pious fiction, of course, that Edward himself was acting 'by the advice and assent of our most entirely beloved uncle the duke of Gloucester, protector and defender of our realm' or 'by the advice of our council'. Gloucester 'exercised this authority', wrote the Crowland Continuator, 'with the consent and the good will of all the lords, commanding and forbidding in everything like another King, as occasion demanded'.[21] The very fact that the King's signature was occasionally required, presumably aware of what he was sanctioning and why, is evidence both that he was being inducted into government – he was more than a dry-stamp – and that his sign manual already carried particular authority. Edward V himself had resided first at the bishop of London's palace and was then moved, between 9 and 16 May, to the Tower. Although it was Buckingham's suggestion, his proposal being 'accepted verbally by all, even by those who did not wish it', the Tower was the obvious choice. Lodging the King in the bishop's palace or even at the priory of St John at Clerkenwell was eccentric and burdensome. If Westminster was inappropriate, given the proximity of his mother in sanctuary, and if Greenwich, Eltham, Kennington, Windsor or other Thames-side palaces outside the metropolis were inconvenient, then the Tower it must be. It was secure, had up-to-date apartments, in which kings and queens regularly stayed, and it had not acquired the sinister reputation that Richard III and the Tudors were to give it. It certainly had not for Edward, who had familiar attendants such as his physician John Argentine, received visitors, and was frequently observed shooting and playing in the gardens with his brother Richard. What the move also signalled, of course, is that the young King was distanced from the day-to-day operation of the central departments at Westminster.

That day-to-day operation always seems to have been brief and intermittent. The patent roll of Edward V has a very unfinished look. Only six membranes long, some blank on obverse or reverse, it is not continuous, entries having clearly been made in batches, and records acts almost exclusively between 14 May, when justices of assize were appointed to four home counties, and 9 June. It suggests that normal rule during Gloucester's protectorate lasted for only a month and the second week of June marked a crisis that suspended normal government until the change of monarch was effected. The financial memoranda also cease about that date. Most patents were warranted by the privy seal but can also be traced back to Edward V's signet register. [22] This suggests not that the King was actively making decisions, but that Gloucester found it convenient to use a seal unfettered by the council and a keeper of ministerial rank. Letters under the signet sent to those outside government, apparently kept in a third register, are lost. We know that Gloucester himself, 'brother and uncle of kings', wrote letters and issued instructions in his own right.

The new regime was anxious to stress continuity between the new and the old. The new King, like his father, was a Yorkist, inherited the allegiance of all and the particular loyalty due to the Yorkist establishment, and was anxious to exact it. The new protector was the late King's brother and one of his most trusted adherents. He had been responsible for the King's principal success in his last years, victory in Scotland and the capture of Berwick, and surely it was he who pushed Berwick up the political agenda. Gloucester's retainer Henry Percy, Earl of Northumberland was contracted for a year to command Berwick, with a garrison of 600 men who cost £438 a month in pay. Presumably it was Gloucester, who had seen Berwick, not the councillors who had not, still less the King (whatever the memoranda say) who certainly had not, who also decided on a building programme to bring the fortress up to standard. The resident English population was to be raised by about 500.

> It was thought by the King's grace that there should be at least 120 houses made at Berwick this year, which would cost by estimation 20 mark a house, which draweth in all to £1,600 ...
> Item that timber should be had to Berwick for making of the hall within the castle and other chambers there.
> Item it was thought by the King's grace that £1,000 should do much to the repair of the two walls of Berwick and castle of the same.

The total cost was to be £2,600, of which £640 was paid in cash to the master porter and to the diplomat Dr Alexander Lee.[23] Given the difficulties of the regime in paying its bills, it may be that observation of these transactions explains the jaundiced view of Berwick of one such councillor, the Crowland Continuator. 'This trifling gain, or perhaps more accurately loss (for the maintenance of Berwick costs 10,000 marks a year) diminished the substance of the King and kingdom by more than £100,000 at this time'.[24]

What can best be studied now, thanks to the fortunate survival of a book of memoranda, are the financial problems of the regime and how they were solved. Of course Gloucester as protector had to be interested, yet these were primarily technical matters, involving liaison between the exchequer and council and ultimately adjudicated by them. It was 'your good lordships' who 'will command what's to be done'. Edward IV left no surplus, revenues and expenses were in precarious balance, and one key source of revenue – the customs – ended with his death. Although the regime tried still to levy it, on the basis that it would be re-granted by parliament, the mercers of London objected on 3 June and collection ceased. The council borrowed from the King's ministers (twice), from Edward IV's estate, which paid for his funeral, and from others, on the security of a future clerical tenth to be voted by convocation (the clerical parliament) summoned on 16 May and by pledges of the King's jewels. Gloucester himself contributed £800 towards the King's household and travel expenses. Royal wards were sold, such as Anne Salvan for 1,000 marks, and other windfalls were juggled against regular liabilities. At one point they listed the following charges:

1 The progress of Edward V, Gloucester, Buckingham and others from Northampton to London.
2 Money to those sent to safeguard different parts of the realm.
3 The costs of sending ships to sea to break up the Wydeville fleet.
4 The King's household.
5 Edward IV's funeral.
6 Edward IV's month's mind.
7 The coronation.
8 The payment of the Calais crew from 7 July until 29 September.
9 The wages of the Berwick garrison for May.
10 The rigging and setting forth of the *Anthony*.
11 The keeping of the King's ships.
12 'The *Grace Dieu* to be remembered that she perish not'
13 The charges of the Lord Protector.

Gloucester, like his father, was probably due both expenses and lavish pay. And when the May wages for Berwick were met, they had to worry about June and July. It was all very hand to mouth.

Ironically one of the early charges, listed here, was the despatch of naval forces to deal with those of the Wydevilles that they had prepared the previous month.

Item a letter to Edward Brampton, John Welles and Thomas Grey to go to the sea with ships to take Sir Edward Wydeville. Item a letter to William Berkeley, William Uvedale and Roger Kelsall to victual and furnish the said ships, with a clause to receive all that will come [to terms] except the marquis [of Dorset], Sir Edward Wydeville, and Robert Ratcliff. This clause also is in the letter above. [25]

Wydeville was lying off the Downs. Although the counter-force was indeed prepared, no fighting resulted, for Richard's tactic of promising pardons to those who deserted achieved the desired result peacefully.

Despite claims to continuity, the protectorate did initially bring about significant changes in personnel. Hastings and Stanley retained their authority both within the royal household, in Calais and their localities, which the Wydevilles might have altered; the King's principal ministers, major local offices, lesser household offices and the hierarchy in Wales all being changed. At the top, Archbishop Rotherham, chancellor 1474-83 and perhaps too committed to the Queen, was replaced by John Russell, Bishop of Lincoln. A churchman of similar qualifications, already keeper of the privy seal and the principal diplomat of Edward IV's second reign, this was the normal promotion for a man about whom nothing unfavourable is recorded. 'A wise man and a good and of much experience', writes More, 'he was one of the best learned men undoubtedly that England had at this time'. [26] His own replacement, Dr John Gunthorpe, Dean of Wells was similar in type. As for the treasury, vacated on death by Essex, unusually an insider was promoted, John Wood, hitherto under-treasurer. These appear a-political (and uncontroversial) appointments of career civil servants. We cannot know for sure what happened to the royal household, since appointments and dismissals by the chief officers are recorded nowhere else. Yet it appears that the household of Edward IV was allowed to continue and served Edward V. His household as Prince, whose members had served in the expectation of graduating into his household as King, had been dismissed at Stony Stratford. Most were disappointed. Even though continued, many of Edward IV's household men were to prove loyal to his son rather than to his brother.

Much the same applied to those who had ruled in Wales for the Prince. There was no longer a council of the marches. Most of its powers were transferred en bloc on 15 May to Buckingham, already one of the principal lords marcher, who thus became more powerful in Wales than anybody before him – even greater than William Herbert, Earl of Pembroke, Edward IV's right-hand man in the 1460s. The duke was appointed chief justice and chamberlain both of north and south Wales, constable of all castles, steward and receiver of all lordships and master forester of all chases of the crown, principality, duchy of Lancaster and earldom of March in Wales. Like the Prince before him, Buckingham received

the oversight of our subjects now being or hereafter in south Wales, north Wales, and in the marches of Wales and in the counties of Hereford [and] Shropshire ... and also power and discretion in our name for our defence and the defence of our realm and for the defence and keeping of our peace and in the said parts to assemble all our subjects defensibly arrayed and therein convey or send to such place or places and from time to time as shall be thought to the said duke expedient.

Perhaps a French invasion was feared, but more probably a Wydeville revival was being pre-empted. Sweeping though they were, such powers were no greater than those theoretically of Prince Edward but actually exercised by his council on his behalf. But there was more:

We, considering that the said duke shall bear and sustain costs and expenses in executing the said authority and power to him committed, have granted to the said duke that he have and retain in his own hands of such money as he shall receive to our use by reason of the said office[s] ... such sum or sums of money as he shall expend or lay out in executing the said authority committed to him in form above said.

Royal auditors were to allow such expenses. Buckingham was being given carte blanche over all the revenues that the King possessed in Wales. Since he held all the principal offices and spent the receipts, it was logical that he was now allowed to command the chancellor of March, now Richard's favourite William Catesby following the death of Richard Martin, Bishop of St David's; on 11 May the see was conferred on Gloucester's northern admirer Thomas Langton. Moreover, Buckingham's authority was enforced. Letters were despatched to the people of Caernarvon to be supportive of Buckingham as sheriff, to remove Hugh Bulkeley from the constableship of Conway, to the keeper of Bewdley to hand over all munitions to the duke, and for the castle of Ludlow and its contents to be delivered to him.[27] If somewhat indigestible therefore and inevitably exercised by deputies, perhaps sometimes the same personnel in practice, Buckingham's new hegemony superseded the whole structure of authority and all the offices that had owed obedience to Edward V as Prince of Wales. The power-base that the Wydeville regime had constructed him in Wales since 1473 had been demolished.

It was for his services to Gloucester, at Stony Stratford and since, that Buckingham was being so strikingly advanced. It was argued, of course, that these services had also been to the young Edward V. His advance displaced others. Inevitably there were casualties, here and elsewhere. The custody of several castles in the Solent area were changed. Other Wydeville posts were re-allocated to Richard's future and presumably current adherents, Rivers indeed being treated as though attainted. His office as chief butler of England was conferred on Gloucester's friend Lord Lovell. A mysterious instruction 'to the bishop of Exeter to deliver the duchess of Exeter unto my lord of Buckingham' probably relates to Anne St Leger, daughter of Edward V's aunt Anne, who had been scheduled to marry Dorset's son and heir. Was she destined instead for

Buckingham's son Edward, later 3rd duke? Buckingham had ambitions in the West Country, in Dorset and Wiltshire, where his authority was as great as in Wales. Lord Howard became chief steward of the duchy of Lancaster, Arundel became master of the game south of the Trent, and Dynham became chief steward of the duchy of Cornwall. Rivers' seat of the Mote at Maidstone was seized. Two northerners, William Malliverer and Miles Metcalf, were granted respectively all the offices at More End (Northants.) and the chief justiciarship of the palatinate of Lancaster.[28] It was a sign of what was to follow. These were to prove amongst Richard's most trusted partisans. They were being rewarded as dependants of Gloucester rather than for services to Edward V.

On Friday 13 June, we are told, there was a divided council. One was meeting at Westminster: this was the administrative council, featuring Lord Treasurer Wood and the other insiders, most probably the Crowland Continuator also. The other, at the Tower, was preparing for the coronation. It is apparent that much more time was being devoted to this, to the knightings and feastings that went with it, and perhaps also parliament. It was at this council that the crisis that led to Edward's deposition began to break.

The Deposition of Edward V [29]

Gloucester's first coup had placed him temporarily in the saddle and had set planning in motion for Edward V's coronation on 22 June and for the opening of parliament by the newly crowned King on 24 June. This combination ensured a good attendance for both occasions and the fullest endorsement of Edward's succession. Elections were organised throughout the kingdom in response to royal writs. A parliament was required at the beginning of every reign to vote the new King his customs revenues. In this case, with a King so young, parliament could also be expected to approve arrangements for government. In early May the necessary decisions about the form that government took during Edward's majority had been deferred. Gloucester's protectorate was scheduled to expire. Yet the speech of opening that Bishop Russell drafted appears to contain proposals to prolong Gloucester's power beyond the coronation. It was also critical of Rivers and the Wydevilles. Perhaps Richard intended seeking their attainder. Parliament was to be the venue for a trial of strength. Would the Lords do as they were directed, for the Commons could be expected to follow their lead, or would they resist such extreme measures? Despite the unpopularity of the Wydevilles, they numbered many kinsmen and dependants amongst the peerage and Elizabeth was still a queen. Parliament, in short, offered the Wydevilles a chance to recover.

That Russell had already drafted his speech by 16-17 June,[30] when both coronation and parliament were postponed to November, indicates a sudden change of plan. So, indeed, the government itself alleged. An atmosphere of crisis comes over in some cryptic notes amongst the Cely papers:[31] evidently the author did not know what to fear. The first signs of it emerge in Gloucester's two letters of Saturday 10 and Sunday 11 June to the corporation of York and Ralph Lord Neville, both trusted supporters during his rule of the north; no doubt others were sent that do not survive. 'Come unto us in London in all the diligence you can possible', the city was urged,

> with as many as you can make defensible arrayed, there to aid and assist us against the Queen, her blood, adherents and affinity, which have intended and daily do intend to murder and utterly destroy us and our cousin the duke of Buckingham and the old royal blood of this our realm.[32]

Evidently the letters were secret. None of our sources, even the eyewitnesses (the Crowland Continuator and Mancini) report any such plot in London or Gloucester's fears. Of course the plot must have been secret. Gloucester did not act alone. Buckingham probably knew of his letters; possibly also Hastings. What Hastings evidently did not predict, else he would not have let himself be caught out, was that on Friday 13 June Gloucester would charge *him* with participation, with plotting with the Queen, and he would be arrested and executed at the Tower without trial. Three other councillors were also imprisoned: Lord Steward Stanley; Bishop Morton, master of the rolls; and the Bishop King, the King's secretary. Security was heightened, crowd control measures were instated and the City gates were guarded, but the coronation was not at once postponed. It was to ensure Prince Richard's attendance at his brother's coronation that on 16 June Cardinal Bourchier removed him from his mother's custody at Westminster Abbey to join Edward in the Tower. That day or next day both coronation and parliament were cancelled. The following Sunday Dr Ralph Shaa was preaching the illegitimacy that debarred Edward V from kingship. The dates are too close to be coincidence.

Obviously Elizabeth remained implacably opposed to Gloucester's protectorate and unwilling to trust his re-assurances. She had not abandoned hope of wresting the young Edward V from Gloucester's grasp or of rehabilitating her sons and brothers. She had good grounds for plotting, yet, in retrospect, the forthcoming parliament was her best hope. If the council was unwilling to take decisive action against them, how much more so would be the Lords, who included more Wydeville connections and more uncommitted peers. A plot is not implausible, but it is unsubstantiated. Apart from the letters emanating from Gloucester, we have only the duke's charges against Hastings. There is nothing to confirm his story. Hastings' fall indicates a split within the regime. What could have provoked it? Hastings appears to have had everything to gain from his alliance with Gloucester. If he was plotting against the duke and even allying himself with Elizabeth, his long-time foe, he must have had the strongest reasons for changing sides. What united him and the two dukes, hostility to the Wydevilles, was less powerful than what now divided them. Similarly for Gloucester to destroy his key supporter, who had helped make him Lord Protector, was to cut off his nose to spite his face.

The explanation traditionally advanced, from 1483 onwards, that Hastings' commitment to Gloucester stopped short of the throne, is surely correct. Hastings, however self-interested, had a lifetime of service and friendship to Edward IV and would resist to the utmost the deposition of his son Edward V. That threat could drive him into alliance with the Queen, if the plot existed. More probably, however, Gloucester was staging a pre-emptive strike. Just as at Stony Stratford, sociability was a cover for ruthlessness. This time the victim's survival was not left to chance. And the summons of the northern army looked several moves ahead, to when the capacity to overawe the City, the council and the Lords would be needed.

If Gloucester was to usurp the throne, he could not leave Edward V's heir Prince Richard at liberty. He was bound to become the focus for plots, particularly if his brother were to die. It was because Edward of Lancaster was still free – and more dangerous as the Lancastrian claimant than as the heir of the Lancastrian claimant – that Edward IV had preserved Henry VI alive from his capture in 1465 until after the prince's death in 1471. Similarly during the summer King Richard was to find it necessary to blockade Westminster Abbey to prevent Edward V's sisters being spirited away. Undoubtedly Prince Richard's presence was necessary at the coronation if the right note of unity was to be struck, as those removing him from sanctuary pointed out, but of course the coronation was cancelled forthwith. With both the King and heir in Gloucester's power, both securely within the Tower, he could safely embark on his push for the throne. On Sunday 22 June Shaa preached his sermon at St Paul's Cross. On Wednesday 25 June the Duke of Buckingham put the case to the citizens of London at the Guildhall and they progressed to Baynards Castle to elect Gloucester as king. Edward V was no longer king. Next day, Thursday 26 June, Gloucester acceded as Richard III: he was crowned on 6 July. Elaborate verbatim reports survive, particularly in More's *History*, but these cannot be authentic. Reconstructed long after the event, they may or may not faithfully record what was said.

Edward V played no part in any of this. At best, he was a passive and powerless observer, at worst unaware of what was happening or why. His attendants were Gloucester's creatures, who could be trusted to keep him securely. He was aware, of course, of the arrival of his brother on 16 June, and was presumably notified of the postponement of the coronation and the opening of parliament, both of which – from modern parallels – surely required some rehearsing. His deposition alleged nothing against him in person, no evil government or sin, merely defects that preceded his conception and that he could do nothing about. How far these were real reasons, how far pretexts to keep his mother's kindred out of power and/or to enable Uncle Richard to succeed, historians are not agreed. What is clear, however, is that at this point his father's licentiousness during his first reign, explored in chapter 2, fatally undermined the fortunes of his son. Someone was needed to exploit the legacy and was found in Gloucester, both as manipulator of opinion and man of action.

Titulus Regius, the act of the 1484 parliament that approved Richard III's title, purports to record the petition to the duke that was approved and presented to him by the non-parliamentary assembly that elected him on 25 June 1483. This appears to be true: few or no changes were made to it. What survives, however, is a highly elaborate and polished document, not one run up unofficially on the spur of the moment as seems to have been claimed. The Crowland Continuator states that it supposedly originated in the north, but that the author was well-known and was in London at the time. How one wishes that the chronicler was less reticent and had named names! This suggests perhaps that the intended impression in 1483 was that the petition had popular support in the north, like that of 1469 nominally from Robin of Redesdale but actually from Warwick, but that we lack the contextual evidence. The author, obviously a cultivated man of legal background, could indeed have been Robert Stillington, Bishop of Bath and Wells and disgraced chancellor of Edward IV, to whom, as we have seen, the precontract story was later attributed.[33] Stillington hailed from Acaster in Yorkshire and was thus a northerner, although *Titulus Regius*, as we have it, is not in a northern dialect.

Titulus Regius develops further the depiction of a lax, corrupt and incompetent regime dominated by the Wydevilles that Gloucester had been creating and decrying even before his protectorate began. Everyone must deplore such a regime, to which Edward V was heir and from which Gloucester, who purported to have been exiled in the north, was distanced. He could cleanse the Augean stable. The title to the throne that *Titulus Regius* presented on his behalf was based on the disqualification of more senior members of the House of York, the offspring of Edward IV and Clarence. Clarence's son Warwick was excluded because Clarence himself had been attainted by parliament and debarred from inheritance, which was true enough, although such barriers had not in practice prevented two previous contestants from becoming kings. Richard's claim arose, however, only because those of Edward V and his siblings were discounted. Against them, *Titulus Regius* alleged, was the invalidity of Edward V's marriage. Not only was it clandestine, unapproved by the Lords, and procured by the sorcery of the Queen's mother and Edward V's grandmother Jacquetta Duchess of Bedford, but it was invalid because the groom had not been free to marry, being already contracted to Lady Eleanor Butler.

> Which premises being true, as in very truth they be true, it appears and follows self-evidently that the said King Edward during his life and the said Elizabeth lived together sinfully and damnably in adultery, against the law of God and the Church ... Also it appears self-evidently and follows that all the issue and children of the said King are bastards and unable to inherit or claim anything by inheritance according to the law and custom of England.

Because his parents were not married, Edward V was illegitimate and could not be king. At this point the notorious promiscuity of the King's father during the 1460s directly impinged on politics and served to remove Edward V from his throne.[34]

What *Titulus Regius* did not say, but which was stated elsewhere at the time, was that he was also disqualified because his father Edward IV was not legitimate either, not the offspring of his father Richard Duke of York, and hence unable to convey the Mortimer title to the crown to Edward V.[35] Gloucester however was legitimate: not only did he resemble York in appearance, as Edward IV did not, but he was safely born in England, whereas the births of Edward IV at Rouen and Clarence at Dublin could not be vouched for. Supposedly this allegation was omitted from *Titulus Regius* to avoid offending the Duchess Cecily, mother of Edward IV, Clarence and Richard III, but it offended her nevertheless. After his own accession Richard attributed the bastardy of Edward V to his own birth, not his father's, who was a legitimate king. It was never the official reason: Richard recognised Edward IV as king.

Fifteenth-century English land law did indeed debar bastards from inheritance. The law of succession to the crown, however, was not necessarily identical to general inheritance law – witness the succession of Henry IV in 1399! William the Conqueror was an obvious example of a bastard who had become king, albeit a rather distant precedent. Later in 1483 Henry Tudor was to lay claim to the English crown and to secure a substantial measure of acceptance as heir of John of Gaunt's legitimate bastards the Beauforts: two years later he was to be king. If short of precedents, therefore, bastardy was not as complete a bar as *Titulus Regius* suggests. Moreover the argument implies that title to the crown merely depended on hereditary priority – as York of course had asserted with his pedigree in 1460 – but this was only one ground, the others being conquest and acclamation. Whether a bastard or not – and recent research has suggested that he may have been – Edward IV's title rested on both these. He was undoubtedly king of England. It was perverse to trace one's claim from Richard Duke of York, who was never a king, rather than from his son, who reigned for over twenty years. Defects in Edward IV's own birth could not discount any title that Edward V had inherited from him. Whatever his own legitimacy or that of his grandfather, Edward V had succeeded without question, had been recognised by the royal council, had received oaths of fealty from his uncles Gloucester and Buckingham, the citizens of London and York and many others. He was the King – is rightly included in the list of English kings – and was not disqualified by subsequent doubts about his birth. That said, there were no doubt many Englishmen to whom the argument was addressed for whom this was a technical point and who considered that illegitimacy and adultery were reason enough why Edward should not be allowed to reign.

Titulus Regius sought to discredit Edward IV's marriage as clandestine, not approved by the Lords, procured by sorcery and because of the precontract. The first two grounds can be dismissed quickly. Certainly Edward's marriage was secret, not in the face of the Church, but this alone was insufficient ground to set it aside. Similarly the validity of the marriage did not depend on approval by his subjects. The sorcery charge is more serious. It was probably intended to signify that Edward did not consent of his own free will, which would indeed have invalidated the marriage. Most serious was the precontract story, which alone made it to the chronicles, although two different ladies were cited as Edward's partners. If valid and consummated, as it must have been, such a contract would have invalidated the King's marriage to his Queen and illegitimated their children. Once Eleanor Butler was dead, in 1468, and Margaret Lucy was dead, in 1466, Edward and Elizabeth would have been free to marry and subsequent children, including the princes, would have been legitimate, but no such remarriage ever took place. As the Crowland Continuator says, it was not for parliament to try such issues but the church courts, which was not allowed. Parliament however met in 1484, the issue being decided the previous year.

DNA testing might one day enable us to test Edward IV's legitimacy, if we thought it worthwhile, but we have no easy way (or, indeed, any way) to demonstrate whether the charges of sorcery or the precontract were valid. The sorcery charge dates back to 1469, as we have seen, but Jacquetta was acquitted in 1470, admittedly primarily on political grounds. Apparently, acquittal did not altogether clear her name. *Titulus Regius* invokes notoriety here – 'as the common opinion of the people and the publique voice and fame is through all this land' – but evidence was also claimed to exist: 'and hereafter, if and as the case shall require, shall be proved in time and place convenient'.[36] Albeit unrevealing, papers from Jacquetta's 1469 trial survived, but her accuser had died in 1476. It seems highly improbable therefore that enough evidence could have been assembled in 1483 to satisfy even a fifteenth-century audience. So far as we know, it was never produced. Recent historical success in identifying which Eleanor Butler was intended, moreover, does not prove the case. Eleanor never substantiated her case in her lifetime – did she ever put it? – and she was fifteen years dead in 1483. If Stillington did indeed say this and if it was true, it would have invalidated the marriage. That Edward IV appears to have undergone several such ceremonies, however, makes it more likely.

It follows therefore that Edward V could have been illegitimate, but he remained nevertheless a king. Many people, perhaps most, still thought that he was. Right was insufficient, however. That so many people supported him – as revealed by Buckingham's rebellion later the same year – did not help him; rather it may have sealed his fate. And in the meantime, backed by overwhelming force and confirmed by the established constitutional formalities that all usurpers manufactured on such occasions, Gloucester was able to set his nephew Edward V aside and make himself King.

7

THE LAST KING

An Ex-King and His Future

Edward V's significance changed decisively when his reign ended on 25 June 1483. At that point he became, in our parlance, an ex-king. To Richard III and his supporters, if one accepts Richard III's arguments, he had never been a king at all. Richard called him 'Edward bastard, late called King Edward V', and reminisced about 'the time we stood protector of our realm, Edward bastard son to our entirely beloved brother Edward IV was called king of this our realm'.[1] He was disqualified by his birth, from the moment of his birth, indeed from his conception, even from before his conception and his parents' marriage. Edward V did not revert to being Prince of Wales or indeed a prince since, by the same arguments, he had never been a prince at all and did not now become one. He was still the son of his parents, his father unquestionably being a king, but his mother not a queen. No longer Queen Elizabeth, she was Dame Elizabeth Grey, as Richard III called her. Edward V was now merely a bastard, a royal bastard admittedly, but no better than those other obscure bastards fathered by Edward IV, without any pretensions to legitimacy or entitlements. He had altogether lost his royal rank and status and had no right to inherit anything that his father had left behind. Edward, his brother Richard, and their sisters were, at best, genteel, without prospects, and were dependent for the future on the bounty of their uncle King Richard. All this might have changed next year, in 1484, when Richard III came to terms with Queen Elizabeth and agreed to provide respectably for her daughters, if the princes had been included in the deal. In fact, they were not and could not be, since that agreement presumed their deaths. Had they still been alive, no deal would have been possible.

Hence it is often stated by those sympathetic to Richard III that he had nothing to fear from Edward V and his brother. How could he have? Were they not bastards, disqualified from the succession? It is a valid argument. However it presumes, firstly, that it was this view that universally prevailed, secondly that bastards could not be kings and, thirdly, that it was possible for kings to cease to be kings.

To start with the last point, contemporaries thought not. Once a king, always a king. A king might lose his throne, yet retain his status. Mary Queen of Scots in the next century remained a queen after losing her kingdom. Late medieval Europe was littered with kings without kingdoms, such as Jerusalem, Cyprus, Sicily and Navarre. Henry VI lost two thrones, yet never ceased to be a king. Edward V is rightly included on the list of English kings because, for eleven weeks, he had been recognised as the king by the royal council and everyone else who mattered. His rule in England ended on 25 June, not his kingship. How could God's deputy resign his charge? He could not, so Shakespeare's Richard II was to declare. The binding oaths of allegiance that all had tendered to Richard II and to Henry VI had been serious obstacles to their depositions that were overcome, in Richard's case, only by his supposedly voluntary abdication and the release of his subjects from their oaths, and in Henry's by exposing the misapprehensions about his title that had existed when the oaths were sworn. Edward V, of course, was too young to repudiate the allegiance due to him. In his case, the Calais garrison was told that their oaths had been made on the mistaken presumption that he was legitimate, a copy of *Titulus Regius* being sent to them as evidence.[2]

On the second point, kings could, of course, be illegitimate. William the Conqueror himself had been a bastard; so too was Henry of Trastamara, the fourteenth-century King of Castile, King

Ferrante of Naples and others. Assertions of bastardy did not make Edward's contemporary Joanna la Beltraneja less than dangerous to her aunt Queen Isabella of Castile. Henry VIII's offspring were to be routinely bastardised and legitimated again by acts of parliament. Of course a bastard could be a king – even a known bastard.

On the first point, it is obvious that many did not accept that Richard's title had refuted Edward's, that Edward V was illegitimate, or that such illegitimacy disqualified him from kingship. Some, certainly Edward IV's Queen and her family, had always dissented. The assembly of notables that had elected King Richard – certainly led by Buckingham and perhaps overawed by the northern army encamped at Finsbury Fields – may have been coerced and may have acted reluctantly under duress. Later sources in retrospect indicate so. If convinced then, many rapidly changed their minds, as soon as the threat was withdrawn. Witness alone Buckingham's rebellion in the autumn right across southern England, which sought initially to replace Edward V on his throne. Here is ample evidence that Richard's arguments were not decisive. Bastard or not, Edward V remained a potent political force and the greatest threat to his uncle's fledgling regime.

Why the Deed Was Done

Edward's future, for so long leading inexorably to the throne, and now, as interpreted by his uncle, so shadowy, unpromising and uncertain, was actually ominous and portentous. Former kings had a poor life expectancy. To their successors, as in pre-revolutionary Russia, they were *bacilli*, genies that must not be allowed out of their bottle. No pretender or claimant to the diadem was more dangerous that he who had already worn it. Former kings were the constant focus of plots. It was not necessary for them to be active conspirators themselves. However vicious, inadequate, degenerate or simple, ex-kings retained their aura of kingship and remained the ideal figureheads for any revolt. Actions could be taken in their name. The people were notoriously unstable and could not be relied upon to act rationally. Ex-kings therefore had to be confined, as strictly as possible, and forever. Given the porous nature of late medieval prisons, the scope for armed uprisings and the uncertain loyalties so characteristic of civil war, no monarch could guarantee keeping his predecessor safe forever more. Preventing them from plotting was little help since, as we have seen, their active complicity was unnecessary. They had merely to exist.

Inevitably, therefore, all usurpers disposed of their predecessors. Odd kings could not be left hanging around. England's deposed monarchs had always died mysteriously (and almost certainly violently) within a year of losing their throne – in Henry VI's case after his third deposition. Edward II perished at Berkeley Castle, Richard II at Pontefract and Henry VI in the Tower. Their titles, as the eldest son of King Edward I, as the eldest son of the eldest son of King Edward III and as the eldest son of King Henry V, could not be gainsaid. Was not each indisputably the heir of the previous king, also unquestioned? Was not each long before his accession designated as heir? Had not they all been elected, acclaimed and crowned? The latter two, like Edward V, had acceded as children. Had not the great council in 1471 sworn allegiance to the infant Edward V, had not parliament in 1472 acknowledged him as heir, and had not another great council done homage to him in 1477? Admittedly Edward V was not crowned – he was the king who never wore his crown, as the panel painting in Bishop Oliver King's chantry at Windsor portrays him, but coronation did not make a king. It merely set the seal and hence could be long postponed. Henry VI reigned for seven years before his coronation. Edward V, similarly, was the eldest son of his father. He had been Prince of Wales from 1471, after the destruction of all Lancastrian rivals that made Edward IV ten years into his reign at last uncontested. Ever since then he had been invested with all the panoply of the King's eldest son, and was unquestionably heir presumptive to the throne. Everybody who mattered, including the King's two brothers, had publicly acknowledged him as such. He had received oaths of allegiance from all the King's vassals. There had been no doubt about his accession. To Richard III therefore he remained a threat.

Yet Edward V was a child. Children have always been loved, valued, and cherished,[3] yet their lives used to be much more precarious than nowadays. They were expendable. Infant deaths were unremarkable commonplaces, nobody's fault, and children were habitually set to work. We are far more romantic about childhood today and far more protective than previous generations. Witness our stress on child abuse, which certainly formerly existed, but which passed almost unremarked until the late twentieth century. Nowadays child abuse is *the* offence that cannot be purged. We tend to think of Edward V as an innocent and harmless child and therefore regard his murder as an unnecessary act of vicious cruelty. Contemporaries shared some of these sentiments, yet they knew he was not harmless. As limited physically and intellectually as any twelve-year-old, Edward was a symbol of extraordinary power. More than a symbol indeed, he was an instrument – a ballistic missile – that, as long as he lived, could at any time be used to strike at and to destroy King Richard III, King Richard's government and his regime. With Edward V in their hands, or even outside their hands, plotters – principled or unscrupulous, altruistic or self-interested – possessed a cause and figurehead, with which many, perhaps the majority, sympathised and often enough were willing to fight for and to risk their lives. 'For beyond doubt', later remarked Polydore Vergil, with some exaggeration, 'the entire population would have risen in arms to defend them'.[4] Personally innocent Edward may have been, but there can be little doubt that he approved of those, who backed his claim and would have escaped into their hands if he could. His personal incapacity to lead and fight, though a serious weakness, was much less important than his symbolic significance.

Moreover, Edward V was a growing threat. Time marched on. The boy that was Edward V was destined to grow up, to progress rapidly from the twelve-year-old child to a sixteen-year-old adolescent, mature enough in contemporary parlance to rule as well as reign, to an eighteen-, twenty-one-, or twenty-five-year-old adult able first to function politically and militarily and then to command, direct and rule. So, too, was his ten-year-old brother Richard. From being dependent on others, tools that could be manipulated or figureheads for their schemes, the two boys could become politically active in their own rights, able to escape, conspire, machinate, rebel, or rule. Their future potential was graphically illustrated by the obscure (but well-connected) Henry Tudor later in 1483, who proved his value to insurgents as an adult male, royal figurehead and fiancé in marriage alliances. Potentially Edward was an idol of the multitude – able, like his father, grandfather, uncle Clarence and cousin Warwick to invoke mass popular support – and, as a former king, more dangerous than any of them. His uncle Richard III could not leave the future to chance. To confine them and keep them single was not enough. The future had to be faced. The only way out was for them to die. Killing them, moreover, was justifiable. It promised peace, order and the public good as well as Richard's good. Reason of state dictated their deaths. It was in the public interest. It made good practical sense. However Richard reached his throne, moreover, he himself *was* the king and can have been in no doubt about his own right to rule.

Thus, all usurpers have to dispose of their predecessors. Late medieval English usurpers wanted nevertheless to avoid the opprobrium, always of regicide and of disposing of helpless prisoners in their charge, perhaps also patricide in Edward II's case, martyrdom in Henry VI's, or infanticide in that of King John's nephew Arthur. They dared not proceed in accordance with the law, through formal trials that offered their victims a stage, an audience, or mere publicity. Summary elimination, without trial or judgement, was what was required. Usurpers cared about their public images. If badly handled, such killings could be propaganda disasters. Murder therefore had to be done secretly. For future opposition to be disarmed and the political potential of the former monarch as a figurehead to be decisively quelled, the *fact* of death had to be public and unquestioned. It was valueless if it remained concealed. The body had to be displayed, generally nude. Therefore death had to be by some means that left no visible mark on the corpse. This was the case with Richard II and also with Henry VI, whose body allegedly (but incredibly) bled when on display. Such pantomimes were not altogether successful. A pseudo-Richard II, William of Trumpington, was fomenting discontent and disorder until 1417. A cult grew up around Henry VI, like earlier political saints, miracles being performed at his tomb and pilgrims resorting to it in lucrative numbers. Informed opinion realised that the deposed monarch was indeed dead. No particular discredit or adverse political consequences accrued to the usurper responsible – although some ascribed Henry IV's crippling illnesses to his political sins.

Regicide was a crime and a sin. If the princes were slain, it was unquestionably murder. However politically desirable or expedient, there was no proper legal process: no form of trial, however summary, and no judgement. It was also a sin. 'Thou shalt commit no murder', states the sixth commandment. Whoever was responsible, whether by authorising or actually committing the deed, was answerable to God at the Last Judgement. Reason of state was no excuse. But the worldly advantages could be worth the price: both of damnation, which even hindsight cannot yet reveal, and of earthly retribution and eternal infamy, which Edward III, Henry IV, and Edward IV had all escaped. The alternative, the loss of throne, status and worse, could not be contemplated.

Here, therefore, was the model that in due course Richard III was surely bound to follow. It was expected, the Crowland Continuator reports, by supporters of Edward V who had taken sanctuary.[5] But the fate of the princes differs in several important particulars from previous models. They certainly died. They were certainly murdered. However necessary and politically desirable, their deaths offended against human law – there was no trial, even a summary one, and no judgement – and against divine law. Whoever was responsible, hitman or king, was answerable for their deaths as sins to God and had no conceivable defence. The deaths of the princes were never publicly announced. Their bodies were never publicly displayed. There are several possible reasons why. Richard, in fact, accrued all the disadvantages – the opprobrium and notoriety that previous usurpers had generally escaped – without it ever being demonstrated conclusively that they were dead. That was the worry of his successor, Henry VII, who must already have believed them dead before his accession. He did not change his mind, but seems to have uncovered no proof. Henry could not refute the challenge of Perkin Warbeck, who claimed to be Prince Richard from 1491, as easily as he did Lambert Simnel, who pretended to be Clarence's son in Warwick in 1486, because the real princes could not be produced as evidence, either alive or dead. Hence there has been much debate, both at the time and since, about what befell the 'Two Little Princes in the Tower' and at whose hands.

Debate at the time was about precisely how the deed was done. In England at least there was scarcely any doubt *who* did it: Richard. It remains an obvious presumption that he had them murdered. He had the strongest of motives and, since they were in his custody, the opportunity. Who else could both dispose of them and conceal the fact? For rebels and plotters, in contrast, the princes were useful as focuses for discontent and were undoubtedly much more valuable to them alive than dead. They were the best possible weapon against their uncle. Those against Richard therefore had the strongest of motives to keep the princes alive. Unless, the one proviso, the plotter concerned actually wanted not merely to remove Richard, but to put *himself* on the throne. In that case, the superior claims of the princes to everyone else's posed an obstacle to him and needed to be removed. This, of course, is the argument that supporters of Richard III have made for centuries both about Buckingham and Henry Tudor. If Buckingham was after the throne for himself, he needed both to eliminate the princes (if they were not already dead) *and* to secure the backing of their supporters before striking against Richard. If the princes were still living when Henry secured the Tower, he had to dispose of them if he was to continue to reign himself. What Buckingham in

1483 and Tudor in 1485 had in common with Richard was that none of them could have allowed the princes to live.

Somebody, or some people, did know what happened, of course, but they kept their knowledge private. Without proof of the fates of the princes, it was possible in 1491-7 for enemies of the Tudors to present Perkin Warbeck as Richard Duke of York, the younger of the princes, a pretence sufficiently convincing to secure him recognition as Richard IV at Dublin (though the Irish had also crowned Lambert Simnel as Edward VI!), to win him the support of several monarchs, and even the hand of a well-born Scottish lady. His story was false. In actual fact Warbeck was a pretender.[6] Both princes were dead, including Edward V. Nobody ever dared to impersonate Edward: far too many people had known him alive. There is no contemporary evidence that the princes outlived Richard's reign – of any sort that historians can take seriously and certainly none that is not fiction – that the princes survived into the reign of their nephew Henry VIII and into Sir Thomas More's household.

For five centuries it was historical orthodoxy that Richard III slew his nephews. Only Buckingham was cited as an alternative in his own day. One historian per century perversely has defended the wickedest of English kings and uncles against the majority view until the twentieth century, when the contrary became fashionable and popular. The evidence for Richard's guilt would never stand up in a court of law, so it has been claimed. Perhaps indeed it would not in our modern courts of law, to which no statements or forensic evidence could be available and at which no witnesses could attend, but even today murderers can be convicted without a body, if motive, opportunity and circumstance suffice. Acquittal by television does not convince.[7] In a fifteenth-century court the evidence might well have sufficed – indeed late medieval jurors were selected from those who knew the truth – but of course kings could not be put on trial. Rex v. Rex! However damning the evidence at the time, Richard III could never have been prosecuted or convicted.

The death of Richard III in battle also meant that he could not be brought to book. There was no need, therefore, to keep the case file. Who could doubt his guilt? Most of the evidence, moreover, was surely circumstantial, if suggestive. It consisted principally of the complete and permanent disappearance of the princes from the Tower during Richard's reign. We cannot tell which, if any, of a score of contemporary historians had access to the first hand information that alone deserves our respect. The princes perished in secret: a secret that was maintained during Richard's reign and for very different reasons thereafter. To admit to killing the princes, a past king, the brothers of the current queen, the king's sisters-in-law and their influential husbands, was surely to invite arrest, trial, execution, or, at the very least, revenge. Such an admission was eventually made, by Sir James Tyrell, in 1502: we have a circumstantial account supposedly derived from it, which indicts Richard, but which supporters of Richard III have chosen to discard as Tudor propaganda. Even the bones that were dug up in the Tower in 1674, identified as those of the princes, and confirmed as such in the 1930s by the best medical opinion of the day, cannot convince those who do not wish to believe.

All sources need to be carefully scrutinised and tested. If our sources have been relentlessly attacked by those who do not like what they say, there are also legitimate grounds for scepticism. Tyrell may have had good reason to lie. Those who recorded the story were biased towards the Tudors – who wanted the princes not only dead and buried, but publicly seen to be so. If the bones were those of the princes, it remains to be demonstrated. However sophisticated the scientific analysis they probably cannot answer all our questions. Any answers have to be sought from the historians of the time with all their well-known deficiencies.

When the Deed Was Done

There is no record of the princes alive after Richard III's reign. Only a misdated passage in the London chronicles, attributable most probably to the wrong mayoral year, refers to them in 1484.[8]

No fifteenth-century security system could have concealed them indefinitely if alive. They died therefore prematurely, as children. What befell them raises four key questions: why, how and when did the princes die; and at whose hands. The proposition that they died naturally, from disease such as sweating sickness, has never carried much weight. For both to die, simultaneously, in some way that their doctor could not be allowed to reveal, constitutes an unlikely set of coincidences. Therefore they died violently, many sources suggesting how and the reasons being too obvious for debate on why. That leaves who and when. Modern commentators are preoccupied with who was to blame, whether Richard III or whoever else to whom the fault could be transferred – Buckingham, Henry VII, or even Surrey. Debating who in a vacuum has always been inconclusive, since the sources do not agree. The key to the conundrum is when, since to that question a concrete answer can be found.

Richard Duke of York joined his brother Edward V in the Tower of London on 16 June 1483. Some Tudor sources date the end of Edward's life to 22 June, several days before the official end of his reign on 25 June, but there seem no reasonable grounds for believing this.[9] Those who approved Richard's accession, and all the chroniclers of it, presumed at that date that both princes were still alive. It was apparently to release them and reinstate them that an obscure plot was concocted in July and scotched.[10] This may also have been an initial objective of the rising of the Yorkist establishment in the autumn right across southern England, which, the Crowland Continuator reports, was rendered pointless by accounts of the princes' deaths. 'A rumour arose that King Edward's sons, by some unknown manner of violent destruction, had met their fates'.[11] The banner of rebellion was raised at Bodmin on 2 November (Edward V's thirteenth birthday) on behalf of a new king[12] – an imprecise phrase, that presumably meant somebody new, rather than the revival of a former king, Edward V. However that may be, the acknowledgement by Yorkist exiles on Christmas Day 1483 of Henry VII as their king, on the strength of his promise to marry Elizabeth of York,[13] indicates that they believed the princes were dead. Their rights had always taken priority over hers. It was with this fear in mind that Richard's enemies had plotted to secure the princesses during the summer and that the king had set John Nesfield to blockade them in Westminster Abbey. Even before his usurpation he had confined Clarence's son Warwick, 'for he feared', reported Mancini, 'that [even] if the entire progeny of King Edward [IV] became extinct, yet this child, who was also of royal blood, would still embarrass him'.[14] The same message is implied in the agreement a few months later of Queen Elizabeth with Richard III.[15] The princes were dead and nothing more was to hoped of them. The interests of the living, the Queen and her daughters, the Prince's mother and sisters, had to be cared for now. Henry Tudor referred to Richard as a *homicide* in letters to actual or hoped-for supporters in England – he had no need to explain what he meant – and the act of attainder against his deceased rival referred to 'the shedding of infants' blood', which contemporaries cannot have found mysterious or ambiguous.[16] Besides the text of the act, there was surely a speech explaining the government's case that is now lost. We do not know if this passage was debated, but others were. The punishment of Richard's army, supporters of the actual king, was highly controversial. Henry VII himself, we are told, insisted on their attainder. The act did not pass on the nod.[17]

All such evidence, of course, is circumstantial. It cannot tell us what actually happened to the princes. What it does show, however, is that from the winter of 1483 (Christmas Day), probably from 2 November, and most likely several weeks earlier, those who most wanted the princes alive – their kinsfolk and opponents of Richard – had reluctantly accepted that they were dead and had therefore moved on to plan B. The princes were politically dead, if not actually dead: henceforth politics managed without them. Nothing ever happened to change their supporters' minds. If some had doubts, like Sir William Stanley, who was executed in 1495, it was because he could not be sure. Everything pointed to their deaths, but he had no proof.

When he first arrived in London, at the Bishop of London's palace, and afterwards in the Tower, Edward V received visitors. His brother joined him – and, by implication, even after his deposition both boys were seen playing with bows and arrows in the garden of the Tower.[18] That phase, however, seems to have been brief. They were increasingly closely confined, reported the Italian Mancini, so that they could be seen only 'behind the bars and windows' and eventually not at all. Their own attendants were withdrawn – by that, trusted members of their own households must be meant – one of the last being their physician, Dr John Argentine, who was Mancini's informant.[19] Eighteen were to be paid – presumably paid off – soon after 9 July 1483.[20] That probably carries us no further than the end of July, when Mancini went abroad, by which time there was no longer any public access to or reports of the princes. Mancini makes no reference to the unsuccessful plot late in July and must surely have done so had he still been around. Writing in December, he was in no doubt that something happened: 'already' – before he departed – 'there was a suspicion that he [Edward V] had been done away with', but he admitted that he did not know. 'Whether, however, he has been done away, and by what manner of death, so far I have not at all discovered'. Clearly Mancini's testimony is not evidence that the princes were indeed murdered or when. Nor indeed are reports that Edward expected to die. He was old enough to understand, whereas his brother Richard, only ten, was not: he only wanted to play, wrote the Frenchman Molinet. Edward V 'was very melancholic, recognizing the malice of his uncle'. Similarly Argentine told Mancini of Edward's preparations. 'The young king, like a victim preferred for sacrifice, sought remission of his sins by daily confession and penance, because he believed that death was facing him'.[21] How could he not? Edward V was no prophet, but he knew his history. How could he be allowed to stay alive? If he was to die, at least his soul could be saved. Across half a millennium the pathos for the terror of this helpless boy awaiting violent death, still screams to us. What it all means, nevertheless, is that there is no concrete evidence that the princes were still living after August 1483.

There was an obvious parallel in France to the English situation since King Louis XI also died in 1483 and was succeeded by a child, Elizabeth of York's erstwhile fiancé, the thirteen-year-old Charles VIII. It was a parallel very much in the mind of the Chancellor of France, Guillaume de Rochefort, when he addressed the estates general at Tours on 15 January 1484. We must not allow what has happened in England to occur here, he said: 'Look [at] what has happened since the death of King Edward [IV]: how his children, already big and courageous, have been put to death with impunity, and the royal crown [has been] transferred to their murderer by the favour of the people'.[22] Making revelations about the princes was not the point of the speech, which was not a deliberate attempt to whip up hostility against England. They were throwaway lines to illustrate his point. Nothing ulterior hung on it: it deserves all the more weight. Obviously De Rochefort expected his audience to recognise what he was talking about and to share his sentiment. Had he also concrete evidence behind it? Chancellors, we might suppose, do not make frivolous and unfounded assertions. Even fifteenth-century states had special sources of information not available to private citizens. The French government was as well-placed to find out as any of our other informants. France had a pressing need to establish the real situation. It had been on the brink of war with Edward IV and was itself now much weakened by an under-age king. To the suggestion that De Rochefort's informant was Mancini, who was in touch with him, and can thus be discounted as an independent source, we need note only that they say different things. Much later it was reported that Louis XI before his death had been informed of the princes' deaths by Edward IV's chaplain Thomas Ward.[23] After De Rochefort, of course, a host of historians, English and foreign, declared that the princes were dead. Many wrote under the Tudors – only two years after the supposed events, of course, but a crucial two years and after the change of regime. However they differ not at all in what they say. Apart from the Warbeck pretence, which was conclusively refuted at the time, all our sources agree both that the princes died violently and that they perished during Richard's reign. Those that attempt any chronological precision place their deaths early in Richard's reign.

We are faced therefore with three types of evidence that coincide. By the end of 1483, and probably several months earlier, politicians worked on the basis that the princes were dead. Sometime in July is the last recorded sighting of them as still alive. Secondly, within four months, by November and probably earlier, they were politically dead: their demise was presumed and politics operated on that presumption. Thirdly, six months later, on 15 January 1484, it was first announced that the princes had been murdered. Endless chroniclers took up the theme. It was a topic of European interest, which attracted comment and speculation from Danzig to Spain. The princes perished in a dozen different ways according to these accounts – individually none of which is conclusive. But together they are. Contemporaries were unanimous about when the princes died.

If the princes were slain during Richard's reign, almost certainly in 1483, most probably in the summer, our sources also narrow the culprits down. Only two are mentioned: Richard III and Buckingham. Nobody else is mentioned. As historians, we are not entitled to fly in the face of such evidence or to prefer alternatives lacking in contemporary support. Regrettably Henry Tudor cannot be on our list. Not only did no contemporary suggest him, but he lacked the opportunity – being in exile abroad – and the event almost certainly happened before he had a serious interest in the crown. It was only Tudor sources writing under Henry VIII, More and Vergil, who commence his claim in August 1483, which is not conceivable if Buckingham's rebellion initially intended restoring the princes. Because Tudor was recognised by the princes' erstwhile supporters at Christmas 1483 and eventually acceded in 1485, these Tudor historians anticipated his candidacy by several months.[24]

Who Did the Deed

If King Richard was the obvious suspect and was actually blamed by most, Buckingham alone was cited by contemporaries as an alternative. Both were the princes' uncles. Most of Buckingham's accusers are foreigners: Commynes blames Richard three times and also Buckingham, 'who had put the two children to death'; the Netherlandish *Divisie Chronicle*, which cites the duke as murderer among three options, the others being starvation and the escape of Prince Richard; and Molinet, who talks of them being smothered.[25] As foreigners abroad, none were eyewitnesses or on the spot, but may nevertheless have had access to privileged information and may have published what their English informants dared not. If so, they did not recognise it as conclusive, as their offering of several alternatives indicates. How, therefore, can we? The first English account indicting Buckingham was apparently by an anonymous London citizen: surviving in a later copy, it may first have been written about 1488. It states that 'King Edward IV's sons were put to death by the *vise* of the Duke of Buckingham'. What the original text had for *vise*, we cannot tell: the modern editor thought *advice*,[26] by the advice of the duke – but it could be short for *device*, Jeremy Potter suggested: the device of the duke of Buckingham – his own plan. In either case, our source is brief and cursory, replete with spelling and other errors and ambiguities, of which the *vise* is one, and does not look particularly authoritative. It does clarify our two options with Buckingham. If he was involved – and most accounts, please note, omit him – was he acting as agent for Richard III or on his own behalf?

Those anxious to exonerate Richard III stress that Buckingham was acting for himself. Having made Richard king, Buckingham rebelled in the autumn. He wanted the throne for himself, they argue. As great-great-grandson and heir of Edward III's youngest son Thomas of Woodstock, whose coat of arms he had recently adopted, and co-heir through his mother of the Beauforts, thus through two female lines inferior to that of York,

Buckingham was certainly on the succession list, though well down it, I suggest. Why he rebelled we cannot at present tell: later Tudor accounts mislead. If out for himself, Buckingham needed to remove the princes as preferred candidates, to avoid any blame himself and to place it instead on Richard, thereby encouraging the princes' own supporters to join him in rebellion against Richard as their slayer and back him instead. It sounds ludicrous, but no less than any other explanation for the duke's actions. This possibility is not discounted by what little we know about events: the rumours of the Prince's deaths and the blaming of the king, both perhaps leaked by Buckingham, and Richard's failure (and the failure of any other contemporary English account) to blame the duke. Yet this is to argue unnecessarily from silence about what can be explained in other ways. If Buckingham killed the princes, their deaths certainly occurred before 3 November, when he was executed, and probably before 12 October, by which time he had rebelled, and after which he and his agents lost access to them. Buckingham was apparently with the King on progress until 27 August, at Pontefract, after which he proceeded via Stafford to his castle of Brecon in Wales, apparently without visiting Westminster: he did not deliver an extremely valuable warrant from Richard, which he would surely have done if he could.[27] He does not seem to have had the opportunity to slay the princes himself, but of course he need not have done it in person: perhaps, as Potter suggests, Buckingham's status as constable of England could secure his men access to the princes.[28] Some authority would have been necessary for the princes' keepers, fearful of royal wrath, to have relinquished their charges. Thereafter, however, the story becomes incredible. How could the princes' fate have been concealed for any length of time from their keepers or from a king, for whom their security was a most pressing concern? If the princes were dead, not at Richard's hand, must the King not have publicised it and pursued the perpetrators, even if Buckingham's ultimate responsibility was concealed? If Buckingham's complicity was known, must it not have featured in the surviving proclamations against him? If the boys had merely disappeared, must not Richard have instituted a wholesale search? Yet none of these alternatives, we can be confident, occurred.

Alternatively Buckingham was acting as adviser or agent of the king. If he counselled the king to kill the princes, he surely recommended what was the most sensible course and obvious to all – to Edward V himself and to those Yorkists whose attempt to secure his sisters thereby drew the same message forcibly to the king's attention. Kings could and did reject advice: advice leaves the king responsible. If Buckingham acted as the king's agent, it does not relieve Richard of the responsibility. Buckingham shared the sin and perhaps also the blame, though the Nuremberg trials had not yet rejected acting on orders as defence. Why someone so senior should have acted is another issue: to misquote More, why should the king impose such a 'butcherly office' on a man of the highest rank and birth, when he had countless underlings?[29] The lieutenant of the Tower, Sir Robert Brackenbury, or a trusted retainer like Tyrell would have seen to it.

Buckingham's responsibility, therefore, seems as incredible today as it did to most contemporaries. The king's enemies' first priority was to unseat Richard, for which the princes were their most powerful instrument, and only afterwards to divide the spoils. Without the princes, they were initially confused, divided and ineffective. It was the king who possessed the motive, means and opportunity. The why and how are obvious. The burden of proof rests on those who wish to show otherwise.

If Richard killed the princes, then he had three aims. First of all, he wished to destroy them. Secondly, and imperatively, he had to publicise their deaths. Plots on their behalf would continue as long as they were thought alive and might indeed continue if their deaths were not public, proven and undeniable. And thirdly, ideally, he wished to avoid the blame. This last consideration may have mattered least: Richard cannot have appreciated what uniquely effective propaganda the despatch of the children was to be made against him. Strangely the bodies of the princes never were so exhibited. Why? Maybe they had wounds that showed. That, however, seems unlikely. Their incarceration after Richard's accession indicates that their deaths were premeditated. There was no need for such violent means when drowning, smothering, or poisoning – all of them contemporary suggestions – were easy enough. Alternatively it was for political reasons, perhaps changing political reasons. If they were killed to remove their threat to Richard, it was sensible to disarm the opposition by publishing their fates. Perhaps that was the rumour reported by the Crowland Continuator: Polydore Vergil, much later, says so explicitly.[30] Exposing the children's corpses could have excited sympathy for them. It was enough, surely, that they were missing and presumed killed. If Richard slew them, surely he did so to deprive his opponents of a leader. Once they found one unexpectedly in Henry Tudor, he was confounded. To reveal that the princes were still alive could have enlisted any doubters to their cause – a more formidable combination than he already faced. Moreover, once the murder of the princes had been made a charge against him – and we cannot know whether this charge was made against him even during Buckingham's rebellion, for which no rebel manifestos survive – to reveal their deaths would again have strengthened the case against him. In this scenario, Richard had either arranged the princes' deaths before the rebellion and concealed it or did so after the rebellion broke out, then revealed it to disarm his opponents. In either case, his scheme went disastrously wrong.

The evidence related above is circumstantial thus far, but it points to only one conclusion: that Richard III had the princes killed. We have yet to consider the one explicit account that we do possess: Tyrell's tale.

Tyrell's Tale

That Sir James Tyrell killed the princes in the Tower was the historical orthodoxy until after the Second World War. It was the story of

Shakespeare, who culled it from Sir Thomas More. Like all such Tudor propaganda, it has been discounted by Ricardians and has become too difficult to defend, besides unnecessary, for academics. It is not inherently unlikely. From Ipswich, the son of a leading local family, Tyrell fought for Edward IV at Tewkesbury and was already one of Richard's most trusted retainers by 1473. After Richard's accession, he was one of his most indispensable supporters. He was needed everywhere: in government, where he was chamberlain of the exchequer and a royal councillor; at court, where he was a knight of the body, master of the horse and henxmen; in the far west, where he was steward of the duchy of Cornwall; in south Wales, where he was constable of Cardiff and sheriff of Glamorgan; and in Calais, where he commanded Guines Castle. In practice, of course, he could not be everywhere, therefore missed Bosworth, and survived to pursue a no less distinguished career under Henry VII.[31] There is nobody to whom King Richard was more likely to turn for the highly sensitive task of eliminating the princes.

There are three sources that blame Tyrell. 'Of which cruel deed Sir James Tyrell was reported to be the doer', states the *Great Chronicle of London*, which was uncertain how it was performed, 'but others put that weight upon an old servant of King Richard named [blank]'.[32] This records what the chronicler had heard and was evidently not, to his own mind, conclusive. Polydore Vergil tells how Richard instructed Sir Robert Brackenbury, custodian of the Tower, to eliminate the princes. When he refused, the task was assigned to Tyrell, who did the deed. Vergil was not sure how it was done, what happened to the bodies, or what were his sources.[33] Essentially this is also More's account, which is however more elaborate and dramatic. The King was on progress in the West Midlands, presumably in August 1483, when the decision was made. The murder was supervised by Tyrell, but actually done at night and in secret by Miles Forest and John Deighton. The bodies were concealed under a heap of stones, but subsequently, so More adds, they were dug up and interred secretly by Brackenbury's chaplain in a secret place. His source, More states, was Tyrell and

Deighton, both of whom were interrogated under Henry VII 'and confessed the murder in manner above-written'.[34] Additional to these – but naming no names – is the *Chronique* of Jean Molinet (d.1507). It incorporates other material. Whilst wrongly naming the princes as Peter and George, his account of their smothering by the captain of the Tower, their discussions with their murderers, their burial and subsequent more honourable reinterment suggests that he had access to the same story, perhaps in or after 1502, certainly garbled and more probably oral than text-based.[35]

That three (or four?) independent writers tell the same story is usually evidence enough for historians. In this case, it has not been. Our sources are late – three of them probably not earlier than Henry VIII – and their sources also appear late. They could all derive from a single original. Sir Thomas More states that Tyrell confessed when on trial for treason – a different treason against Henry VII. The charge was that he had imagined the death of the king and had conspired to make Edmund de la Pole, Earl of Suffolk, king instead. This had happened in the parish of St Lawrence Poultry, Dowgate ward, London three years before, on 1 July 1499: he had afterwards committed himself to the earl, met with him at Antwerp, written to him and received letters from him. Most of the others tried with him had more recent treasons to their debit. What excited the King was a second flight into exile by Earl Edmund and perhaps also the death of his heir Prince Arthur on 2 April 1502: although the arrests were in February, the commission to try them was issued only on 1 April and met at the London Guildhall on 2 May. The accused were produced from the Tower. All with one exception admitted that they could not deny the charge and that they were guilty of treason, and so were condemned to be returned to the Tower, drawn to Tyburn, there to be hanged, beheaded and quartered, and their heads and bodies disposed as the king determined.[36] There may of course have been more impressive evidence than the charges suggest, but that did not come out in the trial. Was there some sort of deal? If so, the plea bargain did not save Tyrell's life, nor yet protect him from attainder nor his estate from forfeiture, but he had handed over Guines, his son escaped execution and was allowed to treat for return of his inheritance, and Tyrell's own sentence was commuted to beheading at the Tower – a more honourable death for an aristocrat.[37] Was his confession to the murder of the princes part of the price? Or did Tyrell confess because, facing death, he wanted to clear his soul?

If Tyrell spoke to his spiritual adviser, his confession did not remain secret. There is no copy among his trial records, nor was a proclamation enrolled on the close roll, nor does any copy apparently feature anywhere in the public records or elsewhere. This is not particularly surprising when we are missing so much that was once scattered broadcast – the rebel manifestos of 1483, 1485 and most of the 1490s for instance – and when the relative abundance for 1450-71 owes much to the copies of a single man (apparently John Vale).

Yet it seems likely that the confession was circulated or posted up. None of the London chronicles that share material with the *Great Chronicle* blame Tyrell. This suggests the story is after *c.*1497, when they were composed and before *c.*1512, its own date. After 1502 looks feasible. The very vagueness of the story and its reliance on 'reports' indicates that the story was in circulation. Vergil and More, however, give more detailed accounts, perhaps derived independently from different copies of a confession or borrowed from one another. Vergil was not in doubt about the authenticity of his source: 'which business he thoroughly performed', he wrote.[38] That More gives more detail about how the murder was done may be because he knew directly about the confessions both of Tyrell and of Deighton, whom Vergil does not mention, and/or because of additional information – it is he who records that 'whither the bodies were removed they could nothing tell'. It is also obvious that More tidied any confessions up, making the tale more literary and dramatic. More took liberty with his sources, but he was generally very well informed and did not invent them. It follows therefore that there were indeed confessions.

But were such confessions authentic? We know of their existence and their story only through later narratives. How much we need the confessions themselves! If we had them, of course, they could not prove Tyrell's tale to be true. There was good reason for inventing it in 1502. With his first son Arthur and his third son Edmund already dead, Henry VII had even more good reason to want the princes conclusively buried. In return for their confessions he may have made concessions to Tyrell and agreed to leave Deighton unmolested. Tyrell had good reason to tell him what he wanted to know, true or false. On More and Molinet's evidence, Henry could not find the bodies to confirm their story. Deighton, however, had no pressing reason to confess. If he did so, and if his confession agreed with Tyrell's, his testimony deserves credit as independent – unless the interrogators asked leading questions, or put the words in the witnesses' mouths. Frankly we cannot know. There is nothing about the tale that clashes with other data. The princes were eliminated by their uncle.

Afterlife

Death was not the end. Edward V died centuries ago, yet – unlike most of his contemporaries – he is not forgotten.

When Richard III removed Edward V from public sight and if he subsequently slew him, he did it to remove the danger that the former King posed. If there was no Edward V – or if there was thought to be no Edward V – the enduring threats that he posed to the King himself, his family, followers, government and regime would be allayed. How wrong he was. Probably Edward V was not more threatening to Richard than he had been before, but he was dangerous nevertheless. For many he still symbolised the rightful line that Richard had set aside: it was as his heir, the senior representative of the rightful Yorkist line, that his sister was selected to be Henry Tudor's queen. Exchanging the princes for their sisters did not help Richard. Murdering his nieces, which he does not seem to have contemplated, was a step too far; even marrying Elizabeth proved beyond him. Moreover, the two princes now had a new symbolic importance. They were Richard's victims. They were innocent infants, comparable to the Holy Innocents murdered by King Herod, and their fate was attributable to him. Richard seems never to have dared to justify their deaths – to argue that their deaths, at whoever's hands, was politically fortunate, justifiable, or in the public interest. He had to declare in public his agreement with their mother and to deny in public any intention of marrying their sister, but he never, to our knowledge, denied in public that he had killed the princes. Richard was blamed during his own life and during his own reign for the deaths of the princes. It damaged his reputation by tarnishing him with sin. It branded him in his own day both as a tyrant and a monster. It was a crucial element in the propaganda against him – so crucial that it became commonplace.[39] What a pity we lack the letters, manifestos and placards that made it so!

Richard had thought it advantageous to conceal what had befallen the princes. He cannot have anticipated what effective propaganda would be made of it. Neither Edward III for the death of his father, nor Henry IV for that of Richard II, or even Edward IV, for the martyrdom of Henry VI, suffered serious polit-ical damage from disposing of such dangerous political opponents. We cannot be sure how successfully it was exploited. Was it the murder of the princes – and the other charges that were made against Richard – that alienated former supporters and subjects so that his army at Bosworth was the smallest of any English king during the Wars of the Roses? If it was: we have no headcount. Was it such considerations that caused Northumberland to hold back his men in battle, if he did? Did it deter the Yorkist exiles of 1483 from making their peace with Richard? Was it their fate that recruited an army for the obscure Henry Tudor, besides his Scottish and French mercenaries? We cannot possibly tell. All that we can be certain of is that Henry (and those about him) thought it a key element in his campaign.

Once Richard was dead, moreover, the fate of the princes was a key element in the propaganda that justified the Tudor dynasty, its continuation and its authority. They were symbols of why the Tudors must be supported. Their fate is the core of a moral narrative that runs from the attainder of Richard III through the narratives of Vergil and More, of Hall, Holinshed and Shakespeare, and thence into the mainstream histories, children's textbooks and historical understanding of generations of English people and English speakers everywhere. 'Richard III was a wicked king because he murdered his nephews the princes' – this impacts on us all. Perhaps he did not, but the truth remains that, beyond doubt, he deprived Edward V of his throne. Inadvertently as revenge, Edward V destroyed his uncle's reputation, if not perhaps for all time, at least for five centuries. If today we are more sympathetic to Richard – the achievement of half a century of revisionists and especially the Richard III Society! – there are still as many if not more unthinking attacks on him than defences across the English-speaking world.[40] Edward V has been better known – and more pitied – since his death. Sadly, this can often still be the case for other monarchs today.

Of course, the memory of the princes has been constantly revived by speculation about what happened to them, even by those who were sure. What happened to their bodies and where are their graves? It is an interest that started early. It was presumably in response to these questions that Tyrell and Deighton said that they did not know and it was certainly of interest to More who passed the message on to us. In 1674 it was conclusively answered when the bones of two boys of the right age were dug up under a stairway in the White Tower, were identified as those of the princes and reinterred as those of the princes. Strangely they are incomplete and presumably were so when first interred. Anatomical examination of these bones in 1933 by Lawrence Tanner and William Wright confirmed that they were indeed the princes, that they had died in August 1483 and suggested that they were smothered. It may be so. The evidence, however, is far from conclusive. Many people were buried on the site, some even before the Tower was built, several other sets of children's bones were found beforehand, and nothing was found with the bones conclusively to identify them with those of the princes. Attempts to refine the 1933 autopsy with more up-to-date methods have failed as Hammond and White have indicated. [41] Theya Mollason's brave attempt to stretch the evidence further, by indicating family resemblances with the remains of Anne Mowbray, [42] was inconclusive for many reasons: not least because Anne Mowbray, Prince Richard's child wife, shared her common descent with the princes through Ralph Earl of Westmorland (d.1425) and his twenty-five children with most of the late fifteenth-century nobility! For some years modern carbon-dating offered hope of locating them to approximately the right period. Now ever more refined genetic finger-printing offers scope for establishing their identity precisely. If not the princes, we must search elsewhere. If they are the right bodies, modern anatomical skills ought to locate their deaths within or beyond the reign – where it already appears certain that they belong. That they were buried in unmarked graves suggests even more forcibly that the boys had been murdered – that nobody seriously doubts. To establish how they died from any surviving remains still seems highly improbable: Wright, a professor of anatomy, would surely have identified any wound or injury not resulting from damage in digging. If these bones are those of the princes, they perished from some means that left no visible sign on those bones that remain, such as the poisoning, smothering, and drowning suggested by contemporaries. Exhumation and analysis will not dispel all the mysteries.

Yet Edward V was much more than an archaeological deposit, a forensic project, a literary exemplar, a historical mystery, or an inconvenience to be palmed off on some half-forgotten nobleman. He was a historical reality. He was also a Christian who believed in eternal life. As he knelt in the Tower, in trepidation of death, Edward V cannot have supposed that his killer could escape eternal damnation. We cannot answer that question. Earthly retribution he may not have expected. Yet within two years both claimants for his murder, Richard III and Buckingham, met violent ends. Their agents may have taken longer. 'But see how God remembers all the crimes we have committed', wrote Vergil. 'At length even Sir James Tyrell came to the scaffold'.[43] If Edward V suffered for who he was, his cruel fate brought him all the vengeance on earth that anybody could desire – and perhaps also hereafter. Surely the terrified boy besought God both for mercy during his life and salvation after his death. The former was denied; the latter was a matter of faith that not everybody can share. Edward V was aware of many chantries that already included him in their prayers. Many more after his death were to be added to the total. Nothing has been passed down against his character. Our sole witnesses report a youth of high promise well-suited to fulfil his predestined role. Yet Edward V comes down to us not as an individual – certainly not mature and fully formed – but as a symbol, a succession of symbols, shaped by birth, circumstance and misfortune for a succession of roles over which he could exercise little control. He was the hope of his parents, his dynasty and his nation, as valued as any other prince who actually ascended the throne. Five centuries on his fate still astonishes people everywhere.

PEDIGREES AND MAP

1 THE HOUSE OF YORK IN 1461

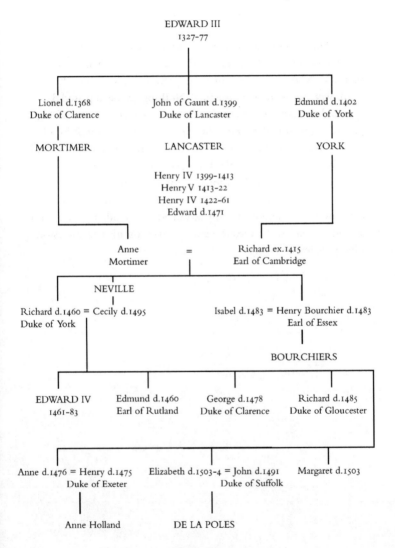

EDWARD III
1327–77

Lionel d.1368
Duke of Clarence

MORTIMER

John of Gaunt d.1399
Duke of Lancaster

LANCASTER

Henry IV 1399–1413
Henry V 1413–22
Henry IV 1422–61
Edward d.1471

Edmund d.1402
Duke of York

YORK

Anne
Mortimer

=

Richard ex.1415
Earl of Cambridge

NEVILLE

Richard d.1460 = Cecily d.1495
Duke of York

Isabel d.1483 = Henry Bourchier d.1483
Earl of Essex

BOURCHIERS

EDWARD IV
1461–83

Edmund d.1460
Earl of Rutland

George d.1478
Duke of Clarence

Richard d.1485
Duke of Gloucester

Anne d.1476 = Henry d.1475
Duke of Exeter

Elizabeth d.1503–4 = John d.1491
Duke of Suffolk

Margaret d.1503

Anne Holland

DE LA POLES

2 LADIES OF THE PRECONTRACT 1461–4

a) Lady Eleanor Butler

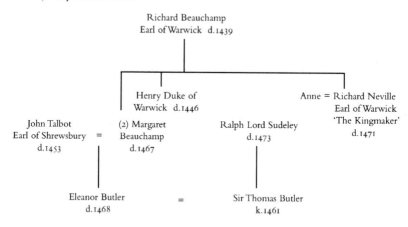

Richard Beauchamp
Earl of Warwick d.1439

Henry Duke of
Warwick d.1446

Anne = Richard Neville
Earl of Warwick
'The Kingmaker'
d.1471

John Talbot
Earl of Shrewsbury =
d.1453

(2) Margaret
Beauchamp
d.1467

Ralph Lord Sudeley
d.1473

Eleanor Butler
d.1468

=

Sir Thomas Butler
k.1461

b) Lady Margaret Lucy

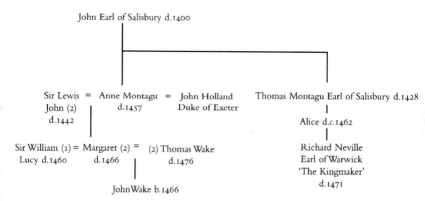

John Earl of Salisbury d.1400

Sir Lewis = Anne Montagu = John Holland
John (2)   d.1457   Duke of Exeter
d.1442

Thomas Montagu Earl of Salisbury d.1428

Alice d.c.1462

Sir William (1) = Margaret (2) = (2) Thomas Wake
Lucy d.1460   d.1466   d.1476

Richard Neville
Earl of Warwick
'The Kingmaker'
d.1471

John Wake b.1466

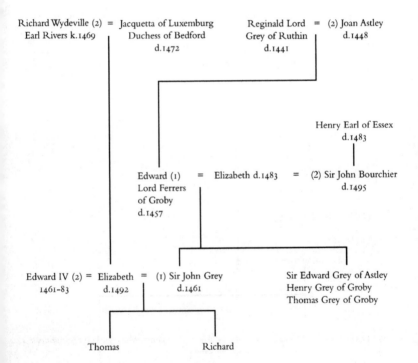

Richard Wydeville (2) = Jacquetta of Luxemburg
Earl Rivers k.1469   Duchess of Bedford
                              d.1472

Reginald Lord = (2) Joan Astley
Grey of Ruthin   d.1448
d.1441

Henry Earl of Essex
d.1483

Edward (1) = Elizabeth d.1483 = (2) Sir John Bourchier
Lord Ferrers   d.1495
of Groby
d.1457

Edward IV (2) = Elizabeth = (1) Sir John Grey
1461-83   d.1492   d.1461

Sir Edward Grey of Astley
Henry Grey of Groby
Thomas Grey of Groby

Thomas   Richard

4 THE PATERNAL FAMILY OF EDWARD V c.1480

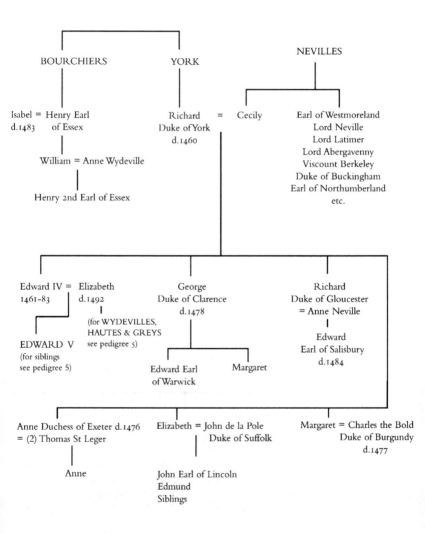

5 THE MATERNAL FAMILY OF EDWARD V *c.*1480

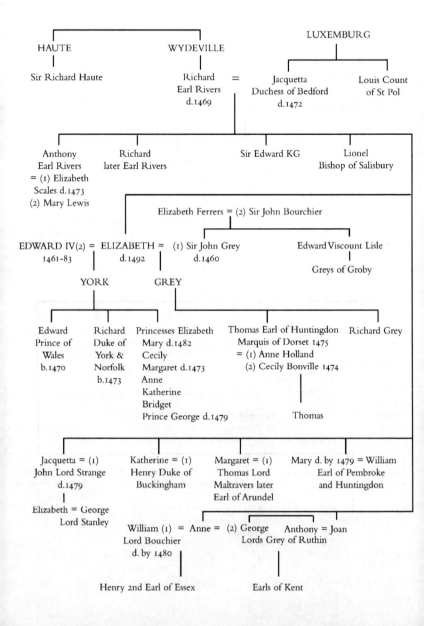

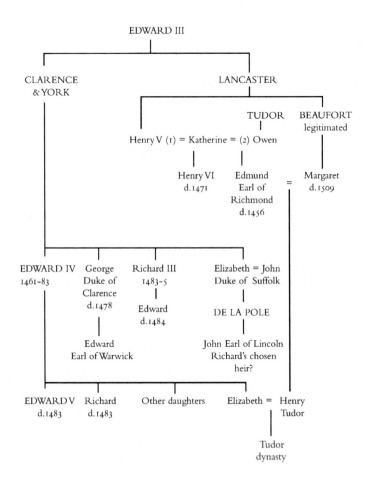

MAP OF LATE YORKIST WALES

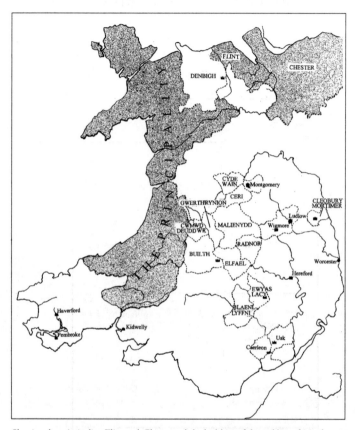

Showing the principality, Flint and Chester and the lordships of the earldom of March

FURTHER READING

LIVES

Edward V has no other modern biography. He is an important part of the reigns of the other Yorkist kings, whose lives should therefore be consulted: C.L. Scofield, *The Life and Reign of Edward IV*, vol. 2 (1923); C.D. Ross, *Edward IV* (2nd edn, Yale, 1997) and *Richard III* (2nd edn, Yale, 1999), are especially reliable. R.E. Horrox, *Richard III: A Study of Service* (Cambridge, 1989) contains much on those around Edward V. The definitive book on Perkin Warbeck, who pretended to be the younger of the Princes, is I. Arthurson, *The Perkin Warbeck Conspiracy 1491-1499* (Stroud, 1994). A.J. Pollard, *Late Medieval England 1399-1509* (Harlow, 2001) is the most comprehensive recent narrative. A medley of crucial snippets, especially those assembled by A.F. Sutton and L. Visser-Fuchs, are collected in the last twenty years of *The Ricardian*. An alternative provocative overview is M.K. Jones, *Bosworth, 1485: Psychology of a Battle* (Stroud, 2002). *Fifteenth-century England, 1399-1504: Studies in politics and society,* ed. S.B. Chrimes, C.D. Ross and R.A. Griffiths (Manchester, 1972)

SOURCES

The most valuable narratives are *The Crowland Chronicle Continuations 1459-86*, ed. N. Pronay and J. Cox (1986); D. Mancini, *The Usurpation of Richard III*, ed. C.A.J. Armstrong (Oxford, 1969); T. More, *The History of King Richard III*, ed. R. Sylvester (Yale, 1963). A considerable amount of material is contained in *Rolls of Parliament*, vol. 6 (Record Commission, 1783) and in *British Library Harleian Manuscript 433*, ed. P.W. Hammond and R.E. Horrox (4 vols., Upminster, 1979-83). Most of the relatively few other records in print are in K. Dockray (ed), *Richard III: A Reader* (Stroud, 1988) and A.R. Myers (ed.), *English Historical Documents*, iv, 1327-1485 (1969). A mass of unprinted estate accounts and petitions at the Public Record Office deserve further analysis.

2 THE LEGACY OF EDWARD V

For the House of York, see especially P.A. Johnson, *Duke Richard of York 1411-60* (Oxford, 1986); C.D. Ross, *Edward IV* (1974); and T.B. Pugh, 'The Estates, Finances, and Regal Aspirations of Richard Plantagenet (1411-60), Duke of York', *Revolution and Consumption in Late Medieval England*, ed. M.A. Hicks (Woodbridge, 2001). The authoritative work on the politics of 1461-71 is now M.A. Hicks, *Warwick the Kingmaker* (Oxford, 1998). The story of Edward IV's sexual adventures relies principally on More, *Richard III*; *The Coronation of Elizabeth Woodville*, ed. G. Smith (1934); J. Ashdown-Hill, 'Edward IV's Uncrowned Queen: The Lady Eleanor Talbot, Lady Butler', *The Ricardian* 139 (1997) and (less authoritative) 'The Elusive Mistress: Elizabeth Lucy and her Family', *The Ricardian* 145 (1999), and sources cited below. For the Wydevilles, see J.R. Lander, 'Marriage and Politics in the Fifteenth Century: The Nevilles and the Wydevilles', *Crown and Nobility 1450-1509* (1976); M.A. Hicks, 'The Changing Role of the Wydevilles in Yorkist Politics to 1483', *Patronage, Pedigree and Power in Late Medieval England*, ed. C.D. Ross (Gloucester, 1979), reprinted in my *Richard III and his Rivals* (1991). Margaret Lucy's brass is reproduced in H.L. Elliott, 'FitzLewis of West Horndon and Ingrave', *Trans. Essex. Arch. Soc.*Vi.1 (1896), 28-53.

3 HEIR PRESUMPTIVE

For Edward IV's upbringing, see N. Orme, 'The Education of Edward V', *Bulletin of the Institute of Historical Research* 57 (1984), which includes his household ordinances, to be supplemented by *The Household of Edward IV*, ed. A.R. Myers (Manchester, 1959). For Gruthuyse's visit, see C.L. Kingsford, *English Historical Literature in the Fifteenth Century* (London, 1913), and for the Prince's estates, council and staff, see *Rolls of Parliament*, vol. 6, and *Calendar of the Patent Rolls 1467-85*. There is useful material in R.A. Griffiths, 'Wales and the Marches', *Fifteenth-century England, 1399-1509: Politics and Society* (Manchester, 1972); Hicks, 'Changing Role of the Wydevilles; D.E. Lowe, 'The Council of the Prince of Wales and the Decline of the Herbert Family during the Second Reign of Edward IV (1471-83)', *Bulletin of the Board of Celtic Studies* 27 (1976-8) ; and D.E. Lowe 'Patronage and Politics, Edward IV, the Wydevills, and the Council of the Prince of Wales, 1471-1483', in ibid. 29 (1980-2).

4 PRINCE OF WALES

This chapter derives principally from Lowe's two articles cited above. R.A. Griffiths provides the context in his 'Wales and the Marches' *Fifteenth-century England, 1399-1509: Politics and Society* (Manchester, 1972) and definitive data on office-holding in the southern principality in his *Principality of Wales in the Latter Middle Ages*, I (Cardiff, 1972). His 'Ludlow during the Wars of the Roses', *Ludlow Castle: its History and Buildings* (Almeley, 2000) has been valuable in conjunction with M.A. Faraday, *Ludlow 1085-1660* (Chichester, 1991). For the interpretation, see also Hicks, 'Changing Role of the Wydevilles'.

5 POLITICS OF THE FAMILY

The principal sources are Edward IV's will in *Excerpta Historica*, ed. S. Bentley (1833) and the *Rolls of Parliament*, vol. 6. Earlier discussion of court faction and Yorkist land politics in Edward IV's second reign are contained in M.A. Hicks, 'Changing Role of the Wydevilles'; *False, Fleeting, Perjur'd Clarence* (rev edn, 1992); *Richard III* (2nd edn., 2000); E.W. Ives, 'Andrew Dymmock and the Papers of Anthony, Earl Rivers, 1482-3', *Bulletin of the Institute of Historical Research* 41 (1968); and Lowe, 'Patronage and Politics'.

6 KING AT LAST

The best account of the usurpation is now Hicks, *Richard III*. Apart from the *Crowland Chronicle Continuations* and Mancini's *Usurpation of Richard III*, the principal records are collected in *Richard III: The Road to Bosworth Field*, ed. P.W. Hammond and A.F. Sutton (1985). Apart from the standard chancery calendars, Edward V's government is uniquely well-documented in *British Library Harleian Manuscript* 433, ed. P.W. Hammond and R.E. Horrox (4 vols, Upminster, 1979-83), esp vols 1 and 3 and in 'Financial Memoranda of the Reign of Edward V', ed. R.E. Horrox, *Camden Miscellany*, xxix (1987).

7 THE LAST KING

The relevant accounts are Mancini, *Crowland Chronicle Continuations*, and More, *Richard III*, or are collected in K. Dockray, *Richard III: A Reader* (Gloucester, 1988); see also L. Visser-Fuchs, 'English Events in Caspar Weinreich's Danzig Chronicle 1461-1495', *The Ricardian* 8 (1986). For plots against Richard in 1483, see especially Hicks, *Richard III*; Hicks, 'Unweaving the Web: The Plot of July 1483 against Richard III and its Wider Significance', *The Ricardian* 114 (1991); and I. Arthurson and N. Kingwell, 'The Proclamation of Henry Tudor as King of England, 3 November 1483', *Historical Research* 63 (1990). The original autopsy of the bones is in L. Tanner and W. Wright, 'Recent Investigations regarding the Fate of the Princes at Westminster abbey', *Archaeologia* 34 (1934). The fullest recent discussions are in P.W. Hammond and W.J. White, 'The Sons of Edward IV: 'A Re-Examination of the Evidence on their Deaths and the on the Bones at Westminster Abbey', *Richard III: Loyalty, Lordship and Law*, ed. P.W. Hammond (Gloucester, 1986), and A.J. Pollard, *Richard III and the Princes in the Tower* (Stroud, 1991), ch. 5.

ABBREVIATIONS

BL	British Library, London
BRUC	A.B. Emden, *A Biographical Register of the University of Cambridge* (Cambridge, 1963)
BRUO	A.B. Emden, *A Biographical Register of the University of Oxford* (3 vols Oxford 1957-9)
BIHR	*Bulletin of the Institute of Historical Research*
	Biographies J.C. Wedgwood, *History of Parliament, 1439-1509 Biographies* (1936)
CCR	*Calendar of the Close Rolls*
CChR	*Calendar of the Charter Rolls 1427-1516*
CFR	*Calendar of the Fine Rolls*
CLB	*The Coventry Leet Book or Mayor's Register*, ed. M.D. Harris (Early English Text Society, 4 parts, 1908-13)
CPR	*Calendar of the Patent Rolls*
Commynes	P. de Commynes, *Mémoires* ed. J. Calmette & G. Durville, 3 vols. (Paris, 1923-5)
Crowland	*The Crowland Chronicle Continuations 1459-86*, ed. N. Pronay and J. Cox (1986);
EHR	*English Historical Review*
GEC	*The Complete Peerage of England, etc*, ed. H.V. Gibbs and others, 13 vols (1910-59)
Hammond & Sutton	P.W. Hammond & A.F. Sutton, *Richard III: The Road to Bosworth Field* (1985)
Harley 433	*British Library Harleian Manuscript* 433, ed. P.W. Hammond and R.E. Horrox (4 vols., Upminster, 1979-83).
Hicks, *Clarence*	M.A. Hicks, *False, Fleeting, Perjur'd Clarence: George Duke of Clarence 1449-1478* (Gloucester, 1978)
Hicks, *Richard III*	M.A. Hicks, *Richard III* (2nd edn. 2000)
Hicks, *Warwick*	M.A. Hicks, *Warwick the Kingmaker* (Oxford, 1998).
Hicks, *Wydevilles*	M.A. Hicks, 'The Changing Role of the Wydevilles in Yorkist Politics to 1483', *Richard III and his Rivals: Magnates and their Motives during the Wars of the Roses* (1991)
Lowe 1	D.E. Lowe, 'The Council of the Prince of Wales and the Decline of the Herbert family during the Second Reign of Edward IV (1471-83', *Bulletin of the Board of Celtic Studies* 27 (1976-8)
Lowe 2	D.E. Lowe, 'Patronage and Politics, Edward IV, the Wydevills, and the Council of the Prince of Wales, 1471-1483', in ibid. 29 (1980-2).

Mancini   D. Mancini, *The Usurpation of Richard III,* ed. C.A.J. Armstrong, 2nd edn, (Oxford, 1969)

Memoranda   'Financial Memoranda of the Reign of Edward V', ed. R.E. Horrox, *Camden Miscellany* 29 (1987).

More   T. More, *The History of King Richard III and Selections from the English and Latin Poems,* ed. R.Sylvester (New Haven, 1976).

Orme   N. Orme, 'The Education of Edward V', *Bulletin of the Institute of Historical Research* 57 (1984)

PRO   Public Record Office, Kew

RDP   *Report from the Lords' Committee touching the Dignity of a Peer,* 5 vols (1820-39)

Ross, *Edward IV*   C.D. Ross, *Edward IV* (2nd edn Yale, 1997)

Ross, *Richard III*   C.D. Ross, *Richard III* (2nd edn Yale, 1999)

RP   *Rolls of Parliament,* 6 vols (Record Commission, 1783)

Scofield, *Edward V*   C.L. Scofield, *The Life and Reign of King Edward the Fourth,* 2 vols *Edward IV* (1923)

Vergil 1   *Three Books of Polydore Vergil's English History,* ed. H. Ellis, Camden Soc. xxix (1844)

Vergil 2   *The Anglica Historica of Polydore Vergil 1485-1537,* ed. D. Hay, Camden 3rd ser. lxxiv (1950)

NOTES

I WHO WAS EDWARD V?

1 I. Arthurson, *The Perkin Warbeck Conspiracy 1491-99* (Stroud, 1994), vii.
2 Orme, 119.

2 THE LEGACY OF EDWARD V

1 A.J. Pollard, *Late Medieval England 1399-1509* (2000), 332.
2 For Duke Richard, see especially P.A. Johnson, *Duke Richard of York 1411-60* (Oxford, 1988); T.B. Pugh, 'The Estates, Finances, & Regal Aspirations of Richard Plantagenet (1411-60), Duke of York', *Revolution & Consumption in Late Medieval England*, ed. M.A. Hicks (Woodbridge, 2001), 76.
3 I.M.W. Harvey, *Jack Cade's Rebellion of 1450* (Oxford, 1991), 78; E. Powell, 'The Strange Death of Sir John Mortimer: Politics & the Law of Treason in Lancastrian England', *Rulers & Ruled in Late Medieval England*, ed. R.E. Archer & S.K. Walker (Oxford, 1995), ch. 6.
4 *GEC* i.341; iv.281; W. Dugdale, *Monasticon Anglicanum*, ed. W. Thomas, 8 vols (1830), ii.62.
5 Commynes, ii.50.
6 M.K. Jones, *Bosworth 1485: Psychology of a Battle* (Stroud, 2002), 67-70.
7 A heraldic source *c.*1475 records that the King was actually baptised in Rouen cathedral. BL Add MS 6113 f. 49v. A godmother was the highly respectable Elizabeth Lady Say, Lord Sudeley's sister and mother of Sir Thomas Montgomery. At birth Edward may not have been York's eldest son.
8 M.A. Hicks, *Richard III as Duke of Gloucester: A Study in Character*, Borthwick Paper 70 (1986), 27, 33.
9 Ross, *Richard III*, 138; *Harley* 433ii, 271; Hammond & Sutton, 167-8; R.E. Horrox, *Richard III: A Study of Service* (Cambridge, 1989), 41. John could have been conceived at Pontefract *c.*1465-8 when Richard was residing with his predecessor Warwick.
10 Scofield, *Edward IV*, ii.150; *Calendar of State Papers Milanese*, ed. A.B. Hinds (1912), i.124.
11 C. Given-Wilson & A. Curteis, *The Royal Bastards of Medieval England* (1984), 8, 160.
12 Commynes, i.203.
13 Hammond & Sutton, 146, 209.
14 *Crowland*, 150-3; *Historical Collections of a Citizen of London*, ed. J. Gairdner, Camden Soc. n.s. xvii (1876), 226.
15 PRO E 101/412/8 m. 3. The boy was not named and seems unidentifiable.
16 Mancini, 66-7.
17 Commynes, i.203; Vergil 1, 117.

18 More, 5, 73.

19 *Chronicles of the White Rose of York*, ed. J.A. Giles (1843), 19; for the next sentence, see Commynes, i. 203.

20 Commynes, i.203.

21 Vergili, 117. Margaret Lucy gave Warwick as her address in 1462, PRO C 67/45 m.33; see below.

22 More, 22. For what follows, see ibid. 73.

23 *GEC* viii.63-8; PRO C 1/664/ 11; *The Lisle Letters*, ed. M. St Claire Byrne, 6 vols (Chicago, 1981), i. 140. The most recent efforts, impressive if inconclusive, are Byrne, *Lisle Letters*, passim; Ashdown-Hill, 'Elizabeth Lucy'.

24 A.F. Sutton, L. Visser-Fuchs, 'The Royal Burials of the House of York at Windsor: II', *The Ricardian* 144 (1999), 456. We cannot be certain whether Grace was her forename or surname.

25 PRO DURH 3/54/22 m. 8; *John Leland's Itinerary*, ed. J. Chandler (Stroud, 1993), 337; R. Surtees, *History & Antiquities of the County Palatine of Durham*, 4 vols (1816-40), ii. 141; Byrne, *Lisle Letters*, 140n, 141n. They had eight children. As Richard Lord Lumley (d.1510), married in 1489, was thirty and more in 1508 and his own son John Lord Lumley was eighteen in 1510, Richard must have been born in the mid 1470s to a teenaged bride conceived very early in the 1460s, *GEC* viii.271-3; J.W. Clay, *Extinct & Dormant Peerages of the Northern Counties of England* (1913), 130; *Calendar of Inquisitions post mortem, Henry VII*, iii, nos. 360, 432; *Testamenta Eboracensia*, ed. J. Raine, iii, Surtees Soc. lv (1864), 355; *Forty-Fourth Report of the Deputy Keeper of the Public Record Office* (1883), 45; see also *Biographies*, 563.

26 More, 56.

27 Hammond & Sutton, 156.

28 College of Arms, Butler roll; D. Winkless, 'Medieval Sudeley part 2: The Fifteenth Century Roll Chronicle of the Kings of England, with the Sudeley & Boteler Pedigree', *Family History* 10 (1977), 17, 34n. For what follows, see J. Ashdown-Hill, 'Edward IV's Uncrowned Queen: Lady Eleanor Talbot, Lady Butler', *The Ricardian* 139 (1997), 166-90; *GEC* ix. 422; xii(1), 421n; C. Carpenter, *Locality & Polity* (Cambridge, 1992), 463.

29 Commynes, ii. 232, 305.

30 H.A. Kelly, 'The Case against Edward IV's Marriage & Offspring: Secrecy; Witchcraft; Secrecy; Precontract', *The Ricardian* 142 (1998), 329.

31 Commynes, ii.232; see also ibid. ii.305. The much later indictment of Stillington by the imperial ambassador Chapuys most probably derives from Commynes, *Letters & Papers, Henry VIII*, vi. 618; see also ibid. viii.281.

32 *CPR 1467-77*, 133; *CFR 1461-71*, 215; PRO C 140/29/4/2.

33 More, 65-6. Note A.F. Pollard's documentation of the early sixteenth-century Elizabeth Lucy, 'The Making of Sir Thomas More's *Richard III*, *Historical Essays in honour of James Tait*, ed. J.G. Edwards, V.H. Galbraith & E.F. Jacob (Manchester, 1933), 231, 232n; also *Letters & Papers illustrative of the Reigns of Richard III & Henry VII*, ed. J. Gairdner, Rolls Series, 2 vols. (1861-3), ii.239.

34 PRO PROB 11/4 (PCC 11 Stockton); A. Payne, 'The Salisbury Roll of Arms, 1463', *England in the Fifteenth Century*, ed. D. Williams (Woodbridge, 1987), 197.

35 It was delivered to chancery only on 16 Nov. 1463 by Thomas Pachet, PRO C 140/8/18/1; *GEC* viii. 262; *CCR 1461-8*, 5.

36 'Annales rerum anglicarum', *Letters & Papers illustrative of the Wars of the English in France*, ed. J. Stevenson, Rolls Series, 2 vols (1864), ii(2), 783; PRO C 67/45 m.33; Vergil 1, 117.

37 *Calendar of Papal Registers*, 1458-71, 405; *CPR* 1461-7, 491; *CCR* 1461-8, 271, 273; PRO C 1/31/298 (which makes it clear her husband was Thomas, not John, as in *Biographies*, 912); C 4/2/6-7. Both suits began with Neville as Bishop of Exeter and ended when he was archbishop. For Danvers, see *Biographies*, 256-7.

38 *GEC* viii. 263; PRO C 140/20/6/1-16; *CPR* 1467-77, 598; W.E. Hampton, *Monuments of the Wars of the Roses* (Upminster, 1979), no. 76; W.E. Hampton, 'Roger Wake of Blisworth', *Richard III: Crown & People*, ed. J. Petre (1985), 160n.5.

39 Mancini, 96-7.

40 Hicks, *Warwick*, 199-200.

41 Commynes, ii. 248.

42 More, 63.

43 Mancini, 60-1; L. Visser-Fuchs, 'English Events in Caspar Weinreich's Chronicle 1461-95', *The Ricardian* 95 (1986), 312.

44 Weinreich also records speculation about how her husband Sir John Grey had been killed, ibid. 313.

45 Ibid.

46 *Ingulph's Chronicle of the Abbey of Croyland*, ed. H.T. Riley (1859), 439.

47 *The Great Chronicle of London,* ed. A.H. Thomas & I.D. Thornley (1938), 202; Mancini, 96-7; for what follows, see Vergil 1, 116-17.

48 R. Fabian, *New Chronicles of England & France*, ed. H. Ellis (1811), 654; for the next sentence, see Vergil 1, 117.

49 Scofield, *Edward IV*, i.332-3.

50 At Northampton Art Gallery.

51 Hammond & Sutton, 156.

52 PRO E 163/29/11, indicated to me by Prof. Rawcliffe, who kindly supplied me with a transcript; for Eborall, see *BRUO* i. 623.

53 *White Rose*, 16.

54 C. Fahy, 'The Marriage of Edward IV & Elizabeth Woodville: A New Italian Source', *EHR* lxxvi (1966), 660-72; for what follows, see Mancini, 60-1; More, 62.

55 *Death & Dissent: Two Fifteenth-Century Chronicles,* ed. L. Matheson (Woodbridge, 1999), 95; *Historical Collections*, 226; *Great Chronicle*, 202; *Chronicles of London*, ed. C.L. Kingsford (1906), 179; *White Rose*, 16; T. Perez-Higuera, *Art of Time* (1998), 196; *The Riverside Chaucer*, ed. A Burgess, 3rd edn (Oxford, 1987), 160-1.

56 Hammond & Sutton, 156; *RP* vi.232.

57 *Fabian's Chronicle*, 654.

58 *GEC* v.356-60; G. Smith, *The Coronation of Elizabeth Woodville* (1935), 29-31; More, 62; PRO C 1/27/267-71; C 253/38/83, 90, 264-5; CP 25(1)/294/74/5; A.R. Myers, *Crown, Household & Parliament in 15th-Century England* (1983), 264; Carpenter, *Locality & Polity*, 469.

59 *GEC* v.360n; PRO CP 25(1)/294/74/7; see also *CCR* 1468-76, no. 1382.

60 Historic Manuscripts Commission, 78 *Hastings*, i.301-2. Regrettably, this item is not among the Hastings MSS at the Huntington Library, California.

61 PRO DL 37/33/27.

62 *CPR* 1461-7, 327; PRO C 81/1495/32.

63 *Fabian's Chronicle*, 654.

64 Commynes, ii.305.

65 Hammond & Sutton, 156.

66 *Calendar of State Papers Venetian*, ed. R. Brown (1864), i.114; *Milanese*, i.113–14.

67 Mancini, 60–1; More, 65.

68 *Crowland*, 114–15.

69 Ibid.; *Ingulph's Chronicle*, 445.

70 *Death & Dissent*, 95; J. Waurin, *Recueil des Chroniques et Anchiennes Istoires de l'Angleterre*, ed. W. & E.L.C.P. Hardy, 5 vols, Rolls Series (1891), v.456.

71 Hicks, *Clarence*, 34–6, 60; 'Wydevilles', 214–16.

72 Commynes, ii.50; see also J.Calmette & G. Périnelle, *Louis XI et l'Angleterre 1461–83* (Paris, 1930), 307.

73 *RP* vi.232.

74 *GEC* vii.478; *CFR* 1461–71, 264; G. Baker, *History & Antiquities of the County of Northampton*, part V, ii (1841), 204.

75 *RP* vi. 232; Hicks, *Clarence*, 48.

76 *The Arrivall of Edward IV*, ed. J. Bruce, Camden Soc. i (1836), 17; *Political Poems and Songs*, ed. T. Wright, 2 vols, Rolls Series (1861), ii. 274; *Crowland,* 122–3; Kingsford, *London Chronicles*, 183.

3 HEIR PRESUMPTIVE

1   PRO C 66/532 m. 15.

2   *CPR* 1467–77, 283; *RP* vi.9–14; *CChR*, 239; PRO C 67/532 m. 15.

3   C.L. Kingsford, *English Historical Literature in the Fifteenth Century* (1913), 380.

4   *RDP* v. 419, 421–2; *CChR*, 239; see also *CPR* 1476–85, 59–60, 94, 273, 339; PRO E 28/91/4.

5   *Foedera*, xi.714; *CCR* 1468–76, no. 858.

6   BL Add MS 6113 f. 74v.

7   Kingsford, 382; *RP* vi. 1–6. For Allington, see J.S. Roskell, *Parliament and Politics in Late Medieval England*, iii (1983), 369–81.

8   Kingsford, 383–8.

9   PRO E 101/ 412/8 mm.1–3. This is attached to a misplaced writ dated 5 Oct. 1477 to the barons of the exchequer.

10 *CPR* 1467–77, 361, 365; H. C[hitty], 'An Incident in the Life of Edward V', *Notes & Queries* 11th ser. 11 (1915), 221–2; Winchester College MS 1544.

11 Lowe, 289; BL Add. Ch. 26,786; *CCR* 1468–76, nos. 722, 849; PRO SC 6/1305/13 m.6.

12 BL Add. Ms 6113 f. 107v; *RDP* v. 402–4; *CChR*, 249.

13 *CLB*, 390–3; *Register of the Gild of Holy Trinity etc of Coventry*, ed. M.D. Harris, Dugdale Soc. 13 (1935), 69n.

14 *CPR* 1467–77, 455.

15 *CLB,* 391, 504; PRO SC 6/782/5 m.1; /1225/8 m. 5; SC 6/1305/13 m.6; CHES 2/154 m.3; H.Owen & Blakeway, *History & Antiquities of Shrewsbury*, 2 vols. (1825), i.232; *Registrum Thome Myllyng, Episcopi Herefordiensis, 1474–92*, ed. A.T. Bannister, Canterbury & York Soc. xxvi (1920), 33.

16 Lowe 1, 288; PRO E 101/412/9–11; BL Harley MS 158 ff. 119v, 120v; Add MS 6113 ff. 97v–8, 111–12.

17 BL Add MS 6113 f. 49v.
18 *Foedera*, xii.110, 128, 134, 138, 147. In general, Ross, *Edward IV*, chs. 9 & 10.
19 *Foedera*, xii.142; Ross, *Edward IV*, 246-7.
20 *Foedera*, xii.13-14; *CPR* 1467-77, 499, 534-5; Scofield, *Edward IV*, ii.125.
21 *Excerpta Historica*, ed. S. Bentley (1833), 366-79.
22 PRO C 66/532 m.15; *CPR* 1467-77, 417.
23 PRO C 66/ 531 m. 3; /532 m. 15; *CPR* 1467-77, 401.
24 PRO C 66/531 m. 3, /532 mm. 15, 17 calendared in *CPR* 1467-77, 401, 414, 417.
25 Orme, 120; *CPR* 1467-77, 358; 1476-85, 241. Unless otherwise stated, this section
    is based on Orme, 119-28.
26 *CPR* 1467-77, 414, 455; PRO C 66/532 m.17; H. Chitty, 'Incident', 221. For
    Vaughan's career, see *Biographies*, 902-3.
27 *CPR* 1467-77, 283; Chitty, 'Incident', 221; for Dacre, see Hicks, *Clarence*, 149.
28 *The Household of Edward IV*, ed. A.R. Myers (Manchester, 1959), 126-7.
29 *CPR* 1467-77, 417; Orme, 126-8.
30 Lowe2, 553-5; PRO C 66/532 m.15; E 159/254, *communia*, Mich. 17 Edw. IV.
31 Ross, *Edward IV*, 278, 289-90.
32 *CPR* 1467-77, 401; PRO C 66/531 m.3; Lowe1, 291; Lowe2, 557; *BRUC*, 4-6.
33 N. Orme, *From Childhood to Chivalry* (1984), 117.
34 *Calendar of Papal Registers*, 1471-84, 569, 638; *BRUO* i.553; ii.798-9. For Giles, see
    CPR 1467-77, 592. Since Richard seems to have lived with his mother, perhaps
    Giles' service to Edward had already ceased or for Richard had yet to begin.
35 *Great Chronicle*, 234; Mancini, 70-1.
36 Mancini, 92-3; A.F. Sutton & L. Visser-Fuchs, *Richard III's Books* (Stroud, 1997), 178.
37 *CPR* 1467-77, 283, 451; 1476-85, 58, 308; Mancini, 92-3; Lowe1, 281; Lowe2, 556,
    559. N.H. Nicolas, 'On the Badge & Mottoes of the Prince of Wales', *Archaeologia*
    xxxi (1846), 369.
38 *CPR* 1467-77, 361, 365; *RP* vi.15; PRO C 66/532 m.15.
39 PRO SC 6/1217/6; SC 6/1225/8; SC 6/782/5.
40 PRO SC 6/ 816/8.
41 Myers, *Household*, 94.
42 PRO DL 29/616/9887.
43 *CPR* 1476-85, 59-60, 94, 339; Pugh, 'Duke of York', 76.
44 Ross, *Edward IV*, 385.
45 Harley 433, i.3. On 14 May 1483, *after* his accession and Gloucester's appointment as
    protector, the post was revived for the duke's retainer William Catesby, ibid. i.6-7.
46 PRO SC 8/344/1281. A saving for him suggests that he was already in post by
    October 1472, *RP* vi. 16.
47 Hicks, 'Wydevilles', 77.
48 *CPR* 1467-77, 283, 366; PRO C 66/ 531 m.3.
49 Chitty, 'Incident', 221-2.
50 PRO SC 8/344, /345; Lowe1, 282-4.
51 Hicks, 'Wydevilles', 77. He was the Prince's chancellor probably only for the
    duchy of Cornwall, PRO SC 8/344/1281.
52 *Reg. Myllyng*, 33.
53 Lowe1, 278, 284-5; Lowe2, 538; Orme, 128n; PRO E 163/8/36.

1   *CPR* 1467-77, 283, 366; Orme, 128.
2   E.g. More, 14; but see P. Williams, *The Council in the Marches of Wales under Elizabeth I* (Cardiff, 1958), 7-8.
3   *CPR* 1467-77, 283.
4   Ibid. 366.
5   PRO DL 37/41/6, 17, 18.
6   Hicks, *Clarence*, 149.
7   *Biographies*, 9, 350-1; *BRUO* ii.1236-7; Hicks, 'Wydevilles', 77; *CPR* 1467-77, 262.
8   Lowe2, 550-1, 555.
9   *Crowland*, 132-3.
10 *CLB*, 391.
11 Lowe2, 556.
12 Orme, 128n.
13 *Original Letters illustrative of English History,* ed. H. Ellis, 11 vols (1824-46), 1st ser. i. 9-10; *Excerpta Historica,* 8-9.
14 Ellis, *Letters*, i(i), 9-10.
15 Pugh, 'Duke of York', 76.
16 Ellis, *Letters*, i(i), 11-13.
17 PRO E 28/90/48.
18 *Leland's Itinerary*, 386. The next three paragraphs are based on *Ludlow Castle: its History & Buildings*, ed. R. Shoesmith & A. Johnson (Almeley, 2000); M.A. Faraday, *Ludlow 1085-1660: A Social, Economic & Political History* (Chichester, 1991*); CChR,* 155.
19 PRO SC 966/13-19.
20 Ibid. /15; *Leland's Itinerary*, 387; *CPR* 1476-85, 473; see also *Biographies*, 58-9, 827-8; C.F. Richmond, 'The Sulyard Papers: The Rewards of a Small Family Archive', *England in the Fifteenth Century*, 199-228.
21 *CPR* 1461-7, 92. For what follows, see N. Baker, *Shrewsbury Abbey: A Medieval Monastery (c.* 2000); Owen & Blakeway, i.231-3; *CChR,* 211-14.
22 Owen & Blakeway, i.230n, which establishes the year and place; 17 Aug. is not in doubt. It was also at the Shrewsbury Blackfriars that Elizabeth Countess Rivers, who died on 2 Sep. 1473, was interred, College of Arms Roll 12/22; *GEC* xi. 24.
23 Owen & Blakeway, ii.125; PRO SC 6/782/5 m.7.
24 *CPR* 1467-77, 54-5, 365; 1476-85, 74.
25 *CChR*, 229-32.
26 More, 14. For what follows, see M.A. Hicks, *English Political Culture in the Fifteenth Century* (2002), ch. 7.
27 *RP* vi. 8.
28 PRO E 28/90/48.
29 PRO E 315/40/75.
30 *RP* vi.8.
31 *RP* vi.159.
32 PRO E 315/40/75; R.A. Griffiths, 'Wales & the Marches', *fifeenth-century England,* 158-60; Lowe2, 548-9; PRO KB 9/ 329sqq.
33 Lowe1, 288.

34 *CPR* 1467-77, 574.
35 Owen & Blakeway, i.232.
36 *CLB*, 420-506, esp. 499; Lowe 1, 286-8.
37 Lowe 1, 286.
38 Orme, 128n; *CPR* 1467-77, 449; PRO C 66/533 m.13.
39 *RP* vi. 159.
40 C.S.L. Davies, 'The Crofts: Creation & Defence of a Family Enterprise under the Yorkists & Henry VII', *Historical Research* lxviii (1995), 246n.
41 Hicks, *Clarence*, 38-9, 56; PRO DL 37/41/6.
42 *RP* vi.46. Sir Roger Kynaston was similarly exempted for offices in north Wales, ibid.
43 PRO SC 6/1305/13 m.6d.
44 *RDP* v.419; *CChR*, 250; *RP* vi.202-4; T.B. Pugh, 'The magnates, knights & gentry', *15th-cent. England*, 111.
45 Hicks, 'Wydevilles', 226-7; PRO DL 42/19 f. 11; C 81/1662/23, 24. For the dates, compare *CLB*, 497.
46 Lowe 1, 292.
47 *CPR* 1467-77, 574; 1476-85, 5; *Calendar of Fine Rolls* 1471-85, no. 607.
48 Lowe 1, 288-9; Lowe 2, 555; PRO DL 42/19 f. 31v; R.A. Griffiths, *The Principality of Wales in the Later Middle Ages*, i (Cardiff, 1972), 160-1, 187-9; *CPR* 1467-77, 451; 1476-85, 288.
49 PRO SC 6/1209/18, 19; see also BL Add Ch. 8526 for a signet letter addressed to the lieutenant justice of north Wales.
50 Lowe 1, 278-81, 295.
51 Unfortunately this file seen by the author in the 1970s has not been found.
52 E.g. Hicks, *Clarence*, 94; *CPR* 1476-85, 7; PRO SC 6/782/5 m. 4.
53 Lowe 2, 560.
54 PRO DL 37/46/18.
55 PRO SC 6/782/5 m.8; Owen & Blakeway, i.231-2; Orme, passim.
56 Lowe 1, 289, 291; Hicks, 'Wydevilles', 77; Hicks, *Clarence*, 154-5; E.W. Ives, 'Andrew Dymmock and the Papers of Anthony, Earl Rivers, 1482-3', *BIHR* xli (1968), 222-3.
57 PRO SC 6/635/10337 m.17; *CLB*, 492-3, 504.
58 Owen & Blakeway, i. 231n. The Prince sent a Frenchman there via Shrewsbury in 1478-9, ibid. i.232.
59 BL Add MS 6113 f.107v; KB 8/1/ 19; KB 9/343/74, /344/55; SC 6/782/ 2 rot. 4; F. Grose & T. Astle, *Antiquarian Repertory*, ed. E. Jeffrey (4 vols 2nd edn. 1808), 385; *pace* Lowe 2, 552.
60 Davies, 'Crofts', 241-9; M.K. Jones, 'Sir William Stanley of Holt: Politics & Family Allegiance in the Late Fifteenth Century', *Welsh History Review* 14 (1988), 6-9.
61 *CPR* 1467-77, 410; 1476-85, 10, 222.
62 Lowe 2, 569-70.
63 W.B. Baker, 'Appendix', *Archaeologia* xx.581.

5 POLITICS OF THE FAMILY

1 *RP* vi.168.
2 Hicks, *Clarence*, chs 1 & 2; *CChR*, 217.

3   *Excerpta Historica*, pp.366-79; M.H.N. Stansfield, 'John Holland, Duke of Exeter & Earl of Huntingdon (d.1447), & the Costs of the Hundred Years War', *Profit, Piety & the Professions in Later Medieval England*, ed. M.A. Hicks (Gloucester, 1990), 105.

4   PRO E 101/412/11; *Privy Purse Expenses of Elizabeth of York*, ed. N.H. Nicolas (1830), 157; see also *CPR* 1476-85, 179.

5   Hicks, *Clarence*, 149, 152.

6   Hicks, 'Wydevilles', 221, 226.

7   *Excerpta Historica,* 366-79.

8   *Registrum Thome Bourgchier, Cantuariensis Archiepiscopi, 1454-86*, ed. F.R.H. Du Boulay, Canterbury & York Soc. 54 (1957), 52-3.

9   Hicks, *Clarence*, 143-6; *RDP* v. 405-7.

10   Ibid. 156-7; BL Add MS 6113 ff.15-v; PRO DL 29/454/7312; C 49/40/9/2, 3, 4; *RP* vi.168.

11   *RP* vi.206-7.

12   It is suggestive that there are two incomplete copies, College of Arms MS L8a f. 16v; BL Add MS 6113 ff.15-v.

13   Hicks, 'Wydevilles', 220-1; *CCR* 1468-76, no. 1382.

14   'Annales Rerum Anglicarum', 786.

15   Stansfield, 'John Holland', 105, 111.

16   *RDP* v.391-2, 402-4; *CPR* 1467-77, 582; *CChR,* 239, 249.

17   *RP* vi.106-8; *RDP* v.402-4.

18   *RP* vi.215-17; *CCR* 1476-85, 36.

19   *RP* vi.106-8.

20   As T.B. Pugh long ago indicated, *15th-cent. England*, 112.

21   PRO DL 29/584/9253.

6 KING AT LAST

1   Mancini, 92-3.

2   Historic Manuscripts Commission 11th *Report Appendix III, MSS of the Boroughs of Southampton & King's Lynn*, 170. Unless otherwise stated, this chapter is based on Hicks, *Richard III*, ch. 3.

3   Mancini, 74-5.

4   Ibid., 72-3.

5   Ibid., 74-5.

6   *Crowland*, 155; see also Mancini, 74-5; More, 18.

7   Mancini, 76-9; *Crowland*, 156-7.

8   More, 20-1.

9   P. Tudor-Craig, *Richard III*, National Portrait Gallery (1973), p.66.

10   Horrox, *Richard III*, 96.

11   More, 23.

12   *Crowland*, 156-7.

13   Mancini, 84-5.

14   *Crowland*, 158-9.

15   *Memoranda,* 209; *Reg. Bourgchier*, 52-3. The late king's goods were not of course confiscated, *pace* Jones, *Bosworth*, 85-6, but were applied to pious works for the good of his soul (including repayment of debts, including public debts), not

necessarily what Edward had devised. Allowance was made for future repayments to his estate of monies applied to current expenses, *Memoranda*, 221.

16 *Memoranda*, 211, 216, 220.
17 *CPR* 1476-85, p. 350-1, 353-5; *CCR* 1476-85, p. 308; *CFR* 1471-85, nos. 256-8; . PRO C 66/551 mm. 1-6; C 54/334 m.1d; *Foedera*, xii. 179.
18 *Lynn MSS*, 170; Horrox, *Richard III*, 96; *Harley* 433, i.3-4.
19 PRO C 81/1641/1. *Harley MS* i.16-17 dates his appointment to 16 May.
20 PRO C 81/1529 /1-4; C 81/1528/1-3; BL Add. Ch. 5987, 19398; see also *Harley* 433 iii.4.
21 *Crowland*, 156-9.
22 PRO C 66/551; *Harley* 433 i.3-65; ii.1-21.
23 *Memoranda*, 214-15, 225; see also ibid.210.
24 *Crowland*, 148-9.
25 *Memoranda*, 229-30
26 More, 25. For these & other appointments, see Ross, *Richard III*, 76-7.
27 *CPR* 1476-85, 349-50, 356; *Harley* 433 i.8-18, 30-2; iii.2; PRO PSO 1/561/2834-5, 2840.
28 *Memoranda*, passim, esp. 217n, 229-30; *Harley* 433 iii.2.
29 Unless otherwise stated, this section is based on Hicks, *Richard III*, ch. 3 & sources reprinted in Hammond & Sutton. The argument in Jones, *Bosworth*, ch. 4, that the Duchess Cecily asserted Edward IV's bastardy (and her adultery) in 1483 and backed Richard's claim is not accepted.
30 S.B. Chrimes, *English Constitutional Ideas in the Fifteenth Century* (Cambridge, 1934).
31 *The Cely Letters 1472-88*, ed. A. Hanham, Early English Text Society 253 (1975), 184-5.
32 Hammond & Sutton, 103.
33 *Crowland*, p.161; for Stillington, see *BRUC*, ii.1777-9.
34 Hammond & Sutton, 156.
35 Jones, *Bosworth*, 67-70.
36 Hammond & Sutton, 156.

7 THE LAST KING

1 PRO E 404/78/2/3, 24.
2 *Harley* 433 iii. 29.
3 L. Attreed, 'From Pearl Maiden to Tower Princes', *Journal of Medieval History* (1983).
4 Vergil2, 126-7.
5 *Crowland*, 162-3.
6 Arthurson, *Warbeck Conspiracy*, 2.
7 *The Trial of Richard III*, ed. R. Drewett & M. Redhead (Gloucester, 1985).
8 *Great Chronicle*, 234.
9 M.A. Hicks, 'Did Edward V Outlive his Reign or did he Outreign his Life?' *The Ricardian* 108 (1990), 342 -5.
10 M.A. Hicks, 'Unweaving the Web: The Plot of July 1483 against Richard III & its wider significance', *The Ricardian* 114 (1991), 106-9.
11 *Crowland*, 162-3.

12 I. Arthurson & N. Kingwell, 'The Proclamation of Henry Tudor as King of England, 3 November 1483', *Historical Research* lxiii (1990), 105.

13 Vergil 1, 203.

14 *Crowland*, 162-3; Mancini, 88-9.

15 Hammond & Sutton, 165-6.

16 *RP* vi.276; R.E. Horrox, 'Henry Tudor's Letters to England during Richard III's Reign', *The Ricardian* 80 (1983), 155-8.

17 *Parliamentary Texts of the Later Middle Ages*, ed. N. Pronay & J. Taylor (Oxford, 1980).

18 *Great Chron.* 234.

19 Mancini, 92-3.

20 *Harley* 433 iii.2.

21 Mancini, 92-93.

22 K. Dockray, *Richard III: A Reader* (Gloucester, 1988), 91.

23 P.W. Hammond & W.J. White, 'The Sons of Edward IV: A Re-Examination of the Evidence on their Deaths & the Bones in Westminster Abbey', *Richard III: Loyalty, Lordship & Law* (1986), 109.

24 As explained in Hicks, *Richard III*, 155-9. *Crowland,* 162-3, borrows the Tudor version

25 Hammond & White, 'Sons of Edward IV', 110-11.

26 R.F. Green, 'The Historical Notes of a London Citizen 1483-88', *EHR* xcvi (1981), 588; see also Dockray, 93.

27 *Harley* 433 ii. 2-4; Hicks, *Richard III*, 138, 157.

28 J. Potter, *Good King Richard?* (1983), 134.

29 More, 9.

30 Vergil 1, 189.

31 *Biographies*, 889-92.

32 *Great Chronicle*, 236-7.

33 Vergil 1, 188-9.

34 More, 85-9.

35 J. Molinet, *Chroniques*, ed. J.A. Buchon, ii (1828), 402-3; Hammond & White, 'Sons of Edward IV', 135n43, also dates the story relatively late.

36 PRO KB 9/ 79/9, 10, 19; *RP* vi.545; for the rest of the plot, see also PRO KB 9/79/7-8.

37 *RP* vi.526; *The Reign of Henry VII from Contemporary Sources*, ed. A.F. Pollard, 3 vols. (1913), i.224.

38 Vergil 2, 26-7. That so careful and sceptical a historian as Vergil had no doubts suggests that he saw evidence that looked authentic.

39 Hicks, *Richard III*, 176-8, 188-9.

40 A section of the *Ricardian Bulletin* each quarter devoted to 'Unlikely attacks' & 'Unlikely Defences' offers interesting insight to people's knowledge of the past.

41 As reviewed in Hammond & White, 'Sons of Edward IV', 117-29.

42 T. Mollason, 'Anne Mowbray and the Princes in the Tower: a study in identity' ' *London Archaeologist*, 5 (1987), 259-62.

43 Vergil 2, 126-7.

LIST OF ILLUSTRATIONS

All illustrations are © Geoffrey Wheeler unless otherwise stated.

INDEX

ABOUT THE AUTHOR

Michael Hicks is Professor of History at King Alfred's College, Winchester. He has written extensively on medieval England and is regarded by many as the leading expert on the Yorkist dynasty. His books include the widely praised *Richard III* and *Anne Neville* both published by Tempus. He is also the author of *Warwick the Kingmaker* and *Edward IV.* He lives in Winchester.

ALSO AVAILABLE BY MICHAEL HICKS

Richard III
'A most important book by the greatest living expert on Richard… A must'
BBC History Magazine
'A fascinating odyssey into English history' **History Today**

£9.99   978 07524 2589 4

Anne Neville: Queen to Richard III
'A masterful and poignant story' **Alison Weir**
'Does little for Richard III's tattered reputation' **BBC History Magazine**

£9.99   978 07524 4129 0

TEMPUS – REVEALING HISTORY

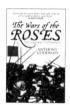

The Wars of the Roses
The Soldiers' Experience
ANTHONY GOODMAN
'A fascinating book' *TLS*
£12.99
0 7524 3731 3

The Vikings
MAGNUS MAGUNSSON
'Serious, engaging history'
BBC History Magazine
£9.99
0 7524 2699 0

William the Conqueror
DAVID BATES
'As expertly woven as the Bayeux Tapestry'
BBC History Magazine
£12.99
0 7524 2960 4

Agincourt: A New History
ANNE CURRY
'A tour de force' *Alison Weir*
'*The* book on the battle' *Richard Holmes*
A BBC History Magazine BOOK OF THE YEAR 2005
£12.99
0 7524 2828 4

Hereward The Last Englishman
PETER REX
'An enthralling work of historical detection'
Robert Lacey
£17.99
0 7524 3318 0

The English Resistance
The Underground War Against the Normans
PETER REX
'An invaluable rehabilitation of an ignored
resistance movement' *The Sunday Times*
£12.99
0 7524 3733 X

Richard III
MICHAEL HICKS
'A most important book by the greatest living
expert on Richard' *Desmond Seward*
£9.99
0 7524 2589 7

The Peasants' Revolt
England's Failed Revolution of 1381
ALASTAIR DUNN
'A stunningly good book... totally absorbing'
Melvyn Bragg
£9.99
0 7524 2965 5

If you are interested in purchasing other books published by Tempus, or in case you have difficulty finding
any Tempus books in your local bookshop, you can also place orders directly through our website:
www.tempus-publishing.com

TEMPUS – REVEALING HISTORY

Quacks Fakers and Charlatans in Medicine
ROY PORTER

'A delightful book' *The Daily Telegraph*
'Hugely entertaining' *BBC History Magazine*

£12.99   0 7524 2590 0

The Tudors
RICHARD REX

'Up-to-date, readable and reliable. The best
introduction to England's most important
dynasty' *David Starkey*
'Vivid, entertaining... quite simply the best short
introduction' *Eamon Duffy*
'Told with enviable narrative skill... a delight for
any reader' *THES*

£9.99   0 7524 3333 4

The Kings & Queens of England
MARK ORMROD

'Of the numerous books on the kings and
queens of England, this is the best'
Alison Weir

£9.99   0 7524 2598 6

The Covent Garden Ladies
Pimp General Jack & the Extraordinary Story of Harris's List
HALLIE RUBENHOLD

'Sex toys, porn... forget Ann Summers, Miss
Love was at it 250 years ago' *The Times*
'Compelling' *The Independent on Sunday*
'Marvellous' *Leonie Frieda*
'Filthy' *The Guardian*

£9.99   0 7524 3739 9

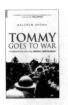

Okinawa 1945
GEORGE FEIFER

'A great book... Feifer's account of the three
sides and their experiences far surpasses most
books about war'
Stephen Ambrose

£17.99   0 7524 3324 5

Tommy Goes To War
MALCOLM BROWN

'A remarkably vivid and frank account of the
British soldier in the trenches'
Max Arthur
'The fury, fear, mud, blood, boredom and
bravery that made up life on the Western Front
are vividly presented and illustrated'
The Sunday Telegraph

£12.99   0 7524 2980 4

Ace of Spies The True Story of Sidney Reilly
ANDREW COOK

'The most definitive biography of the spying
ace yet written... both a compelling narrative
and a myth-shattering *tour de force*'
Simon Sebag Montefiore
'The absolute last word on the subject' *Nigel West*
'Makes poor 007 look like a bit of a wuss'
The Mail on Sunday

£12.99   0 7524 2959 0

Sex Crimes
From Renaissance to Enlightenment
W.M. NAPHY

'Wonderfully scandalous' *Diarmaid MacCulloch*
'A model of pin-sharp scholarship' *The Guardian*

£10.99   0 7524 2977 9

TEMPUS – REVEALING HISTORY

William II Rufus, the Red King
EMMA MASON

'A thoroughly new reappraisal of a much maligned king. The dramatic story of his life is told with great pace and insight'
John Gillingham

£25

0 7524 3528 0

William Wallace The True Story of Braveheart
CHRIS BROWN

'A formidable new biography... sieves through masses of medieval records to distinguish the man from the myth' **Magnus Magnusson**

£17.99

0 7524 3432 2

Elizabeth Wydeville: The Slandered Queen
ARLENE OKERLUND

'A penetrating, thorough and wholly convincing vindication of this unlucky queen'
Sarah Gristwood

'A gripping tale of lust, loss and tragedy'
Alison Weir

A **BBC History Magazine** Book of the Year 2005

£9.99   978 07524 3807 8

The Battle of Hastings 1066
M.K. LAWSON

'Blows away many fundamental assumptions about the battle of Hastings… an exciting and indispensable read' **David Bates**

A **BBC History Magazine** Book of the Year 2003

£12.99   978 07524 4177 1

The Welsh Wars of Independence
DAVID MOORE

'Beautifully written, subtle and remarkably perceptive' **John Davies**

£12.99

978 07524 4128 3

Medieval England
From Hastings to Bosworth
EDMUND KING

'The best illustrated history of medieval England' **John Gillingham**

£12.99

0 7524 2827 5

A Companion to Medieval England
NIGEL SAUL

'Wonderful... everything you could wish to know about life in medieval England'
Heritage Today

£19.99

0 7524 2969 8

The Prince In The Tower
MICHAEL HICKS

'The first time in ages that a publisher has sent me a book I actually want to read' **David Starkey**

£9.99

978 07524 4386 7

TEMPUS – REVEALING HISTORY

D-Day The First 72 Hours
WILLIAM F. BUCKINGHAM

'A compelling narrative' *The Observer*
A *BBC History Magazine* Book of the Year 2004
£9.99   0 7524 2842 X

The London Monster
Terror on the Streets in 1790
JAN BONDESON

'Gripping' *The Guardian*
'Excellent... monster-mania brought a reign of terror to the ill-lit streets of the capital'
The Independent

£9.99   0 7524 3327 X

London
A Historical Companion
KENNETH PANTON

'A readable and reliable work of reference that deserves a place on every Londoner's bookshelf'
Stephen Inwood

£20   0 7524 3434 9

M: MI5's First Spymaster
ANDREW COOK

'Serious spook history' *Andrew Roberts*
'Groundbreaking' *The Sunday Telegraph*
'Brilliantly researched' *Dame Stella Rimington*

£9.99   978 07524 3949 9

Agincourt
A New History
ANNE CURRY

'A highly distinguished and convincing account'
Christopher Hibbert
'A *tour de force*' *Alison Weir*
'*The* book on the battle' *Richard Holmes*
A *BBC History Magazine* Book of the Year 2005
£12.99   0 7524 3813 1

Battle of the Atlantic
MARC MILNER

'The most comprehensive short survey of the U-boat battles' *Sir John Keegan*
'Some events are fortunate in their historian, none more so than the Battle of the Atlantic. Marc Milner is *the* historian of the Atlantic campaign... a compelling narrative' *Andrew Lambert*

£12.99   0 7524 3332 6

The English Resistance
The Underground War Against the Normans
PETER REX

'An invaluable rehabilitation of an ignored resistance movement' *The Sunday Times*
'Peter Rex's scholarship is remarkable'
The Sunday Express
£12.99   0 7524 3733 X

Elizabeth Wydeville: England's Slandered Queen
ARLENE OKERLUND

'A penetrating, thorough and wholly convincing vindication of this unlucky queen'
Sarah Gristwood
'A gripping tale of lust, loss and tragedy'
Alison Weir
A *BBC History Magazine* Book of the Year 2005
£9.99   978 07524 3807 8

If you are interested in purchasing other books published by Tempus, or in case you have difficulty finding any Tempus books in your local bookshop, you can also place orders directly through our website
www.tempus-publishing.com

TEMPUS – REVEALING HISTORY

Britannia's Empire
A Short History of the British Empire
BILL NASSON

'Crisp, economical and witty' *TLS*
'An excellent introduction the subject' *THES*

£12.99   0 7524 3808 5

Madmen
A Social History of Madhouses,
Mad-Doctors & Lunatics
ROY PORTER

'Fascinating'
The Observer

£12.99   0 7524 3730 5

Born to be Gay
A History of Homosexuality
WILLIAM NAPHY

'Fascinating' *The Financial Times*
'Excellent' *Gay Times*

£9.99   0 7524 3694 5

William II
Rufus, the Red King
EMMA MASON
'A thoroughly new reappraisal of a much
maligned king. The dramatic story of his life is
told with great pace and insight'
John Gillingham

£25   0 7524 3528 0

To Kill Rasputin
The Life and Death of Grigori Rasputin
ANDREW COOK

'Andrew Cook is a brilliant investigative historian'
Andrew Roberts
'Astonishing' *The Daily Mail*

£9.99   0 7524 3906 5

The Unwritten Order
Hitler's Role in the Final Solution
PETER LONGERICH

'Compelling' *Richard Evans*
'The finest account to date of the many twists
and turns in Adolf Hitler's anti-semitic obsession'
Richard Overy

£12.99   0 7524 3328 8

Private 12768
Memoir of a Tommy
JOHN JACKSON
FOREWORD BY HEW STRACHAN

'A refreshing new perspective' *The Sunday Times*
'At last we have John Jackson's intensely
personal and heartfelt little book to remind us
there was a view of the Great War other than
Wilfred Owen's' *The Daily Mail*

£9.99   0 7524 3531 0

The Vikings
MAGNUS MAGNUSSON

'Serious, engaging history'
BBC History Magazine

£9.99   0 7524 2699 0

If you are interested in purchasing other books published by Tempus, or in case you have difficulty finding any
Tempus books in your local bookshop, you can also place orders directly through our website

www.tempus-publishing.com

TEMPUS – REVEALING HISTORY

Freaks
JAN BONDESON

'Reveals how these tragic individuals triumphed over their terrible adversity' *The Daily Mail*
'Well written and superbly illustrated'
The Financial Times

£9.99   0 7524 3662 7

King Arthur
CHRISTOPHER HIBBERT

'A pearl of biographers' *New Statesman*
£12.99   978 07524 3933 4

Bollywood
MIHIR BOSE

'Pure entertainment' *The Observer*
'Insightful and often hilarious' *The Sunday Times*
'Gripping' *The Daily Telegraph*

£9.99   978 07524 4382 9

Arnhem
William Buckingham

'Reveals the reason why the daring attack failed'
The Daily Express

£10.99   0 7524 3187 0

Cleopatra
PATRICIA SOUTHERN

'In the absence of Cleopatra's memoirs Patricia Southern's commendably balanced biography will do very well'
The Sunday Telegraph

£9.99   978 07524 4336 2

The Battle of Hastings 1066
M. K. LAWSON

'A *BBC History Magazine* book of the year 2003
'The definitive book on this famous battle'
The Journal of Military History

£12.99   978 07524 4177 1

The Prince In The Tower
MICHAEL HICKS

'The first time in ages that a publisher has sent me a book I actually want to read' *David Starkey*

£9.99   978 07524 4386 7

Loos 1915
NICK LLOYD

'A revealing new account based on meticulous documentary research' *Corelli Barnett*
'Should finally consign Alan Clark's Farrago, *The Donkeys*, to the waste paperbasket'
Hew Strachan
'Plugs a yawning gap in the existing literature... this book will set the agenda for debate of the battle for years to come' *Gary Sheffield*

£25   0 7524 3937 5

If you are interested in purchasing other books published by Tempus, or in case you have difficulty finding any Tempus books in your local bookshop, you can also place orders directly through our website

www.tempus-publishing.com

TEMPUS – REVEALING HISTORY

Private 12768 Memoir of a Tommy
JOHN JACKSON

'Unique... a beautifully written, strikingly honest account of a young man's experience of combat' *Saul David*

'At last we have John Jackson's intensely personal and heartfelt little book to remind us there was a view of the Great War other than Wilfred Owen's' *The Daily Mail*

£9.99   0 7524 3531 0

The German Offensives of 1918
MARTIN KITCHEN

'A lucid, powerfully driven narrative' *Malcolm Brown*
'Comprehensive and authoritative... first class' *Holger H. Herwig*

£13.99   0 7524 3527 2

Verdun 1916
MALCOLM BROWN

'A haunting book which gets closer than any other to that wasteland marked by death' *Richard Holmes*

£9.99   0 7524 2599 4

The Forgotten Front
The East African Campaign 1914–1918
ROSS ANDERSON

'Excellent... fills a yawning gap in the historical record' *The Times Literary Supplement*
'Compelling and authoritative' *Hew Strachan*

£12.99   978 07524 4126 9

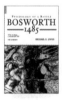

Agincourt
A New History
ANNE CURRY

'A highly distinguished and convincing account' *Christopher Hibbert*
'A *tour de force*' *Alison Weir*
'*The* book on the battle' *Richard Holmes*
A *BBC History Magazine* Book of the Year 2005

£12.99   0 7524 3813 1

The Welsh Wars of Independence
DAVID MOORE

'Beautifully written, subtle and remarkably perceptive' *John Davies*

£12.99   978 07524 4128 3

Bosworth 1485 Psychology of a Battle
MICHAEL K. JONES

'Most exciting... a remarkable tale' *The Guardian*
'Insightful and rich study of the Battle of Bosworth... no longer need Richard play the villain' *The Times Literary Supplement*

£12.99   0 7524 2594 3

The Battle of Hastings 1066
M.K. LAWSON

'Blows away many fundamental assumptions about the battle of Hastings... an exciting and indispensable read' *David Bates*
A *BBC History Magazine* Book of the Year 2003

£12.99   978 07524 4177 1

If you are interested in purchasing other books published by Tempus, or in case you have difficulty finding any Tempus books in your local bookshop, you can also place orders directly through our website

www.tempus-publishing.com

TEMPUS – REVEALING HISTORY

 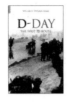 

The Wars of the Roses
The Soldiers' Experience
ANTHONY GOODMAN
'Sheds light on the lot of the common soldier as never before' *Alison Weir*
'A meticulous work'
The Times Literary Supplement

£12.99   0 7524 3731 3

D-Day
The First 72 Hours
WILLIAM F. BUCKINGHAM
'A compelling narrative' *The Observer*
A *BBC History Magazine* Book of the Year 2004

£9.99   0 7524 2842 2

English Battlefields
500 Battlefields that Shaped English History
MICHAEL RAYNER
'A painstaking survey of English battlefields... a first-rate book' *Richard Holmes*
'A fascinating and, for all its factual tone, an atmospheric volume' *The Sunday Telegraph*

£18.99   978 07524 4307 2

Trafalgar Captain Durham of the Defiance: The Man who refused to Miss Trafalgar
HILARY RUBINSTEIN
'A sparkling biography of Nelson's luckiest captain' *Andrew Lambert*

£17.99   0 7524 3435 7

   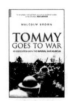

Battle of the Atlantic
MARC MILNER
'The most comprehensive short survey of the U-boat battles' *Sir John Keegan*
'Some events are fortunate in their historian, none more so than the Battle of the Atlantic. Marc Milner is *the* historian of the Atlantic Campaign... a compelling narrative'
Andrew Lambert

£12.99   0 7524 3332 6

Okinawa 1945 The Stalingrad of the Pacific
GEORGE FEIFER
'A great book... Feifer's account of the three sides and their experiences far surpasses most books about war' *Stephen Ambrose*

£17.99   0 7524 3324 5

Gallipoli 1915
TIM TRAVERS
'The most important new history of Gallipoli for forty years... groundbreaking' *Hew Strachan*
'A book of the highest importance to all who would seek to understand the tragedy of the Gallipoli campaign' *The Journal of Military History*

£13.99   0 7524 2972 8

Tommy Goes To War
MALCOLM BROWN
'A remarkably vivid and frank account of the British soldier in the trenches' *Max Arthur*
'The fury, fear, mud, blood, boredom and bravery that made up life on the Western Front are vividly presented and illustrated' *The Sunday Telegraph*

£12.99   0 7524 2980 9

If you are interested in purchasing other books published by Tempus, or in case you have difficulty finding any Tempus books in your local bookshop, you can also place orders directly through our website

www.tempus-publishing.com